DI STÉFANO

Also by Ian Hawkey

Feet of the Chameleon: The Story of African Football

DI STÉFANO

IAN HAWKEY

EBURY
PRESS

1 3 5 7 9 10 8 6 4 2

Ebury Press, an imprint of Ebury Publishing
20 Vauxhall Bridge Road
London SW1V 2SA

Ebury Press is part of the Penguin Random House group of companies whose
addresses can be found at global.penguinrandomhouse.com

Penguin
Random House
UK

First published by Ebury Press in 2016

www.penguin.co.uk

A CIP catalogue record for this book is available from the British Library

ISBN 9780091958558

Printed and bound in Great Britain by Clays Ltd, St Ives PLC

MIX
Paper from
responsible sources
FSC® C018179

Penguin Random House is committed to a sustainable future
for our business, our readers and our planet. This book is
made from Forest Stewardship Council® certified paper.

CONTENTS

PROLOGUE

On a street corner close to the centre of Madrid, nestled into the shoulder of perhaps the most famous stadium in Europe is a small café. Its ceilings are low, the décor functional, the brightness of its strip-lights a little harsh on the eye. But the churros, the long, ridged doughnuts that are the signature elevenses in the capital of Spain, are fresh and the coffee fortifying.

Proximity to the Santiago Bernabéu arena makes the place a convenient ante-room for anybody with an appointment at Real Madrid. It still always seemed a surprise to find the club's honorary president and most celebrated former footballer there, often on his own. Alfredo Di Stéfano's main job, in his later years, was to have the red carpet rolled out for him, to be feted by Real Madrid as the greatest individual who ever played for the most successful club in the world's most popular sport. It would be hard to imagine anyone more instantly recognisable to three or four generations of madrileños than he was. Yet, on red carpet days during one of the most ostentatious periods of Real Madrid's starry history, the first decade of the twentieth century, Di Stéfano would regularly choose this understated café as his retreat, his walking stick hanging on the brass bar just below the counter.

He would sip at his espresso, almost incognito. I first met him there by chance, and then slipped into a habit of seeking him out for half an hour or so before we both set off for work at the stadium: he as the figurehead VIP, the grandee among whose roles, in his seventies and eighties, at modern Madrid was to welcome the multi-million euro recruits into the club, endorsing their status as they posed for photographs and he handed over their new white jerseys; I as a correspondent, posted to Spain by the British newspaper the *Sunday Times* to report on, among other things, Real Madrid's bold, determined, impossible effort to make themselves as dominant as they had been when Di Stéfano graced the Bernabéu pitch, and commanded it in the 1950s and 1960s.

Some people found Di Stéfano gruff and stand-offish. Many of those people were his team-mates and his closest friends. He could certainly be sharp, brusque and held firm opinions, but my experience was usually of a personable man, albeit one who made sure it was he who guided the direction of conversation. That might be along any number of tangents: a jocular grumble about English referees, a bane of his career. It might be his view of the prospects of the contemporary Manchester United team or an off-the-cuff observation about a young footballer who had caught his eye. Di Stéfano had a trove of stories to tell about his own past but never, at least until the very last years of his life, seemed cocooned in them. His enthusiasm for his sport, the essence of it, beyond its commercial paraphernalia, acted as a powerful antidote to grumpiness.

Di Stéfano may, as many argue, be the finest footballer who ever earned a living from the game. He set standards very few have been equipped to emulate. He pushed the boundaries of what it was to be a professional, in how he interpreted the geometry of the pitch, in how to win and to keep winning. He raised the bar for what he and those around him should aspire to. He raised his voice to let others know when they fell short. He pushed at some closed doors beyond the field, too, a truculent trade-unionist who had helped redefine the rights of footballers in his native South America well before Di Stéfano the globetrotter established the European Cup as the summit of the game in an entirely different continent.

Di Stéfano elevated Real Madrid from the higher foothills of Spain's sporting hierarchy into the modern era's pre-eminent club. He gave Spain itself something, a sporting prowess it could parade to the world with pride and a sense of superiority at a time when it was a country reminded by its neighbours, and from within, of its political and economic backwardness. Di Stéfano, the Argentinian who became a Spaniard almost by accident, never sought to be a nation's lodestar, less still to be remembered as the key battle site in what has since become sport's most notorious rivalry, between Barcelona and Real Madrid. But he did more than just live through interesting times, through South American coups and a political kidnapping, through the Cold War and Francoism. He defined his times and his milieu, as much a shaper of a game and a place as Donald Bradman was to cricket and Australia, or Muhammad Ali to boxing and the United States.

At Real Madrid, there is plenty of appreciation of that, even if, for a period he was almost *persona non grata* there, the consequence of a prickly departure once his powers as an athlete had diminished and his sense of his own authority, seldom fragile, had not. But Di Stéfano's story does not begin at the point where he arrived in Europe, tussled over between Catalonia and Castile, nor with the rapid transformations he brought to football in Europe as it began to be televised. The time spent in his hinterland, in Argentina and Colombia, was as eventful as anything that followed, and my research for this book, which began shortly before his death in 2014, focused as much on that as on the stories behind the famous Di Stéfano: the 'complete footballer', the game's first great global superstar, the peerless pioneer.

CHAPTER 1

SPRINTS

As the crow flies, the distance between Calle Salmún Feijóo, the Buenos Aires street which was Alfredo Di Stéfano's first home, and Calle Filiberto, a narrow lane leading off Plaza Garay, is around two kilometres. Take a brisk walk between the two now, through the suburb of Barracas, dipping under the railway line and pausing at an Avenida Brasil heavy with traffic, and the distance will be covered in a little over 20 minutes. By the time the young Di Stéfano had established enough independence to make the trip on his own, he was doing it a great deal quicker.

'He was always running,' Norma Di Stéfano recalls of her older brother. 'He could be a rascal but he was also quite a shy child, quite ordered, as well as energetic.' Alfredito, or Little Alfredo, as he was known around the house, was five years old when Norma was born, three years after her other brother Tulio, and the most eager run he would soon be making was from their home in Barracas to that of their paternal grandparents Miguel and Teresa Di Stéfano on Calle Filiberto. The prospect of a visit to their handsome three-storey house with its substantial garden would put wings in his heels.

His grandparents were very present in the life of Alfredo junior, from his birth on 4 July 1926, the first child of Alfredo Di Stéfano senior and Eulalia Laulhé. Evidently, Miguel Di Stéfano had a talent as a raconteur, a gift for the compelling yarn that, when he was in trusted company, his grandson inherited.

Alfredito loved to listen to his Miguel's adventures. His grandfather had been among more than a million Italians to emigrate to Argentina in the nineteenth century, and settled there via a roundabout route. He was born on the island of Capri, one of at least six children of a family with military connections and some means, thanks to various business interests, including shipping. Miguel Di Stéfano had a difficult relationship with his stepmother, and by the time he was 17 had put a distance between himself and Italy. Following up a commission abroad on behalf of the family business, Miguel settled briefly in the United States, though he soon determined it was at the other end of the Americas that he would build his new life.

His wide-eyed grandson admired his intrepid spirit. Alfredito enjoyed the stories of Miguel's fleet of boats, with their romantic names, like *El Fiel Destino* (True Destiny), and the voyages they made through a South America that promised its new arrivals from Europe all sorts of exciting possibilities, as well as perils. He heard tales of daring and risk, of the hazards of navigating the River Paraná in stormy conditions. Miguel also had funny stories to tell his grandchildren: on one occasion, after he had delivered produce to a remote site, his customers asked for seeds so they could plant and cultivate for themselves the delicious spaghetti the Italians had introduced them to.

Once he had started at school in Barracas, Alfredito would dash as quickly as possible to his grandparents' house after classes, to spend his siesta time there. Most lessons held limited interest to a somewhat mischievous child keen on the outdoors. In time, though, he would enjoy reading, particularly one of Argentina's defining texts, *Martín Fierro*, José Hernández's epic poem about a courageous frontiersman, his duels, his friendships, and the betrayals and setbacks he endured.

Living in Barracas in the mid-1920s felt like living on a frontier of sorts. Di Stéfano's father, Alfredo senior, Miguel's fourth son, had chosen as his first family home a bungalow in Barracas just a few blocks from La Boca, a *barrio* or neighbourhood at the mouth of the Río de la Plata, and even on Calle Salmún Feijóo – then known as Calle Universidad – it could feel that this was a home wrestled from nature. Should the river burst its banks, the danger of flooding was real. Being close to the port also meant a daily reminder that Buenos Aires was a city whose population was swelling rapidly. New immigrants, freshly disembarked, seeking work and opportunity, were conspicuous in Barracas in the 1920s and 1930s.

Alfredo senior had made the most of his opportunities, and worked his way up in the Buenos Aires collective of potato dealers. He spent most of his days at the central marketplace, and some of his evenings making plans for a future outside the city, closer to the farming communities whose representatives he met with regularly. He was a hard worker, and a principled man, keen that his children should grow up industrious and responsible. He could be strict, his children recalled, and protective.

The atmosphere at the big, imposing house on Calle Filiberto was different. Miguel and his wife, Teresa Ciozza, also from Italy but born in the north, were sociable grandparents. Relatives and friends would come round to make use of the outside oven, cooking pizza and focaccia, sometimes to retail to paying customers. Alfredito would clamber up the fig trees in the garden to pick fruit, and, in gleeful conspiracy with his grandfather, conceal some of his harvest from his grandmother, Teresa. Her side of the family had come from Genoa, Miguel would remark with a smile, telling his grandson this meant she had a stingy streak, like all Genoese. In the words of her granddaughter, Norma, Teresa could come across as 'bit straight-laced'. When the grandparents travelled on Sundays to visit Alfredito's family in Barracas, Donna Teresa would not be sprinting, helter-skelter, across Plaza Garay and through Parque España like Alfredito. She would dress smartly. They would catch the number 43 tram. Her son and grandchildren would be there at the tram stop to watch her regal descent from the vehicle.

Alfredo Di Stéfano senior's tastes owed much to his Italian roots. At a time when tango was establishing itself as the national music of Argentina, opera remained his great love. Photos of Enrico Caruso and Titta Ruffo decorated the Barracas home, and he played 78rpm records on what was then a sophisticated gramophone. The house filled with arias of an evening. Meanwhile, not far away, the bars and theatres of the city were animated by a different sound, the rhythm of tango and the voice of its leading artist, Carlos Gardel.

From his father, Alfredito inherited an interest in football, and good genes for the sport. From his mother's side of the family, the young Alfredito inherited other enthusiasms. Eulalia Laulhé was the granddaughter of immigrants from southwest France, not far from Catalonia, and from Ireland. Many of her closer relatives made homes inland of Buenos Aires. Holidaying in his summers outside the city with his maternal cousins and uncles and aunts, Alfredito would learn to ride horses, and develop an appreciation of the countryside. It was to his mother's Irish line of the family that he owed the physical feature that set him a little apart from most of his Argentinian contemporaries and generated several of his nicknames: before Alfredito became 'The Blond Arrow', an instantly recognised shorthand for the rising star of River Plate, he was known to his friends and amateur team-mates as 'El Alemán', 'The German' – again simply because of his light thatch.

Alfredo senior and Eulalia had started their family in a time of relative prosperity in Argentina. When Alfredo junior was born, Buenos Aires was a boom town for those who showed enterprise. Though agricultural exports, a mainstay of national prosperity, had suffered after the outbreak of the First World War in Europe, unemployment remained, officially, low even into the first years of the Great Depression. The national capital became better connected, barrio to barrio, with the founding of the Metro, in addition to the tram network. Social life centred less and less on ghettos of immigrant communities with similar cultural backgrounds and more and more on shared professional or leisure interests. Sport, and particularly football, was gaining a firmer and firmer hold on the public imagination.

Just one block to the south of Calle Universidad stood the Estadio Sportivo Barracas, until the mid-1920s probably the best arena in Buenos Aires. It had hosted a much-celebrated fixture between Argentina and the Olympic champions, Uruguay, in 1924, and by the end of that decade was busy increasing its capacity to answer swelling demand for tickets, and to try and keep up with other grand stadiums being constructed, extended or designed across the city. In August 1928, *El Gráfico*, a popular magazine catering mainly for Argentina's football followers, petitioned the sport's patrons to 'urgently increase the capacity of stadiums'. *El Gráfico*, whose tone tended towards hectoring, added: 'We expect this to come from the clubs because we cannot hope the official authorities, who are always so slow, to do it.' The cry was heard loud and clear. Within the next decade, work was progressing at the sites of what are now River Plate's El Monumental and Boca Juniors's La Bombonera.

Elite club football in Argentina had turned professional at the end of May 1931, following industrial action by players, who at one point marched through Buenos Aires to put their demands for better working conditions to the head of state, General José Félix Uriburu. One of four different presidents in a five-year period of political instability, Uriburu had become accustomed to manifestations of radicalism by organised labour and referred this one to the office of the mayor of Buenos Aires, José Guerrico. Although the players' aspirations for freedom of contract would not be satisfied and indeed would continue to form the basis of a long-running gripe for decades, Guerrico did make some concessions. A streamlined league was formed, centred on clubs from the capital, leading to ever higher standards and the emergence of superstars.

For the opera-loving, hard-working Alfredo senior, the transformation of football from amateur to professional, from a hobby practised by like-minded colleagues and friends to a glamorous, politicised mass entertainment business, would have seemed startling. His own relationship with the sport was deep, but nuanced. He had loved it as a young man, and thrived at it. If you delve around the archives of River Plate, one of the two most celebrated clubs of Argentina, you find his name among the pathfinders of the club's period of greatest growth, a harbinger for the so-called golden era of Argentinian club football.

Alfredo Di Stéfano senior played five competitive matches for River Plate between 1913 and 1915. River played in shirts of vertical red and white stripes in those days and their line-ups featured some Anglo-Saxon surnames, like Simmons and Penney. Di Stéfano senior was a forward, and one good enough to help transform a River team, following a disappointing 1912 Buenos Aires campaign, where they finished lowest of six clubs in the then amateur league, into a more respected opponent. He scored two goals in his three appearances in the zonal group stage of the 1913 championship, in which River were undefeated but finished just shy of Racing Club de Avellaneda at the top of their table. Two years later, Di Stéfano senior, by then aware that a knee problem was going to prevent him from exploiting his talent to the full, appeared once for third-placed River in the far more cumbersome 25-club league, and he played a single match in River's unsuccessful defence of the Buenos Aires Jockey Club's Competencia Cup.

Alfredo senior's appreciation for the sport stayed with him. But his view of the game as a possible profession for any of his offspring would be cautious. He recognised ability in Alfredito and Tulio from an early age. In a 1963 interview, he told the Buenos Aires correspondent of Spain's *ABC* newspaper: 'I knew my son, almost from birth, had everything to become a genuine "crack", a star.' He saw young Alfredito's athletic gifts develop young, noted the 'lightness' of his movements, and presumably noticed the rapidity with which he could dash the 13 or 14 blocks between his own home and that of his grandparents. What Alfredo senior doubted, in the 1930s and early 1940s, was whether football was a proper aspiration or vocation for a young man growing up in Argentina at that time, particularly one with solid alternatives and the kind of comfortable background his father was hard at work building for his family.

He would not have been the only father at the time who thought of football as a chequered career path. One of the most popular Argentinian feature films of the early 1930s, *Los Tres Berretines* (The Three Diversions), captured aspects of the zeitgeist, and did so with a full soundtrack, including dialogue, then a novelty in a country whose cinema industry was only beginning to emerge from the silent era. The film, directed by Enrique Susini, tells the story of a father who owns a shop, of his wife, who loves the movies, and their three sons, all with distinct ambitions, but none of them to follow their dad's line of work. There's Eusebio, who aspires to write tango music, a fashionable pursuit of the time. There's Eduardo, who has made progress as a would-be architect, a savvy choice of career in a country with a rapidly expanding urban population, and space to build. A third son, Lorenzo, meanwhile, worries and infuriates his father with his drive to become a footballer. It strikes him as a frivolous dream, until Lorenzo makes it, and his father has his epiphany, watching his son score a goal in front of a big crowd in an important fixture. Better still, Lorenzo earns a lavish enough salary in his sport to sponsor Eusebio's songwriting, and his new contacts with men in thrall to the sport and its heroes lead to Eduardo being given the job of designing a new stadium.

The part of Lorenzo in *Los Tres Berretines* was played by one Miguel Ángel Lauri, already something of a star well before he went into acting. Lauri had been a player with Estudiantes, the Buenos Aires club. A publicity photograph for the film, published in *Crítica*, a leading newspaper, shows rather splendidly the real-life glamour Lauri had access to as footballer turned movie star. Taken at the headquarters of Estudiantes, it shows Lauri wearing his pale suit, reclining on a bank of grass, surrounded by 16 young women, all in swimsuits.

The Di Stéfanos were River Plate supporters by inheritance. Alfredo senior felt strong links to the club he had represented in their early, amateur era. Norma Di Stéfano remembers the thrill of anticipation as they caught the tram – three children, parents and sometimes other relatives – to River's stadium, an arena they would see expand rapidly. Alfredo junior, a regular spectator from a very young age at Sportivo Barracas matches, reckoned his first River versus Boca Juniors experience in the flesh would have been when he was about seven or eight years old.

By then, the city's most resonant fixture had all the accoutrements of professionalism: stars with auras and their own thrilling backstories. River's leading goalscorer in the early 1930s was Bernabé Ferreyra, alias 'The Beast', a rugged, stocky centre-forward with gelignite in his boots, famous for once shooting so powerfully at a goalkeeper in a tour match in Peru that the poor keeper had been knocked unconscious. River had paid a record 35,000 pesos to Tigre to sign Ferreyra, and to put him on the end of passes supplied by another star they had recruited, Carlos Peucelle, a creative winger whose passing and imaginative reading of a game could stimulate the imagination of an attentive student just as much as Ferreyra's ferocious shot. Alfredito Di Stéfano, talented ball-player, distracted schoolboy, non-stop runner, had his heroes. Peucelle would be one, Ferreyra another, and like many Argentinians of the 1930s, he admired Arsenio Erico, the prolific Paraguayan striker at Independiente.

Sport was his chief passion, but he had others. He enjoyed the cinema, an interest he would maintain all his life, and there were regular excursions to the local bioscope. On one such visit, there was a moment, he came to reflect, that might have sent his life in quite a different direction. At his local picture-house, whenever a child bought a ticket for the main feature, he or she was often entered for a lucky dip. Each ticket bore a unique number and before the screening began, a compére would organise a sort of tombola, picking out the winning number. The game, like bingo, had certain codes, known to the caller and to the audience: number 15 was the 'pretty girl', 44 was known as 'the prison'; 12, 'the soldier'; 22, 'two little ducks'.

Alfredito had gone to see a western with a group of friends, and they swapped and bartered their numbers ahead of the draw.

Alfredito had in his hand number 14 – shorthand: 'the drunkard' – after one of his mates decided he wanted a different number, and, being a rather shy ten-year-old, heard it read out loud by the compere with a mixture of anticipation and embarrassment. He was suddenly the centre of attention, the winner of a prize. It was a good prize, too, for a keen sportsman, though not quite perfect. It was a nice leather ball, only it was oval. He had won a rugby ball.

It is diverting to imagine what might have happened had this become the beginning of a sporting love affair. Rugby had its niche, and strong following in Argentina, legacy of the immigrants from the British Isles who left a mark on much of the country's infrastructure and indeed its landowning class. Organised club rugby claimed several pages in every edition of *El Gráfico*. What it did not do was absorb the pre-teenaged Alfredito Di Stéfano. He and his friends enthusiastically took the new toy into the street, and laughed at the confounding bounce. 'It jumped around like a chicken,' the ball's new owner later recalled.

The more illuminating part of the story is what happened when he took the ball back to his barrio, and showed it to some of the older boys he knew and used to play casual games of football with. A new leather ball represented a valuable possession, but what he presented to the Barracas lads met with their disapproval. Moreover, they believed they should do something about it. A delegation of boys, with Alfredito pushed to the front of the group, the backstreet generals behind him putting on an air of studied menace, returned to the cinema with the oval ball and demanded that the proprietor replace it with a round one. The mob appeared threatening enough that a football was rummaged out of the prize cupboard and handed over instead.

The story stuck with him, a parable for what strength in numbers might achieve. Years later, after Alfredito had become the worldly

Alfredo Di Stéfano, he spoke of the musketeer spirit among the youths of the barrio of Barracas. He said to his friends that ever since he could remember, in times of confrontation, he would repeat to himself the phrase, as a reflex, a touchstone: 'Never back down!'

By the age of eight, he was aware that he had a special gift that was appreciated by older boys, keen that he represented their teams in scratch matches on the street, or on the patches of park space they commandeered. Visit the area around Calle Salmún Feijóo now and the nearest urban space given over to children's activities lurks underneath a motorway flyover. In the early 1930s, there was a good-sized park adjacent to the Águila chocolate factory. Its workers would sometimes play football there, and Águila employees on breaks would often provide a substantial audience for junior kickabouts. The bounce of the ball, often worn and misshapen, tended to be irregular, but there were benefits to that: the sharpening of reflexes, and resourcefulness bringing it under control.

Alfredito the urban footballer was honoured, before his tenth birthday, with a nickname. The older kids christened him 'Minellita', Little Minella, after José María Minella, a central midfield player who had represented Argentina and joined River Plate from Gimnasia y Esgrima La Plata in the mid-1930s. The resemblance was largely physical: Minella was slender, wiry. Like Bernabé Ferreyra, he had a famously fierce shot. Ferreyra might have such force in his right boot he could hospitalise a goalkeeper, but Di Stéfano heard talk that a Minella drive could 'splinter the goalposts'.

To be known as 'Minellita' by your elders felt prestigious. To be a *pibe*, an urchin kid, lining up to play alongside your elders, would have been to feel part of an important tradition for anybody reading the local press in the late 1930s. Argentinian football, enjoying unprecedented popularity and coverage in the expanding medium of radio and across the newspapers, was increasingly self-conscious, looking for signs of self-affirmation, for what might make it unique. Argentina had finished second at the 1928 Olympic football tournament, where Uruguay won the gold medal at their neighbour's expense. That, followed quickly by the advent of a professional club structure, invited all manner of opinion about how the sport should grow, define itself in a young nation aspiring to greater economic self-sufficiency.

The idea of the fearless, enterprising kid, the *pibe* who learned his skills and the codes of companionship on rough patches of urban ground with a fraying ball in his native suburb, became a trope. The day after Argentina's losing Olympic final, in Amsterdam, *Crítica* gave over a whole page to a composition by the poet Raúl González Tuñón lauding the captain of the Argentina team, Luis Monti, and investing him with a uniquely *bonaerense*, Buenos Aires spirit: 'We wait for you, Luis Monti, with our hearts in our hands like an old rag football/We, the raucous lads in the street from La Boca and Barracas, the future champions in a future that is just and fair.' A year later, an editorial in the same newspaper celebrated the fact 'nobody can be any doubt that all the barrios in the city should be proud of being the nurseries of great footballers'.

The boy who would become Argentina's greatest footballer, at least of the first 80 years of the twentieth century, found that belonging to a team helped him cast off what he always maintained was an instinctive shyness. Informal kickabouts in the shadow of the chocolate factory or at Parque Patricios, a few blocks to the west of the family home, would develop into more organised fixtures. The boys of his surrounding blocks got together and called themselves 'Unidos y Venceremos', United, We'll Win, challenged their neighbours to matches and prepared for weekend contests by marching together through the streets and chanting a song they had composed for themselves: 'I hear the sound of the ball. Who knows what will happen? We are the pibes of Barracas, who have come and are here to win.'

And they would not win quietly. Alfredito, younger and much slighter than his older team-mates, would be positioned out on the right wing, to use his speed and dexterity as a dribbler, but he was still well within earshot of the backchat exchanged by the teenagers around him. The Barracas barrio contests he later described were explosive, pugnacious, peppered with insults and often with episodes of violence. The worst offence? Cowardice. Duck out of a challenge and a player would dread being condemned with the cutting phrase: 'You sold yourself out for a sweetie.' Even in these junior contests, spectators sometimes came to blows.

As for the boys, so for the men. Argentinian's professional football, booming in many respects, did not always set a good example for its minors and its amateurs. The sport confronted several crises over the behaviour of its players and spectators in the 1930s. Fencing between the grandstands and the playing areas of the many new or expanded stadia would become a legal requirement, to combat frequent pitch invasions. In October 1933, a referee was attacked by players in the junior ranks of Independiente, an incident that could scarcely be corrected by an instruction for the miscreants to grow up and behave more like their elders. In the same month, River's ground had been closed because of fighting on the pitch during a fixture between their reserves and those of Boca Juniors, while ten footballers had been injured in a brawl during a San Lorenzo versus Talleres game.

As *La Crítica* asked during that heated spring: 'Who is in charge on the pitch? The police, or the referees?' Eduardo Forte, one of the senior Argentinian referees in the era around the switch from supposed amateurism to a professional league, had his own ideas. He was notorious for having produced a knife to defend himself during a confrontation with players and for requiring a police escort away from a Talleres match, a procedure that left four officers requiring treatment for wounds inflicted by stones hurled at Forte.

The solution would be sought from overseas. At the same time that Argentina sought and often marvelled at the increasingly indigenous character of its own football, its administrators came around to an idea that, on the field, it might be best governed by foreigners. Isaac Caswell, an experienced referee from the north of England, was the first to be hired. Several more English officials would follow. They were there to represent neutrality in a sport where suspicion of refereeing bias was widespread among fans, and to deliver British expertise, experience and cool-headedness to inflammable situations.

Analagous tensions pulled at Argentinian society. Alfredito Di Stéfano was growing up in a country where the institutions of authority were regarded with suspicion, where the interests of an aspiring, diverse working class rubbed up against those of the old establishment, landed, moneyed, imperial. Changing governments see-sawed over which group to court. There was in the 1930s an Argentina with a determination to make its own way, to celebrate what made it special; there was also another Argentina, a nation anxious not to be left vulnerable, cut off from the Europe with which most of its citizens felt a bond. And it was a country whose cities, like its stadiums, could seem alarmingly lawless.

CHAPTER 2

THE SMELL
OF DAMP EARTH

There is something defiant about the handsome two-storey house that stands set back from the rest on Avenida Carabobo, in the Buenos Aires district of Flores. On either side are smart blocks of flats, built in the 1960s or 1970s. They apply a certain squeeze on the property in between, and it answers back with the splendour of its garden, creepers that climb up and up, 20 or 30 feet, gripping the wall of the apartment building to its right. The long-term resident of this, the oldest house on the block, relates how, over the decades, she has received a number of offers to allow her patch of real estate to be turned into flats. She always says no. The home has been in her family for close to 70 years, since 1937 – a house cherished, a cache of vivid memories. Some of the plants in the garden she tends carefully have been there since the Di Stéfanos first moved in, when Norma was six.

The house in Barracas that had been the first home for all the children had become a little too small for the growing family, and this chalet, as the Flores house would have been described at the time, offered a great deal more space, not only for the three energetic offspring but for two dogs, a well-populated aviary and a coop for chickens beyond the arbour at the back of the home. The front garden looked almost as lush and well-maintained then as it would remain under Norma's watch well into the next century, with lemon trees, cedars and tall rose bushes shielding the house from the broad avenue. Some creepers were already making their way up the façade and towards the first-floor balcony immediately above the front porch. The iron pole on which the balcony was supported has been replaced with a concrete pillar, quite possibly because it suffered wear and tear in the late 1930s, as one very hyperactive boy, vaulting from the first floor, used to slide down it, like a fireman suddenly called into duty.

Alfredo junior, Norma told me one day in 2015 as she pottered about the pretty garden, could be 'a little devil' as a pre-teenager. She points to where he used to slip down the pole, now a pillar, and to the spot from where he sometimes threw stones at the trams as they rattled their way down Carabobo, chucking the pebbles and quickly concealing himself behind the garden's bushes and trees. Those sorts of mischiefs by Alfredo and his friends made enemies. He provoked the ire of the local butcher, whose shop stood on one nearby corner of Carabobo, and whose window displays would be reorganised by the boys while he wasn't looking. The man once shut Alfredo in his refrigerator, to punish and to frighten him, and he complained about the repeated taunting to the miscreant's mother, Eulalia.

At school Alfredo was given to pranks, like knotting the sleeve ends of a teacher's jacket as it hung, unattended, in the classroom, and giggling as the teacher then struggled to put his arms through them. After their move to Flores, Alfredo went to the Montes de Oca educational institution, where at least one incident led to a fierce confrontation between Alfredo senior, the protective father, and a member of staff who had struck his oldest son for some misdemeanour.

Immediately to the left of the house, an archway reaches over the driveway. That, Norma recalls, made for an adequate, if rather high crossbar for games of football, or at least for the shooting and saving contests all three Di Stéfano children would play, often with Norma put in goal. The rest of their equipment was mostly home-made. Alfredo became adept at turning the malleable packaging materials in which his father collected his freshly starched collars from the nearby Japanese tailor-cum-laundry into usable balls.

Even before the family were installed in the Flores house, Alfredo senior and Eulalia decided she need some help with childcare. As Norma Di Stéfano remembers: 'Usually it would be a girl who would do that sort of work, but at the time, my mother couldn't find one. So we had a young lad who helped around the house.' Enrique Losada was about six years older than Alfredo junior, and a Boca Juniors fan. The three children enjoyed his company, and Alfredo in particular appreciated his enthusiasm for football and his tactical and technical advice. Losada organised drills for the boys, including exercises to strengthen their weaker foot, in Alfredo's case his left. He would never become fully ambidextrous as a player, but would later thank Losada, the cheerful home help, for the tuition and advice that helped give him the advantage of being a two-footed player.

Moving from Barracas to Flores meant a new local team, Imán, and a step into the rugged world of men's football. Imán's headquarters was a local barber's shop where the proprietors had a steady stream of clients and would recruit new players as they talked sport between snips and shaves. Alfredo was initially the youngest member of the side, which included men well into their thirties. Tulio would later turn out for them as well, playing in midfield. Where matches took place would depend on the availability of a ground, or a big enough patch of park, but Imán were serious enough to have their own strip, white with green stripes, and to draw spectators, passers-by and, more regularly, the nuns from a convent next to one of the pitches they used.

Tulio had inherited some of his father's talent for the sport, though also his vulnerability to injury. That would eventually curtail what had been genuine hopes that he might go far in the game. The brothers were close. 'They got on but were quite different in a way,' Norma recalls. 'Tulio was a perhaps calmer and quieter at home. And they competed with each other: Alfredo was always very competitive about everything.' The boys were ticked off by their father for boxing too aggressively with one another. Alfredo disliked losing at anything. He would respond to setbacks by imposing his authority, as older sibling. 'If he ever lost at any sort of game, be it cards, parchís or whatever, to either of us,' remembered Norma, 'he'd say: "What do *you* know about this game, anyway?"'

To his younger brother and sister, Alfredo seemed to know a good deal about a lot of things, and liked to play the sage. In their company, he was a gossip, who often left just enough unsaid to intrigue and tantalise his audience.

Norma recalls in particular some alarming stories he told her and Tulio about a series of incidents which had affected Alfredo senior. It is possible that in the adolescent mind of Alfredito, certain details had become exaggerated, his accounts over-dramatised, but to his sister the vivid descriptions of an attempted extortion against the family seemed very real. Like his grandfather Miguel, the Alfredito who had overcome his shyness could recount a tale, and give it authority. 'Alfredo,' Norma remembers, 'always seemed to know exactly what was going on.'

Later in his life Di Stéfano would describe the same incidents in detail. The menace of the mafia, he called it, and put the dangers felt by his father in the context of the times. The 1930s would come to be known as Argentina's Decada Infame, the infamous decade, chiefly because of its political upheavals, the threats to functioning democracy of the era's military coups and a culture of government and corporate corruption. There was also an element of organised crime, thriving in the cracks created by broader social instability. Communities with Italian roots became most sensitive to it. Certain individuals and families had gathered a notoriety, particularly in the city of Rosario, from where there were lurid reports of vendettas and tussles for control of various areas of commerce. Figures like 'Chicho Grande' Galiffi, and his daughter, the green-eyed, fearless Ágata Cruz Galiffi, one of the masterminds of an attempted bank robbery in 1939 that involved digging a long underground tunnel, became household names. So were Francisco 'Chicho Chico' Marrone and Nicolás Ballestreri. A number of murders and kidnappings for ransom were attributed to these gangs.

Though Rosario remained the stronghold of Argentina's version of the Mob, there were various attempts to establish a presence in the capital, Buenos Aires. There is evidence the techniques of intimidation and patronage used by mafia groups in Italy, and indeed gangsters in Chicago and on the east coast of the United States of America, reached Argentina in the 1920s and 1930s. While some immigrants were arriving from Mussolini's Italy, others were moving south from the America of Prohibition and then the Depression, in search of opportunity. Argentina's organised labour movements and its agricultural collectives looked the sort of institutions a mafia might lucratively penetrate and exploit. A senior official of Buenos Aires's central market for potato farmers, suppliers and distributors, as Alfredo Di Stéfano senior was, would doubtless have heard the story of José Martire, a potato trader who, having defied a number of threats of blackmail from mafia heavies, had a bomb thrown at his house. He survived.

By the early 1930s the head of the Di Stéfano household was himself under threat. Norma was told by her eldest brother that their father had taken to keeping a pistol in his bedroom, and sometimes carried it on him when he set off for work. The enemies against whom he supposed it was worth protecting himself in this way included extortionists. They were demanding a proportion of the income from every truckload of potatoes that left the central market. From time to time, their menace was expressed by a warning shot or two fired at delivery vehicles. According to Alfredito, members, perhaps leaders, of one gang drew up in their Ford in front of the Di Stéfano home in Flores one day, and engaged him and Tulio in conversation, offering them sweets and small change as they chatted. The boys dutifully called for their mother, Eulalia, who emerged from the house clutching the kitchen knife she had been using to prepare a chicken for supper. The gangsters left in a hurry.

Alfredo senior held a position that made him a natural target and he clearly had means. The handsome two-storey on Carabobo spoke of wealth and social standing. A few months after the family had settled there, a pair of smartly dressed men approached Alfredo senior to offer him twice the sum for the house that he had only recently paid for it. He felt suspicious, particularly when they suggested a meeting over a possible sale, to take place at their premises rather than his. His scepticism grew when they expressed reluctance at the idea that the vendor intended to bring along a notary to the meeting, insisting that they preferred Alfredo senior to come alone. He told Eulalia he felt frightened by the encounter, and evidently he said so within earshot of his alert eldest son.

One of the suspected mafiosi in that escapade had given his surname as 'Di Carlo'. Alfredito would recall his look clearly, well over 60 years later: a man of short stature, with a well-trimmed beard. Those features stuck in his mind's eye because of a dramatic episode for the impressionable pre-teenager.

It took place during a train trip to visit cousins in the town of San Nicolás, on the route from Buenos Aires to Rosario. Alfredito, then 11 or 12 years old, was travelling with his father. All of a sudden, he felt sure he spotted the mysterious Di Carlo, seated with three other men at the opposite end of the restaurant car where the Di Stéfanos had taken their places to eat. Young Alfredo would remember the vivid alarm his father showed when his son leaned towards and him and asked softly: 'Isn't that Señor Di Carlo?' The boy was told firmly not to look in the man's direction, to keep quiet, while his father made a surprising, urgent plan for the end of their journey, some four and half hours later.

The story Alfredo recounted to his sister about what happened next, on the Buenos Aires to Rosario train, might have been drawn from the script of a western, or indeed from any one of the films that at that time were attracting large audiences in Argentina; movies like José García Silva's *Asesinos* (Assassins) or Ugo Anselmi's *Bajo La Garra De La Mafia* (In the Grip of the Mafia), or from one of the plays that filled the theatres of Buenos Aires, like *Maffia* and *Don Chicho*. Shortly before the train drew into San Nicolás, late at night, Alfredo senior discreetly placed his luggage just outside the restaurant car. As the train began to slow for the San Nicolás stop and other passengers made ready to disembark, the two Di Stéfanos remained in their seats, as if, like the four men at the other end of the carriage, they were staying on board all the way to Rosario. In a flash, the father grasped his son firmly by the arm, pushed him quickly through the door towards the exit, and, with the wheels still turning, and the platform still some way ahead, clutched his son by his belt, grabbed his suitcase and they jumped off, the pair of them tumbling through a bush and onto the ground until a fence broke their momentum. There they stayed, concealed behind a hedge, until the rest of the San Nicolás passengers had disembarked by more orthodox means. The train rumbled on, with Di Carlo and the other suspected gangsters still on board, headed for Rosario, the Chicago of South America.

When father and son finally reached the home of their relatives, in San Nicolás, they were greeted with curious questions about why they had arrived so late. Alfredo senior explained. He was advised to sort out his difficulties with the mafia, put an end to the fearfulness that was threatening to shape the family's lives. He did so. How? Alfredo junior grew up believing his father had eventually yielded to the extortionists, that for some of his time at the potato market, regular sums were given to the mafia heavies, to their protection racket. Norma is not so sure. 'I don't know if my father paid, or not,' she recalls with a shrug.

Whatever the compromise, the Di Stéfanos had their reasons to uproot again, or at least spend most of their time in a more rural environment, at arm's length from organised crime, the political turbulence and social tensions concentrating in Argentina's mostly densely populated areas. But when Alfredo senior determined that, although they would keep the Flores house, a more bucolic life would best suit the family, he was running against the tide. The Great Depression was impacting on the Argentinian economy.

It negatively affected agricultural exports, and the crisis drove hundreds of thousands from the countryside to the cities in search of an alternative livelihood. Alfredo senior took the opposite path, choosing to go into farming, and bought himself a plot of land around a spacious ranch just outside the town of Los Cardales, about a two-hour journey north-west of Buenos Aires.

It was here that his eldest son would develop several of his passions, notably his love for what he later rather poetically described as 'the smell of damp earth'. But in setting off there he strongly sensed that the move would make the possibility of his becoming an elite footballer, a professional sportsman, far more remote.

Los Cardales used to be known as 'Little Cordoba'. That was an endorsement of its charms. Its clean air is appreciated even today by *bonaerenses* who can afford a second home or bear a long daily commute into the capital. In the first half of the twentieth century it was especially recommended for those whose lungs had suffered in the city, in an era when tuberculosis was liable to shorten lives, painfully. Los Cardales has many delights still, a place of twee boutiques and coffee shops, with country club estates stretching across its outskirts. The Di Stéfanos' former home could pass as one of those, but remains in private hands, largely unchanged since the family occupied it. The farmhouse, with its terracotta-tiled roof, is set back from the main road, a few miles outside the centre of Los Cardales, at the end of a drive of around 400 metres with maize fields either side.

The relocation to the countryside meant significant change for young Alfredo. By the time he was 14 his formal schooling was effectively taking second place to the vocation lined up for him by his father: agriculture. His apprenticeship would be rigorous. He and Tulio worked hard under their parents' watch. They rose before dawn and, heaving large oil lamps through the dark, made their way to the dairy to milk the cows. As the herd grew, so the Di Stéfano boys took on greater responsibilities, eventually supervising the work of hired farmhands. They were tasked with managing the pigs. If that sounds a little grim – and it was certainly arduous, mucky work – there was a certain gaucho glamour to the new life. The boys had to be alert to the threat of rustlers and robbers; they had space to explore, territory to tame. Alfredo would pick thistles and gouge out of them the pulpy fruit whose taste he grew to love. He would let his imagination carry him into adventures. He had by then become a devoted reader of the *Martín Fierro* epics, tales depicting an heroic Argentinian ideal: a courageous, noble, resourceful figure.

The physical demands were considerable. One job the boys took on with some relish would be the breaking-in of horses, a challenge that could carry some perils as well as building up a teenager's thigh, calf and upper body muscles. Alfredo junior had a series of attritional duels and tugs-of-war with a horse named 'Sulki', soon known around the farm as 'Devil' for his wilfulness and rebellious instincts. The steed became a project, a combatant he felt determined to overcome. At least one of young Alfredo's expeditions into town to buy groceries would be abandoned, when, having harnessed Sulki to a tilbury carriage, the horse reared up, broke free of his tether and left the apprentice horse-whisperer ducking away from a carriage wheel that spun violently towards his head.

The Di Stéfanos had arrived in Los Cardales as outsiders, and their new home was located a long walk from the hub of the community. The family aroused some curiosity, particularly at the main gathering point for *cardaleños*, the bar on the corner of Rivadavia Street and 25th of May Avenue, facing Plaza Mitre. The proprietor, one Alfino Di Yorio, had purchased the elegant corner building in the 1920s and adapted it to his needs and passions. Alfino Di Yorio and his sons Titin and Atilio were keen players of pelota, a sport most associated with the Basque region of southern Europe, exported to Argentina during the wave of immigration of the nineteenth century. A little like open-air squash, but using baskets instead of racquets, it needs a sizeable space with a high wall, one of which was constructed at the back of Bar Di Yorio.

At the front, members of the town's amateur football team would gather, over coffees or liquor, to talk about selection, plan fixtures, and sigh about the difficulties they faced in matches against stronger teams from bigger towns. As Alfino's son Atilio, a stalwart of the team from his teens, recounted to his own sons, Alfredo and Alberto, the players became intrigued by the Di Stéfanos. They discovered the new local landowner had turned out in his younger days for River Plate; they saw his two sons had enthusiasm for the game, as well as athleticism, talent and what sounded like a unique practice regime.

Alberto Di Yorio, a vivacious raconteur, describes what first made his father, Atilio, and the other members of the Los Cardales club, interested in the Di Stéfano boys as potential team-mates. 'They used to do these training drills, which seemed almost professional,' he recalls his father telling him. 'Along the drive leading to their farmhouse, there was an avenue of trees planted on either side, at regular intervals. Alfredo senior would stand at one end, giving instructions as the two boys, one of them on either side of the driveway, each dribbled the ball up and down, doing their *gambetas*, their slaloms, back and forth, controlling the ball either side of the trees.' Zig-zagging between the cedars, urged on by his father to strengthen his left foot, Alfredito had, it seemed, brought an impressive sort of sporting professionalism to the rural backwater.

Both Di Stéfano boys were soon deemed far too useful to be corralled for long in Los Cardales's under-18 side. As they had with Imán, the barrio team in Flores, Alfredo and Tulio would spend their weekends with men of various ages, playing and practising, and learning about the region and its rivalries and hierarchies. They heard how matches against the team from the town of Escobar should be approached with caution, and a little awe.

Fixtures were a focus of the town's social life, with a good proportion of residents gathering on the bleachers set up along one of the touchlines of the town's pitch, a short walk from the Bar Di Yorio down Los Cardales's main central avenue. Once Alfredo junior and Tulio were established in the side, Alfredo senior became a distinctive presence, too. He would take up a position on the touchline facing the seated spectators, on his feet throughout and animated. 'My father used to say he was like a "caged lion",' Alberto Di Yorio testifies, a little wide-eyed. 'He would stand and jump around on the opposite side of the pitch from the rest of the people watching, coaching his two sons, shouting at them: "Tulio, do this!" or "Alfredo, get over there!" But he would only ever give instructions to those two. He wasn't trying to coach the team, or take over, just trying to teach his sons the right way of doing things.'

If matches meant some stressful moments for Alfredo senior, his sons' talents made the Di Stéfanos welcome members of the community. Norma gained a reputation as a demanding spectator. As Atilio Di Yorio told his sons, the sister of the starlets used to arrive at the bar with her parents before kick-off, ready to join the other supporters and relatives. She would then announce she would only be going to the game on condition she was given a bag of nuts and sunflower seeds to nibble.

There were other rituals. On matchdays, the Di Stéfanos' journey, some three miles from the farm to the centre of town, would be undertaken jogging by Alfredo and Tulio. The procession made for quite a spectacle. The boys would lead the way, in shorts and football shirts, as if acting as an escort, ahead of the horse-drawn tilbury steered by their father, with Eulalia and Norma seated beside him. 'They were professionals before their time,' explains Alberto Di Yorio. 'They would use those runs as their form of warm-up for the match. None of the others in the team did anything like that.'

The Di Stéfano boys, although younger than their team-mates, raised standards. Alfredo, mostly used on the wing, from where he could put into practice the *gambetas* and feints he rehearsed around the trees of his driveway, contributed a number of goals to Los Cardales's rising reputation in the regional competition. The town would, two decades later, become very proud that it was once the home of Argentina's most celebrated sporting export of the post-war years. In the Bar Di Yorio, the sepia photograph of the 1943 Los Cardales team featuring Alfredo and Tulio Di Stéfano is prominently displayed. There are other souvenirs of Alfredo's later professional career, given by him to the Di Yorio family, with whom he remained in contact long after Titin and Atilio Di Yorio's deaths – but not the boots he wore during his time as the upstart winger of Los Cardales. Those were inherited by Atilio, and duly treasured. They are not preserved as an exhibit in the bar: so reluctant was Atilio to ever replace them, he utterly wore them out.

Los Cardales would never again have as good a team as they did in 1943, with the precocious Di Stéfano brothers in the line-up, the Di Yorio brothers in support, the vocal Alfredo Di Stéfano senior on the touchline. They triumphed in that year's regional championship, and confirmed their first-place finish thanks to a tense victory against those feared rivals, Escobar.

Over the years, a myth took hold that the winning goal came from Alfredito Di Stéfano, then 17, via an inspired overhead kick, of the type he would execute in front of cameras and tens of thousands of witnesses later in his career. But that goal against Escobar apparently had nothing of the magic and spectacle it was adorned with by decades of extended Chinese whispers around a small provincial town. 'The story of the Di Stéfano volley is pure folklore,' reckons Alfredo Di Yorio, careful curator of his father's and uncle's memories. 'That goal came about after a messy, failed clearance in the Escobar defence. It eventually rebounded over the goal-line off my dad's backside.'

CHAPTER 3

WELCOME TO THE MACHINE

If, on the mornings they rose before dawn to the sounds of the farmyard, the Di Stéfanos' decision to up sticks felt like a radical change, theirs was not an absolute exile. The family maintained a connection with Buenos Aires. The house on Avenida Carabobo was still theirs, a base when business or pleasure called Alfredo senior or Eulalia to the capital. Every now and then at weekends the whole troop would catch the tram from Flores to River Plate's imposing new stadium, built with the help of a soft loan endorsed by the Argentinian government, on the same site as today's Monumental arena. One vivid memory that stayed with Alfredo junior was of witnessing River play against the visiting Colo Colo side, from Chile; another, of the time the next day's newspaper pictured him and his father together in the grandstands in the background of an action photograph.

The Di Stéfano children were gripped by the professional game, by River Plate, by the peaks and troughs of River's league rivals, by the elite players of a sport that had developed a self-confidence, amid a growing belief that, in Argentina, some of the best football in the world was being played. In the Bar Di Yorio in Los Cardales, a large radio, a sophisticated model for the period but still with a huge, curled trumpet of a speaker, took up substantial space on the corner of the bar. According to the stories passed down by Titin and Atilio Di Yorio, Alfredo junior would regularly take up a seat with his ear close to the set, to listen to live reports from River's fixtures. Like much of the nation, he was drawn to the vivid descriptions of the commentator Lalo Pelliciari. And like much of Argentina, he felt in thrall to the attacking talent of the River team of the early 1940s.

River had inherited the adhesive nickname 'Los Millonarios' with the coming of professionalism, because of the sums they invested on players like the explosive centre-forward Bernabé 'The Beast' Ferreyra and his creative accomplice, Carlos 'Barullo' (or 'Disorder') Peucelle, who helped the club to three national titles in the 1930s. Peucelle, whose sobriquet was entirely complimentary, pointing to his gifts of improvisation, unpredictability, his capacity to spread chaos through opposition defences, would also be part of the side that won the 1941 title. He would go on to have as great an influence on the next decade in his roles as coach, strategist and sharp-eyed talent-spotter.

Without Peucelle's astute guidance and progressive under-standing of the game there might never have been 'La Máquina', or The Machine, the nickname given to the quintet of footballers, Juan Carlos Muñoz, José Manuel Moreno, Adolfo Pedernera, Ángel Labruna and Félix Loustau who made up the River forward line in the early to mid-1940s, finessing the cerebral style of Peucelle, and making the forceful finishing of Ferreyra look passé and clunky. These five would become an emblem for sporting panache throughout South America. There are various notions about who first coined the term 'La Máquina' for River, although one sturdy claim on the copyright belongs to 'Borocotó', nom de plume of Ricardo Lorenzo Rodríguez, the high-profile journalist from *El Gráfico*, a magazine which by the 1940s was enjoying its golden age as narrator, shaper and sometimes sermoniser of everything to do with Argentinian football.

Once River had been christened 'La Máquina', the nickname stuck. It carried little connotation of grinding efficiency; rather, it celebrated invention. River's front five resembled a machine for the fluency of their movement, the smooth interlocking of their cogs and their precision in passing and opening up space, although not always in their seizing of league titles. La Máquina: in an age of technological advance, where the magic of radio could spread vivid word of great football matches, and bring to the ears of listeners the length and breadth of a nation the latest tangos, here was advanced technology in human, sporting form.

They had charisma, too, the five musketeers of La Máquina. On the right wing was Muñoz. He had strong *pibe* credentials, a backstory and style that easily classified him as a product of rough, urban pitches, and quick-witted, streetwise instincts. He had been spotted playing at unfashionable Dock Sud, one of several Buenos Aires clubs whose prestige had fallen during the transformation from amateur football to professionalism. He was encouraged to move to River by a then ambitious member of the board, Antonio Vespucio Liberti, later River's president. Liberti had seen speed and nimble close control, from a low centre of gravity, in the diminutive Muñoz. He played with his head up and an obvious relish for one-on-one duels. He usually emerged from them with the ball exactly where he wanted it and gave the impression he had already anticipated his next action: a sprint, or a cross, or a return pass. Most of the several times he featured on the cover of *El Gráfico* – to have your portrait on the magazine's cover was an accolade; many players apparently kept as close count of the number of *Gráfico* front pages as of their goals or titles – he is pictured preparing to cross. His eyes and gaze are almost always set in the middle distance, fixing on their target, trusting his right foot to connect sweetly with the ball, sure of his bearings.

'Muñoz's classic manoeuvre was to go past his marker, and then deliver a cross, cut back while at full speed,' recalls Amadeo Carrizo, who established himself as River's goalkeeper in the mid-1940s and kept the position for over 20 years. 'From that manoeuvre, the team scored so many goals.' Indeed, so reliable, so clockwork, so mechanised was La Máquina's impetus from the right wing that the supporters created a rhyming ditty to celebrate the inevitability of the Muñoz assist. '*Sale el sol, sale la luna, centro de Muñoz, gol de Labruna*,' went the rhyme. 'The sun rises, the moon comes up, Muñoz crosses, Labruna scores.' Sometimes, at the stadium, the verse would be accompanied by instruments, if any of the celebrated tango musicians who followed River had come along for the afternoon.

Labruna, operating in principle as the inside-left of the quintet, scored plenty. His figures as a finisher endure into the twenty-first century. Only Arsenio Erico, the Paraguayan whose command of Argentinian penalty areas spanned the 1930s and early 1940s, accumulated more top-flight goals in the country's domestic football than Labruna's 293 for River. Labruna had a greater range to his game than Ferreyra, the barrelly centre-forward of the pre-Máquina River, and a dandy aspect, with his impudent face and neatly trimmed moustache.

Labruna had been associated with River from the age of 8, played for them until he was 41 and would later coach them to a handful of titles in the 1970s. The son of a watchmaker, who apparently pressed his son Ángel to follow him into the trade, he had an uncanny sense of timing, of anticipation. As a child, he had been an able basketball player. His strong thighs, which gave him a high spring from a standing or running start, would be useful in the penalty area. Those crosses from Muñoz, and others, frequently found the head of Labruna as well as his instep.

For colleagues, Labruna had a compelling aura of certainty about his work, and a presence in the dressing-room. He cracked jokes, liked a wager and regaled colleagues with anecdotes of his latest trip to the race track. He had superstitions. Carrizo, who would spend many years facing Labruna's shots in training, defines him as 'a born, instinctive goalscorer. He interpreted very early where every move was going to end up. And that's where he would position himself. He had this ritual, that just before the game started he would need to score with his last shot in practice.' River supporters, like the Di Stéfanos, would learn to observe that moment, take it as an omen. 'He would do that every Sunday, and almost never failed,' adds Carrizo.

'Labruna was the one who finished off the work the others had done,' wrote Peucelle, the River player turned scout and coach. The member of the quintet whom Peucelle perhaps most admired, though, was the left-winger, Loustau. Peucelle had retired himself at 33, once he saw River had a nursery of young players ready to take up the baton of attacking inventiveness he had brought to the team. Peucelle was self-effacing, discreet; Loustau had about him the same mix of the introvert off the pitch and wizard on it. A dozen years as his team-mate persuaded Carrizo that Loustau was 'the finest left-winger Argentina has ever produced'. That's a judgement taking in the entire second half of the twentieth century and the first 15 years of the new millennium. 'He had great speed, but also the ability to brake suddenly, and accelerate fast from a standing start', adds Carrizo.

Loustau acquired the nickname 'Chaplin', after Charlie, icon of the silent movie era, in part because of his posture, his head often leaning to one side. He could also bring great wit to his football. One vivid story about La Máquina's relish for the spectacular gesture comes from an exhibition match they played in Tucumán, in the north-west of the country. So high had been the demand for seats that the stadium was alarmingly overcrowded. Mounted police tried to secure the perimeter of the pitch and at one point, launching one of his runs, Loustau apparently passed the ball between the front and hind legs of a horse that had strayed over the touchline. Loustau himself then ducked under the belly of the creature and emerged, ball at his feet, to take on his next, human opponent.

Like Muñoz on the opposite wing, he had the assets and the confidence to contribute well beyond the space between the touchline and the edge of the penalty area. His capacity for physical endurance was a source of wonder for those who trained with him. To Peucelle, the *pibe* turned project-leader, the slender, wiry Loustau epitomised *lucha*, or struggle, or sheer will to win. 'The capacity for *lucha* is not a physical quality,' explained Peucelle. 'It is a spiritual condition. There are strong people who don't have *lucha*, and there are people who appear weak, for being small, with an enormous capacity for *lucha*. I believe there is no better example of that than Félix Loustau, an exceptional case where the conditions for *lucha* are all brought together. He could look at an opponent as if to say: "Come on then, because when I get to you, you're going to lose this battle."'

Loustau inspired wonder on the pitch, for his guile and for the back-and-forth energy he gave to his wing play, yet colleagues were often mystified about Loustau the private man. Star though he became for tens of thousands, showman though he could be with River's red stripe across his chest, in the off-duty time he was obliged to share with his colleagues he was regarded as remote. During one week, in the prime of River's 1940s excellence, the squad became concerned when for three successive days, Loustau, famed for his diligence, failed to show for training, and indeed, to turn up on the morning of a matchday. So Peucelle travelled to his home in the district of Avellaneda, knocked on the door and found his twinkle-toed left-winger at the top of the stairs with a broom in his hand, carrying out some housework.

'Félix, what's up?' Peucelle asked the player. 'Nothing,' replied Loustau, 'it's just that I got married last Thursday.' Peucelle, entitled to think he knew Loustau as well as anybody who worked with him, was amazed. 'And you didn't tell anyone?' No, came the reply, followed by an assurance that he'd be along for the match that afternoon, where he duly performed to his customary high standards.

Most of the behind-the-scenes stories that intrigued fans of River Plate, like the Di Stéfanos of Flores and Los Cardales, tended to be of a different flavour, and far more racy. They were not about Loustau. The other two members of La Máquina's fabled front five, Pedernera and Moreno, were cut from a very different cloth. Their individual brilliance on the ball and the swagger with which they enjoyed their football made them conspicuous on the pitch. So did their profiles beyond it. One declaration from Moreno, made at the peak of a playing career that lasted until he was 44, has almost come to represent the Argentinian zeitgeist of the 1940s, a decade when, for all the country's political instability, the people could enjoy dazzling entertainment at football stadiums and dance-halls.

'Tango,' Moreno said, 'is the best sort of training. It teaches rhythm, you switch direction while on the run, you're moving all parts of your body, and you're exercising your stomach muscles and your legs.' There may be merit in the analysis, but there were times when Moreno had to offer the argument not so much as a philosophical position, or an advice in physical conditioning, but as an excuse. His bohemian tendencies were famous. He drank. His friends were tango artists and performers on stage and screen. His lovers were film stars and daughters of Argentina's artistic aristocracy. His marriage to the actress Pola Alonso endorsed his celebrity status.

A handsome, tall and imposing man, with slicked back hair, a moustache and a prominent nose that bore the evidence of a break sustained boxing in his teens, Moreno kept his own hours. He was the oldest of La Máquina's quintet, 26 when River won the 1942 league title, and his late nights and epicurean appetites were part of Moreno's legend even as Muñoz, Loustau and Labruna were still making their way up through River's youth ranks.

Part of Moreno's legend comes from the loyalty he inspired among team-mates. In 1939, River Plate disciplined him for what they decided was his unprofessional preparation ahead of a top-of-the-league meeting with Independiente, suspending him after a 3–2 home defeat. Several of his senior colleagues went out on strike in sympathy, refusing to play for the remaining two months of the season. River, in their absence, could not catch Racing, who finished champions. There was one upside to the kerfuffle: Labruna, then 21, was among those accelerated into the first team to cover for the indignant refuseniks. He scored seven goals in nine matches.

Moreno had none of Labruna's one-club devotion to River. By the end of a picaresque career, Moreno had compiled as promiscuous a list of employers as he had romantic liaisons. The son of a policeman, he had grown up a fan of Boca Juniors. Early rejection by that club led to him to River, their chief rivals, but then he left for an adventure playing in Mexico in 1944, returning to a hero's welcome at River two years later. He then hopscotched across Latin America: to Universidad Católica in Chile, where they too had him back enthusiastically for a second spell, either side of a contract with Boca, by which time he was in his 35th year.

But he was hardly tiring by then, or looking to settle into the sort of cosy, domestic life a Loustau might have longed for. Moreno had cachet as an international superstar, and took up offers to play in Uruguay and for a long period in Colombia before he moved on to the next thing, which included a part in the 1960 feature film, *El Crack*, about a young, aspiring footballer. Moreno played a worldly and wise senior, some of whose lines in the dressing-room scenes are delivered while wearing nothing but a pair of swimming briefs. The director José Martínez Suárez anticipated audiences swooning: The torso on display is not that of a man in his forties whom two decades of carousing have left wheezing or flabby.

Some of the tales handed down through four generations about Moreno depict him as almost superhuman. There was the day he defied a doctor's warning that, suffering the toxic after-effects of excessive alcohol consumption, if he took part in River's next match, against Racing Club de Avellaneda, he risked dying on the field. He completed the 90 minutes and, by Loustau's account, outperformed everybody else. There was the afternoon he was struck, during an away game in front of a pugnacious crowd at Tigres, by a large stone smuggled into the ground from the nearby railway line and then hurled with deadly aim at the tallest target in the River forward line. His face bleeding profusely, he refused treatment, explaining: 'If the medics come and give me treatment on the pitch, they'll take me off on a stretcher. I won't give them the satisfaction. Imagine: they'd be singing at every match from now on, "We *got* to Moreno".'

Two-footed, he could shoot with explosive force but preferred, where possible to stroke or glide the ball past the opposing goalkeeper. He was a formidably powerful header of the ball. For Carrizo, the River goalkeeper for Moreno's second spell at the club, he has to be bracketed with the top three or four footballers in Argentina's history. 'He is with the greats, and that's *the* greats,' says Carrizo. That is to say, he should be regarded next to Diego Maradona, Lionel Messi and Di Stéfano.

The secret of La Máquina's fluency was said to be the complicity of the fabled quintet, a telepathic communion. It was not always replicated by their relationships outside the workplace. Loustau kept to himself. Labruna and Pedernera did not get on especially well privately. But Pedernera and Moreno did seem to enjoy one another's company. If anybody could try to keep up with Moreno on a night out, Pedernera seems to have had sufficient social stamina, the required independence of spirit, and bon vivant inclinations.

Pedernera's influence on the way River played in the 1940s, meanwhile, was second to nobody's. 'He regulated the pace of a game,' Carrizo remembers, 'he was a strategist. You look back at the goals scored by La Máquina and so many came from mathematically calculated passes that ended up at Labruna. He struck the ball more precisely than anyone, and could pass it over long distances with such accuracy.'

Pedernera had started his career as a winger, with a magic wand of a left foot. The coach Peucelle had the idea that his broad vision, his sixth sense and his eye for a pass could be better used in a position where he would receive more of the ball, particularly once Loustau had made his case for commandeering River's left flank. So he encouraged Pedernera to take the central role in attack, but not with a brief to play as the most advanced point, as would be expected of the number nine in what was essentially a W-M formation – two defenders, three midfielders, and five across the front line – but with a licence to drop much deeper than was conventional. Peucelle, ever alive to ways to disrupt the straight-line thinking of opponents, trusted Pedernera to give a fresh interpretation to the role. In the twenty-first century, his revision of the centre-forward position might have had him referred to as a 'false nine', dropping deep, picking up possession in midfield.

Peucelle and Pedernera would talk strategy at length, and at times their discussion might have sounded like the discourse of a tango instructor, marking out steps. Peucelle recalled one conversation with Pedernera about the tempo of the team's play like this: 'We were on the subject of the way we linked up and the speed of our passing. Pedernera would say what we need was a principle of three short passes and then launch a longer one. I proposed two short passes, then one long. But the rhythm Aldolfo wanted was best suited to the players. With two short passes you give the others less time to make their runs, and you risk a bit of security, you risk losing the ball, and losing your organisation. The downside is that delay gives defenders the chance to organise themselves.'

Some defenders from River's rivals cottoned on, in time, that the key to interrupting La Máquina might be to suffocate Pedernera, to police his unorthodox movements, even if it meant straying from their own orthodox zones as markers. The theory was one thing, the practice another. One of the world's best markers, the Uruguay captain Obdulio Varela would time and again find himself up against Pedernera, in Uruguay–Argentina matches or meetings between Varela's club, Peñarol, and River, and he ranked him as the best in the world. Just ahead of the 1950 World Cup final, Varela declared that the prospect of facing a glittering Brazil forward line at the Maracanã stadium seemed a far less intimidating prospect than policing River Plate and Argentina's drifting playmaker had been in the decade before. 'Why would I be nervous about Brazil?' Varela asked. 'Remember, I faced Pedernera. I assure you nobody matches his standards.'

In the era of La Máquina, River cherished possession, and they seemed to be innovating. They played with wingers who could interchange positions with inside-forwards, had a number nine who would initiate moves from where the anchor midfielder would normally be sizing up a pass. They were lauded for their mesmeric circulation of the ball, and championed in the pages of *El Gráfico* and *Crítica* for guiding Argentinian football in a sophisticated direction, and markedly away from the direct, straight-lined game associated with the English inventors of the sport.

Equally, they could seem over-indulgent, at least to their supporters. They were The Machine, but also 'Los Caballeros de Angustia', The Knights of Anxiety, not for giving off symptoms of nervousness in their own work, but for those days where, even when outpassing the opposition, they frustrated their audience with a lack of urgency, leaving an impression that the mastering of possession, the racking up of sequences of 15, 16, 17 passes were more rewarding to the players than the conversion of goals, that the seductive dance meant more than the conquest itself. Pedernera would in time suffer for this perception, some River fans identifying him as the man responsible for too much dallying, when he needed more directness. He had many, many gifts, but electric speed was not one, especially in his mature years.

La Máquina had individual record-breakers, like Labruna, in their ranks, but they did not accumulate title after title. The lauded

River Plate of the first half of the 1940s won the championship in 1941 and 1942, but only regained that title again in 1945, after successively finishing behind Boca. The league was sharply competitive at its summit. At the top of the domestic game, Boca, San Lorenzo and Independiente set high standards, both for the football played by their first XI and their nurturing of young talent. Muñoz, Moreno, Pedernera, Labruna and Loustau would be remembered as a special quintet, but they were not a species apart; they just combined so well when they did line up together. And that was not as often as the fame they acquired might suggest. What with injuries, and with Moreno skipping off to Mexico for a season in 1945, those five actually only appeared in the same eleven 18 times over five years.

For a teenager cherishing his trips to River's stadium, or eagerly listening to reports via the radio of the Bar Di Yorio on La Máquina's triumphs and trials, Muñoz, Moreno, Pedernera, Labruna and Loustau seemed an enduring unit. Theirs were names to excite the imagination. Into his eighties, Alfredo Di Stéfano used to answer enquiries about what was the best forward line he ever saw by listing the names most associated with La Máquina: Muñoz. 'El Charro' Moreno. 'El Maestro' Pedernera. Labruna. 'Chaplin' Loustau.

This teenager could identify with all of them, position by position. In his various amateur teams, urban and rural, Alfredito Di Stéfano had played on the right wing, like Muñoz, and on the left wing, like Loustau; he had played inside-forward, like the idol Moreno and the poacher Labruna. He had operated in the middle of the attack, if not in quite as roving or as liberated a role as 'El Maestro' Pedernera. One day, leaving a River fixture, he turned to Tulio, his brother, and said: 'They can really play.' He then added: 'But so can we. We could be doing that one day.'

Out on the farm in Los Cardales, Alfredo di Stéfano senior had plenty of alternative roles for his crack team of sons than as would-be Morenos or Pederneras. The population of the drove of pigs, whose management was specifically delegated to Alfredo junior and Tulio, grew to well over a hundred. The boys stood to gain a significant share of monies raised from the sale of each animal. Their father was introducing them to the business of agriculture with trust, and motivating them with bonuses. If he became excited patrolling the touchline when his boys played football on a Sunday, the rest of the week he was the stern, careful educator in the serious matter of real work.

Football man though he was, and River player though he had been, there was in Alfredo senior a strong resistance to his sons' becoming dreamily carried away about a career in the sport, albeit a sport that changed enormously since he had briefly performed at its elite level. River in the 1940s looked very different than River had in 1913, for a start. Alfredo senior played his handful of matches in a jersey of red and white stripes; River had since adopted the single diagonal red band. In his era, he had represented a club with fewer than 700 members. By the 1940s, River had tens of thousands.

The footballers Alfredo senior knew as contemporaries all needed other jobs, a full-time profession, a proper trade. One, Alejando Luraschi, who had been River's main goalkeeper for three years until 1910 and helped their promotion to the top division, had set himself up as an electrician. An unusually small man for a keeper, Luraschi knew Alfredo senior from way back, but it was somewhat by chance he crossed paths with his family again in 1944. Eulalia had travelled to Buenos Aires to the house in Flores and encountered a problem with the wiring. Luraschi the electrician was summoned to sort it out.

They fell into conversation, and Eulalia described to Luraschi her eldest son's passion for the sport, and for River. She praised his talent. Luraschi, still close to the club, resolved to talk to Peucelle's team of scouts and junior coaches and try to organise a trial for young Alfredo. At some risk of displeasing the head of the household, Eulalia passed on the news to Alfredo junior, who then pestered her each time she travelled to the city, desperate for an update, for the latest from Luraschi the fixer. At last, a letter arrived, requesting the presence of the 17-year-old at River's arena on a warm March afternoon in 1944.

Di Stéfano caught the train down to Buenos Aires. From there he went to the house in Flores, feeling a little apprehensive, caught the tram number 88 to River's stadium, now for the first time as auditioner, not to stand in the audience. The nerves would be soothed a little by spotting a fellow passenger in exactly the same frame of mind, who embarked at the stop by the cemetery, his football boots wrapped in a newspaper. Di Stéfano introduced himself, and learned his fellow candidate for a place in River's youth system went by the name of Salvucci. They were the same age. Both thought that inside-right was where they played at their best. Naturally, as that was the dashing Moreno's position.

By Di Stéfano's estimation, there were around 300 triallists at River's headquarters that day, a daunting number even if they were spread over distinct age groups, effectively trying out for River's third, or fourth, or fifth teams. The elite division of Argentinian football was organised so that a club's junior and reserve teams played one another in parallel with the fixtures of the senior side, with the back-up or youth teams playing curtain-raisers to the main event. The leading clubs ran several teams below the level of the first XI.

Surveying the trial of Di Stéfano, Salvucci and the mass of other teenagers was Peucelle, green-fingered cultivator of football talent, expert in planting seedlings and hothousing them. At the end of the session fewer than ten were invited to return for a second examination. Di Stéfano waited for Salvucci outside and found his new companion equally satisfied. As they left the stadium the pair had been beckoned over by Peucelle, who asked for their details and instructed them to return two days later. They would catch the tram back together and excitedly anticipate the next stage in the adventure.

To Alfredo Di Stéfano senior, the news was not entirely welcome. Once his eldest son then passed through a second trial, to Peucelle and the other River coaches' evident satisfaction, he made his views plain. Playing football in Buenos Aires while the rest of the family were based in Los Cardales represented a distraction, he felt, a time-consuming deviation from their work, and the apprenticeships Alfredo junior was progressing through in the countryside. As Norma Di Stéfano recalls: 'My father simply didn't think football was the right sort of profession.'

The notion of earning a decent living through football seemed remote to the head of the household. Granted, the top of the profession could make a man, if not spectacularly wealthy, more than comfortably off. But there were other concerns in Alfredo senior's mind. He was entitled to regard the lifestyles of some of Argentinian football's new superstar class as a little bohemian. He felt protective, as Alfredo junior would learn as he climbed the rungs of River's hierarchy. Alfredo senior could be a tough negotiator, and his anxiety about the danger of his son being exploited by a sport whose stakeholders included men with an eye on power and profit led him to act cautiously, just as he had when he was made to feel beholden to Buenos Aires mafiosi.

Alfredo senior made his case against his son's committing himself to River Plate, to football. Alfredito would not back down. In the end, the father put a high degree of trust in his 17-year-old son by agreeing he could join the club. Once Di Stéfano had registered himself with River, a threshold moment in his career, he was required to be available, naturally, at weekends for matches with his age-group squad, and for practice at least two days a week. Sometimes that was feasible from Los Cardales, but it made more practical sense for Alfredo to stay overnight in the large house in Avenida Carabobo, and catch the tram to training. The young man was about to become very independent, living much of the time on his own, cooking for himself and organising his timetable.

He picked up a few quirky bachelor habits, like buying a slice of pizza on the way home of an evening, in order to eat it for his breakfast. But there was a single-mindedness, a dedication about him that seems to have steered him clear of choices that might have distracted him from his ambitions to succeed at his sport. He was no monk, evidently, because his social life included occasional, rather formal dates with young women of his age and evenings listening to tango and dancing, though by his own admission he was no dashing Moreno on the dancefloor.

Di Stéfano was initially assigned a place in River's fourth XI, for 17- and 18-year-olds. He would quickly find himself rubbing shoulders with the seniors of La Máquina. An early encounter with Moreno as the wannabes and the first-team's grandees crossed paths at practice left Alfredo with a crumb of counsel. The country's most glamorous footballer approached as the teenager was pulling on his socks, and advised him to take precautions against injury. He had noticed the apprentice did not wrap his ankles in a support bandage. Moreno showed him one, and how to apply it, pulling the fabric hard and taut around the joint. 'You know,' Moreno told Di Stéfano, 'there are some rough, stony grounds you'll be playing on.'

When Moreno, the epitome of sporting machismo, offered advice on some of the hidden perils of the tough environment Di Stéfano was entering and on how to guard against those dangers, it paid to listen. Moreno gave him a further piece of advice: 'Before they get a chance to kill, kill them.' Di Stéfano would remember that, arm himself with it, an axiom for life.

Peucelle, principally overseeing the youth teams and reserves, liked the first team to set an example, to stimulate the wide-eyed initiates: La Máquina as mentors. At that stage Renato Cesarini, a former River striker who had played for Juventus in Italy in the 1930s, held the post of head coach of the first team, but took advice from Peucelle about who might be rising through the ranks. Peucelle's idea was that the tactical and stylistic principles should be consistent through each stratum of the club's system, to make smoother the promotion of younger footballers up a level or two. Peucelle wanted the younger players to aspire to a place alongside Moreno, Pedernera, Labruna, Muñoz and Loustau, but he had also developed some dogmas about how to pace the development of the athletes under his charge. 'The right time to bring up a very young player is when the team is doing well,' he later wrote. 'If the team is in a slump of form, a kid straight out of trials is not going to save it. He'll end up slumping with the rest.

'You should avoid,' he continued, 'incorporating more than one new young player in the senior side at a time, and you have to be careful about too much switching between one level and another. If a young player does keep moving from a reserve team to the first team and back, you have to explain carefully why. You have to keep up their morale.' As motivator and teacher, Peucelle would be cherished by the young Di Stéfano; but the teenager was impatient, too, to move up the ranks.

In 1944 River's Fourths were challenging for the domestic title, feeding off the chase for the senior championship being maintained by La Máquina. Matchdays consisted of several games, so the junior XIs of each club would play in the morning, against the junior XIs of the club who were River's opponents that day, or in the hours before the main event. That meant even the 17-year-olds would often perform in front of decent-sized crowds, spectators who had come to the stadium early.

Di Stéfano made a good early impression, and he stood out because of his blond hair. His contemporary, the goalkeeper Carrizo, who had gained a place in the River Plate Thirds when Di Stéfano joined, recalls him as 'good looking, and he had this startling speed. He was strong, too, physically.' Soon enough, they would be facing one another regularly in practice. It was then Carrizo appreciated other assets to Alfredo's game. 'He had real quality to his finishing, the best in any centre-forward I came across, but he could master any position.'

Peucelle was impressed not only with the teenaged Di Stéfano's versatility, his pace and his shooting, but also his willingness to interpret his position on the field with some of the flexibility Peucelle had himself had as a River player and which Pedernera showed with La Máquina. Di Stéfano had started out as the right-winger for the Fourths, but sometimes he would be picked at centre-forward. From there, he would be encouraged to drop deep and forage for the ball in midfield. He soon tired of being posted on the flank, waiting for passes to come to him, frustrated he could not be more proactive.

Peucelle appreciated there was more to Di Stéfano's game than his acceleration along the right touchline and his eye for goal. He tried to have the younger attacking players evaluate their performances not simply in terms of goals or the number of individual duels they might or might not have won over 90 minutes. After one 9–0 win against modest opposition, Peucelle made a point of congratulating the centre-forward that day, who, remarkably, had not contributed a single goal to the emphatic scoreline. That centre-forward was the novice Di Stéfano. He left the pitch crestfallen that, in what ought to have been an opportunity to impress, gather some handsome statistics for himself, he had somehow contrived to have none of the best lines.

Peucelle, noting not the goals but the movement of River's players, told him otherwise. 'Well done, Alfredo,' said the coach. 'You had a magnificent match. No, you didn't score, but you were running the team out there.' The recipient of that sincere compliment would reflect that it sounded like the least heart-warming congratulations he had ever heard. Later, he understood it was meant sincerely.

River's Fourths often won at a canter. But they had rivals who could hurt them. In Di Stéfano's debut season with the club they finished second in their division. Hard lessons were learned. There would be controversy in the denouement of the championship, after an episode which gave Di Stéfano an insight into the kind of off-field chicanery that was part of the sport in Argentina. Ahead of a potentially decisive fixture against championship rivals Platense Fourths, at San Lorenzo, players from both sides turned up at the ground, having made their way there individually, expecting to find their kit and league-registration documents waiting for them. The usual procedure was for a delegate from the visiting team to have dropped off everything the players would need early in the morning. But the young River players could find none of their registration passes, which they were obliged to present ahead of every match, to prevent teams putting a ringer onto the pitch. Several thousand spectators had turned up, and were then turned away with the explanation the match could not go ahead.

River's officials suspected foul play, that Platense, unable to field their strongest XI because of injuries, had spirited away the River documents. When they were later discovered in a post-box, the sabotage theory gained credibility. The match was replayed, but by then Platense had closer to their full complement of 17- and 18-year-olds available, including the future Italy international winger Eduardo Ricagni. Di Stéfano's River side lost 2–1.

La Máquina, meanwhile, also finished second in 1944, River Plate two points shy of Boca Juniors, amid some mutterings from supporters that perhaps it was time for The Machine's cogs and wheels to be re-oiled – for fresh blood to be introduced.

Where should they look for it? From within. Di Stéfano stood prominent in the queue, despite his young age. At practice, River's coaches gave him more and more opportunities to test himself in the company of the greats he had watched as a fan, read about in the pages of *Crítica* and *El Gráfico*, listened out for on the radio in the Bar Di Yorio. On 7 August 1944, Alfredo Di Stéfano got his first chance to line up with some of them, play for River Plate's first XI, as his father had done for the last time 29 years earlier.

The occasion: a benefit match against San Lorenzo de Almagro on the neutral ground of Chacarita Juniors, to raise funds for victims of an industrial accident. To the River president, Antonio Liberti, the 18-year-old's demeanour immediately beforehand suggested some butterflies. 'It's okay, *pibe*,' Liberti made a point of saying to him. 'Don't be nervous. Let's see how you can play. Remember, you're just the same as all your team-mates today.'

For 35 minutes, Di Stéfano felt that way. Out on the right wing, he would look up and see Labruna, the man who would become River's most prolific goalscorer, making himself visible as the best target of his crosses. Behind Labruna, the centrifuge of La Máquina, the creative, perceptive Pedernera. In defence and midfield were mostly seasoned first-teamers, but also another promoted from the younger ranks. For the apprehensive Alfredo, there was reassurance in hearing the bellowing voice of one the best friends he would make in his early years at River, the tall Néstor 'Pippo' Rossi, anchoring the midfield.

Some 20,000, Di Stéfano reckoned, came to watch, among them his family and friends from Flores. They saw him perform some promising cameos, and ten minutes before half-time they looked on with anguish as he clutched his ankle, in evident pain. He hobbled off the pitch, his landmark first XI debut, a 2–2 draw, disappointingly incomplete. His friends still made a fuss of him. They had clubbed together to have a silver commemorative medal made to mark the date. He still had it among his prized possessions, a sentimental and cherished souvenir he carried around with him to show to people, when he was well into his eighties.

CHAPTER 4

THE BLOND ARROW

His name is there, in the small print, but an unfortunate spelling error might easily cause the cursory reader to miss it in the best preserved written record of what was a landmark day. It is there in the River Plate XI who lined up away at Huracán on 15 July 1945 and included a newcomer to the top division of Argentinian football, a debutant in the cut-and-thrust of what fancied itself as South America's most sophisticated professional league. The honour of slotting into to a forward line with three of the totems of La Máquina spreading their magic across the width and depth of the pitch went to a teenager, less than a fortnight past his 19th birthday. *El Gráfico* magazine, primary chroniclers of the sport, opinion-formers and influential critics struggled to recognise him as the young man who had been making a better and better impression for his displays in the club's junior teams. *El Gráfico* have the debutant down in their report of the events of matchday 12 of the league season not as Alfredo Di Stéfano but as 'D'Estéfano'.

In the course of the next two years, the Argentinian press would call Di Stéfano by many names, most of them flattering, some of them scornful. The period when reporters needed to consult on how the unknown rookie might spell his surname would be short. Granted, Di Stéfano, or D'Estéfano, did not justify big, upper-case headlines that July day as he slotted in on the right wing, looking up when he had the ball to guage towards which post Ángel Labruna might be plotting to ghost in for a cross, or the cunning position Adolfo Pedernera might be looking to take up for maximum effectiveness, thinking two, three passes ahead.

A Juan Carlos Muñoz injury was responsible for Di Stéfano's call-up for his league bow. The debutant's memory was of a solid, respectable showing, in which he tried to maintain his positional discipline, not be too hasty in advancing down the flank without the ball at his feet. His highlight? Striking the crossbar with a volley. He reckoned there were 80,000 at the San Lorenzo stadium to witness the match. The Huracán fans finished the day delighted. River suffered one of only four losses during that campaign, 2–1.

Di Stéfano went back to the junior ranks after that, as anticipated. Muñoz returned to fitness, Labruna rattled in 25 goals from his 29 games and the back-up available from mature, experienced squad members meant that River's coach and manager Carlos Peucelle, mentor and sometimes martinet to the young Di Stéfano, did not need to bring him into the first team again that season. Peucelle paid him special attention, nonetheless, and continued to supply him with the sort of advice that, delivered to a young man in his formative period by a master who had been an idol to him as a player, stuck in his mind forever.

One day Peucelle took Di Stéfano aside and, rather theatrically, held up a football in his hand. 'What's this?' asked the coach.

'A ball, Don Carlos,' answered the student.

'Yes, so why do you think it's like the sun, so hot that you'd better get rid of it fast in case it burns you?' Peucelle enquired. 'In football, you need some pauses. You're doing everything very quickly.'

Being the boy who never did back down, the apprentice argued back: 'But at River, they always tell me you always have to play first touch.'

'Yes,' said the sage Peucelle. 'But you can do that with some pause, by taking your time.'

Di Stéfano had time, but he was of an age when it doesn't always seem so. He was entitled to feel impatient for promotion. He would contribute plenty to River's third team's finishing top of their junior division in 1945, and gave regular notice of out-of-the-ordinary skills. An early Di Stéfano patent would be witnessed by spectators at a game against Independiente: the flying header, meeting the ball with his body parallel to the ground and airborne. A brave goal, too, in the circumstances, risking collision with an advancing goalkeeper. Take Di Stéfano's word for it; press coverage of the junior teams in the feeder leagues was scant at the time, and no cameras were rolling. But he remembered the goal vividly, even a decade later, by which time the sight of him plunging, horizontally, to meet crosses or clearances with a sudden, powerful flex of his thighs had become quite familiar.

The reward for efforts like those, for registering as the briefly glimpsed 'D'Estéfano' in River's first team's 1945 championship season, and for showing evidence of growing adroitly into the profession, was an end-of-year tour to the seaside, to Mar del Plata, the resort city south of the capital. The maestros, like Pedernera, would mingle with selected juniors, like goalkeeper Amadeo Carrizo, the bumptious Pippo Rossi and Rossi's firm friend Di Stéfano. All three had been called up to the first team from the ranks, in their teens, during the campaign. They had a bond. 'We were friends who told jokes to each other, chatted a lot,' recalls Carrizo. Although he and Di Stéfano had moved away from their family homes to become footballers, and had learned about living independently, the trip to Mar del Plata with the champions felt like a rite of passage. Carrizo keeps a photograph of the squad in their white-belted bathing trunks, sun-kissed and smiling, hair wet from swimming in the bracing southern Atlantic. They enjoyed their freedoms. Di Stéfano would return from the trip with stories of convivial nights out, of the odd broken curfew, observed from a balcony of the hotel by the paternal Peucelle, only half on duty, and of the coach gently admonishing the players who forgot their proper bedtimes.

Di Stéfano would be reminded of the tougher aspect of the job as the new season approached. His status in River Plate's hierarchy had risen enough for him to develop a sense of indignation at the level of his pay, a scant 120 pesos a month – he felt his performances with the various junior teams warranted more. So he raised the matter with a River director after practice one day, and backed his argument up with the suggestion he could be tempted to go and play elsewhere unless a fair deal was forthcoming. Peucelle entered the discussion, and made a remark that irked Di Stéfano, as he recounted to the writer Rafael Lorente several years later. The coach said, in earshot of the player, to the director with whom Di Stéfano was in discussion. 'Don't give him anything. He's just a *pibe*, a kid, and his father's got money.'

Di Stéfano took the words as anything but a flippant aside. 'It made me angry to think about how unfair it was, and even more that my father's money was used as a pretext. I saw more and more how the poorer kids were being abused by the club,' he told Lorente.

It would not be the last time Di Stéfano's superiors encountered his bolshie streak. The boy who had fortified himself as a child with the watchwords 'Never back down!', who had seen at close hand his father put under pressure by extortionists, who had heard his father's misgivings about a career in professional football, seethed with righteousness.

He was certainly not alone in coming to a feeling that worker and boss acted as unequal shareholders in his chosen enterprise. This was the Argentina of 1946, three years after a military coup had toppled a corrupt conservative government, and the year in which one of the more charismatic participants in the coup was poised to take the presidency of the country. His name was Juan Domingo Perón, and he was a decorated military man who had come to prominence through his active and studied championing of trade unions and workers' organisations. His popularity had been enhanced by his marriage and partnership with a glamorous radio and film actress, Eva Duarte, whose populist touch struck a chord with the oppressed and exploited of a country Perón had seen was ready for a robust challenge to its landed establishment and for a leader who could galvanise the frustrations of employees. General Perón and his new wife Evita, and their particular brand of power-to the-people politics, would transform the image of Argentina over the next decade.

Ahead of the February elections that swept Perón to power, a sporting event to stir patriotic crowds had been staged in Buenos Aires. The Campeonato Sudamericano, later renamed the Copa América, brought the national teams of Brazil, Uruguay, Paraguay, Chile and Bolivia to the Argentinian capital for a feast of international football. For a month the host nation was able to bask in the glory of being the focal point of the South American game. Argentina, defending champions, won all their five matches in the round-robin system. They had much of La Máquina about them: Labruna scored at a rate of a goal per game, Pedernera finished as player of the tournament. The up-and-coming teenager who had only just holidayed with that pair in Mar del Plata felt close enough to the action to share in the exhilaration. Di Stéfano played in a junior curtain-raiser to a match between Brazil and Paraguay at Independiente's stadium, and, in the stands to watch the likes of Leônidas da Silva and Ademir after he had done his turn on the pitch, he had a serendipitous meeting with a face from the past.

While Alfredo di Stéfano senior, successful agriculturalist and businessman and one-time capable amateur footballer, did indeed have a comfortable income, as Peucelle had observed, he also had some useful connections. They would help his son – still embittered about the confrontation with River's bosses over his junior stipend, impatient to be in the man's game earning a man's wage for it – to call River Plate's bluff. At half-time of Brazil versus Paraguay, he was spotted by an old friend and team-mate of his father, who now worked as a scout for Huracán, a Buenos Aires club with the resources to jostle around the bronze medal position in the league in a good season, and ambitious enough to be busily constructing a new arena.

Huracán were well connected in the mid-1940s. Their president was Colonel Tomás Adolfo Ducó, a heavyweight in the military who, like Perón, had been among the would-be reformers behind the coup of 1943. Ducó's passion for football was at least the equal of his appetite for politics. His club were looking for a centre-forward, and the scout who bumped into Di Stéfano during the Campeonato Sudamericano had heard that this centre-forward had a gripe with River. They chatted. Soon after, the telephone rang in the Di Stéfano house on Avenida Carabobo and Di Stéfano was told that Colonel Ducó had arranged to talk to River Plate about his future, and a possible loan. He felt flattered, and pleasantly surprised. Di Stéfano had calculated that the queue for regular first-team opportunities in the River of La Máquina was still quite long, particularly at centre-forward. It would soon stretch a little longer. José Manuel Moreno, who had taken up a lucrative contract in Mexico, was planning to come home, guaranteeing extra numbers on the gate, and would be back in River's colours later that year.

Di Stéfano's quarrel with River Plate over the small change of 120 pesos was about to take on a new edge. The imposing Colonel Ducó presented himself at the offices of River and, with what Di Stéfano described as 'a little arrogance', presented as a fait accompli a deal in which Huracán would borrow the young striker for the forthcoming championship season and then see where that might lead. Di Stéfano later heard that Ducó at one stage in the negotiations with River reached for the pistol in his holster, though he was willing to concede that may have been an embellishment to a story of robust talks that involved some eye-catching numbers. River's president Antonio Liberti eventually agreed to the loan, but imposed a clause that Huracán would be required to pay River 80,000 pesos should they want to make the transfer permanent.

That made news. The record transfer fee in Argentinian football at the time was 60,000 pesos. One newspaper expressed astonishment at the Di Stéfano buyout figure: he was a teenager, after all, with one senior league match to his name. He was an unknown. Or he had been. The size of that buyout clause meant nobody was going to misspell the Di Stéfano surname from now on.

The buyout was always going to be theoretical. Huracán, committed to building a new stadium that would eventually bear the name of Colonel Ducó, sometimes struggled to pay monthly salaries. Di Stéfano was lucky. He remained officially on the payroll at River, where recognition of his worth had earned him a first professional contract worth a basic 5,000 pesos a year, the sum

Huracán paid up front to River, quite a jump from the pocket money he had complained about just weeks earlier. His father, ever protective, thought elevation to the first team of a competitive first division team – Huracán had finished fifth in the 16-club league in 1945 – a good idea, quite apart from the fact their interest had stimulated River Plate into acknowledging they had a fine prospect in Di Stéfano.

Huracán discovered in Di Stéfano a sharp point for their attack, wiry but strong and very fast. He was quick to pick up on the wavelengths of senior players, like the Argentinian international striker Tucho Méndez, an experienced team-mate in a young squad. They found Di Stéfano courageous. His early weeks would be hampered by a swollen knee, the result of an infection that left him feverish and the joint painfully tender. He played through it. He was full of energy. His coach, a venerable doyen of the club named José Laguna cautioned him to put a brake on his activity, lest he wore himself out, when he saw how the *pibe* threw himself around the pelota court Huracán had on their premises. Newspaper reports began to hint at an out-of-the-ordinary capacity for hard work, for proactively chasing and retrieving as well as creating and finishing.

Di Stéfano found at Huracán confirmation that he had the pedigree for elite professional football but also that its privileges were not always given generously. He had a close-up view of the Wild West character of the sport in Argentina. Football enjoyed ever greater popularity, it was altering the architecture of Buenos Aires, with stadium construction a significant industry. Yet several of his colleagues went unpaid for months in succession, leading some to protest by withdrawing their services until arrears were paid.

Di Stéfano became familiar with a dispiriting ritual that many of his team-mates rehearsed again and again. After a home match they would go to the club treasurer, on the first floor of Huracán's offices, to ask for gate money to be used to pay what they were owed. But often, before they had even climbed the stairs, they would be told it was pointless to come up: there was nothing there for them that day. Di Stéfano felt blessed that his circumstances were different, and that his background had shielded him from some of the privations colleagues from the poorer strata of Argentinian society suffered. 'There were team-mates who had nothing, not even a toothbrush when we travelled away,' he would later relate. 'I was lucky. I earned. They weren't lucky. Those were the days when my instincts to fight for the next man became part of my character.'

Di Stéfano scored 14 goals in the 1946 season for Huracán, of which one of the most elegant was a volley on the turn, scored in a surprise victory against San Lorenzo, who went on to win the league title. The sneakiest goal? A handball, converted with a clenched fist, unnoticed by the referee or apparently the defender from Ferro Carril Oeste who had just scooped a clearance up in the air before Di Stéfano, deliberately, punched it past the goalkeeper with his hand. He presented no mea culpa when the goal was awarded. It was, on the contrary, a piece of *picardía* (cunning, stealth) of which he was quietly proud.

The most dramatic goal? Against River Plate. Di Stéfano had approached the fixture against the club who owned him, the club he supported, but had encountered those fractious moments with earlier that year, with a special zeal, determined to show his best to their directors and to the coach Peucelle. All that pent-up energy would be released in an astonishing start. Immediately from the kick-off, Di Stéfano received a pass from Llamil Simes, and dribbled, at pace, direct to goal. Boom: a low, firm shot and a Huracán lead against the defending champions.

It had taken Di Stéfano some six seconds, he reckoned, to score against River. Their response would be three goals, the last from Pedernera, and no further damage sustained by the title-holders from uppity Huracán or their temporarily exiled colleague. But Di Stéfano had made his point in the 3–1 defeat, and, to a young man who had just turned 20, his goal felt like a significant threshold.

River Plate's estimation of Di Stéfano had certainly changed. At the end of the season, after Huracán's Colonel Ducó had thanked him for his contributions, Ducó's counterpart at River, Antonio Liberti, made an undertaking. Di Stéfano would from then on be a central cog in La Máquina Mark II – a fresh look for River, who had finished third. He would play not on the wing, but at centre-forward. La Máquina, in its most recognised shape, had been partly restored by the return of Moreno from Mexico, but now it would be reconfigured in a significant way. Pedernera was leaving. He too had his disputes with the club's governing junta. Atlanta, a modest club by comparison with River Plate, had offered him an extravagant sum to join them. Di Stéfano would inherit Pedernera's jersey.

River Plate meant broader horizons. His first major assignments as a designated first-team player would be tours, a trip to Brazil; exhibition matches in the interior of Argentina; a tournament in Uruguay that styled itself the 'South American Cities Championship', in which River and Boca Juniors represented Buenos Aires. It was now that Di Stéfano, whose work on the farm had helped make him impressively tough as an athlete, who already had a reputation as a fierce negotiator of higher wages, began to realise he had a phobia: aeroplanes. One journey, south from São Paulo, alarmed him particularly. Having smelled burning, he complained to one of the attendants, hastening, he believed, the pilot's decision to make an unscheduled landing for several hours of repair work.

It was not a one-off, nor was Di Stéfano alone in his fears. Air travel carried risks in the 1940s, and there was scarcely a literate Argentinian older than 18 who did not know how the life of perhaps the country's most celebrated entertainer ended. The singer and composer, the tango artist par excellence, Carlos Gardel, had died at the height of his fame in an air crash in Colombia in 1935. Football too would have its tragedies. Two years into his senior career at River Plate, Di Stéfano would make his first expedition to Europe as a footballer to play in a fund-raising tournament for the victims and bereaved of the Superga accident, the air crash in which most of the Torino squad who had dominated the Italian championship perished when their plane struck a mountain. The apprehension never left him. 'Alfredo had it badly,' recalled his lifelong friend and colleague, Enrique 'Pachín' Pérez Díaz. 'You'd notice how his hands would sweat whenever he was on a plane.'

On the field, the new face of La Máquina would fit in quickly, except that River played a little differently from the classic Máquina era. Off the field, Di Stéfano's new status earned him some perks, and an important blessing from the Argentinian state. Having turned 20, he was obliged to do national, military service, widely known to young Argentinian men as the 'Colimba', an acronym for *correr, limpiar y barrer* – running, cleaning and sweeping – emphasising the menial tasks it entailed for civilians required to report to barracks or sometimes remote outposts for basic military training and dogsbody work. A small number of Argentinian soldiers had fought for the Allies at the tail-end of a Second World War the country had resisted involving itself in, but there was little threat that a young man called up in the years after that conflict would see action. And for a young footballer on the cusp of fame, it proved helpful that when he reported, he was recognised as a River Plate man by an army administrator sympathetic to the club. He was sent to work at the weapons arsenal, his timetable moulded around his commitments to River, although he was also encouraged to turn out for the regiment's team every so often.

River Plate had a championship to recapture, San Lorenzo having won the national title in 1946 while Di Stéfano was growing up as a centre-forward at Huracán. They also had plans for some serious tinkering with the wheels and cogs of La Máquina. Peucelle's role had been redefined: he was no longer first-team coach, a job now taken by José María Minella, whom Di Stéfano had admired as a player and indeed been likened to as a boy in Barracas. Pedernera was gone, and a serious injury prevented Muñoz, the electric right-winger, from dashing up and down the flank he had made his own. Di Stéfano remembered being aware of talk that the playing style would be 'revolutionised'. There would be sceptics. The tone of some of the reporting of the time, in influential prints like *El Gráfico*, was judgemental and rather proprietorial about the football intelligence of La Máquina and the aesthetic standards it had set.

Di Stéfano's impression was that he took a few matches to feel in tune with the senior players around him. His amigo Pippo Rossi had established himself in the River midfield the previous season, showing no symptoms of beginner's timidity. 'He was a general,' said Carrizo of Rossi, 'and indispensable. He would see problems quickly and knew how to deal with them, and communicate. He was the voice of the team, the boss.' Rossi's passing over distance would lubricate the more vertical, less elaborate, lines of attack that, post-Pedernera, the team were inclined to pursue. A young winger, Hugo Reyes, took over Muñoz's duties.

It would have taken a pedantically fussy River supporter to complain about the manner in which the team, post-Máquina, started out the league campaign. It opened with a 5–1 demolition of Lanús, away, and the restructured River again scored five times in the first home match, against Platense. Di Stéfano netted two of the goals. Blond and brisk, he stood out.

The Monumental stadium was still, strictly speaking, unfinished in the late 1940s, a decade on from the first bricks being laid of an ambitious project. It lacked one quarter-circle of grandstand, so spectators packed around a horseshoe shape, and on breezy days, it was supposed that the wind off the Río de la Plata could influence outcomes on the pitch. Certain sectors of the ground had their own voices. Carrizo would prefer keeping goal at the end that put him closer to a partially covered part of the crowd, because a portion of those places were reserved for women fans, and he found them especially supportive. 'They would blow kisses if you had done well,' he recalled.

River did very well for all their supporters, male and female, in 1947. They registered a club record number of goals: 54 in the 15 home fixtures of a league calendar in which the team scored 90 overall, an average of 3 per match. Poor Atlanta, who had brought in Pedernera to provide instant uplift, were hammered 8–0 at the Monumental, a rout in which three members of the River old guard scored – Ángel Labruna, José Manuel Moreno and Loustau – with the new generation featuring too. Rossi struck the first goal, Reyes scored twice, and Di Stéfano hit the last of the afternoon.

By then he was not just being blown kisses by the girls and women at the Centenario end of the stadium; he had a chant specifically dedicated to him, praising the way so many of his goals were engineered and converted. Belted out with urgency and a little menace, like the theme music of a thriller just before the knife plunges, it went: 'Socorro! Socorro! Ahí viene la Saeta, con su propolsión a chorro!' – 'Help! Help! Here comes the Arrow, jet-propelled! Di Stéfano had already been baptised with the nickname 'Saeta Rubia', the Blond Arrow. He was sharp, speedy and lethal.

He scored 27 of River Plate's league goals. None came from penalties, which Di Stéfano would seldom in his career thrust himself forward to take, nor from direct free-kicks, an area where he would later develop considerable expertise. His goals amounted to almost a third of River's towering total, and they reached the final matchday of the season with the title already confirmed, thanks to a five-point lead over Boca Juniors.

So they went to Atlanta, and the last fixture, with nothing to play for. Yet it turned into quite an afternoon for their leading goalscorer. Arriving there, the players sensed a fevered, threatening atmosphere. Word had gone around that River had been offered payment to ease up: Atlanta were bottom of the table, theoretically still able to escape relegation, but had been humiliated by the champions by those eight goals in the previous meeting with River. In a surreal moment, while the River players were being presented with a floral mosaic of their club badge, while a bouquet of Atlanta's club crest was also paraded in front of a hostile crowd, somebody from the home club muttered in earshot of the veteran warrior Moreno, 'If we don't win, you're not getting out of here alive.' A brawl started, prelude to an afternoon of sporadic violence.

The match never finished. River's players had alerted the referee to gaps they saw in the fencing behind the goal they defended in the first half, a concern given the febrile atmosphere. At half-time it was goalless, Di Stéfano having had an effort ruled out for offside. Stones had already been thrown from the grandstands and, as he recalled, more were hurled as he chased a Labruna pass from the centre of the pitch soon after the restart. The assault hastened his decision to shoot early, rather than linger on the ball: he could always outsprint his markers, but, he reckoned, possibly not the missiles chucked at him. His shot – fired from 35 yards out – went in. River's supporters, who had made plain their anger at any suggestion that their team might do favours for the opposition, duly celebrated.

Then there was havoc. The reports of the game in the Buenos Aires prints have Héctor Grisetti, the River goalkeeper that day, struck by various objects thrown from the stands; Labruna was attacked by a spectator who ran onto the field. Many invaded through the spaces in the fencing. One, with his fist clenched, sought out the goalscorer, and struck Di Stéfano with a blow to the jaw strong enough to knock him unconscious. He came round in the dressing-room later, to learn the match had been abandoned after 76 minutes. The score stood, and the best young footballer of the 1947 season was, to his relief, back on his feet for a celebratory dinner that night, the venue a tango hall a safe distance from Atlanta's headquarters.

Incidents like that revealed the monster, the violence, that still stalked Argentinian football. Reflecting on the anarchy at Atlanta, *El Gráfico*'s Félix D. Frascara wrote: 'It is now worth asking why people who might pass their time peacefully anywhere else, come to football.' It might have been worth *asking*, but enough citizens of Buenos Aires were not pausing too long to give an answer. Gates for the successful clubs were healthy. Business was booming.

To be a football star, especially a fresh-faced, charismatic goalscorer, more often meant being invited into the world of celebrity than having to take a punch to the jaw. Di Stéfano, the new star, found that radio and print journalists wanted to hear from him. Within a few months of his becoming league champion with River and the top goalscorer in the country he was also joining an elite band of famous footballers, the maverick bon vivant and matinée idol Moreno prominent among them, who were being recast as actors. Di Stéfano, with his fame, his look of a young Jimmy Cagney, with that pronounced cleft in his strong chin, was invited to play one of the lead roles in *Con los Mismos Colores* (In the Same Colours), a light film, whose script had been devised by Borocotó, the writer who shaped the opinions of readers of *El Gráfico*.

The movie is an uncomplicated story of a trio of young men who become successful footballers, against the odds, and share various urban adventures. Two of them, Di Stéfano's character and one played by the Boca Juniors striker Mario 'El Atómico' Boyé, suffer a fracture to their relationship because of an incident on the field, before patching up their friendship, in a rather syrupy happy ending. The real glamour in *Con los Mismos Colores* is radiated by the well-known actress of the period, Nelly Darén. Darén's attention to her figure, and her rigorously spartan diet, caught the attention of the young Di Stéfano while on set. He also readily acknowledged her superiority as an actor. She plays her part skilfully, while the footballers look a little wooden as they deliver their lines. The movie, which would be interpreted as a parable for the unifying spirit of sport, a lesson for the more excitable followers of rivals Boca and River, had some success locally.

Di Stéfano suited its promoters because he was now a pin-up, youthful, handsome poster-boy for his sport. And he was not just River's great revelation but a national sporting idol. By the end of 1947, Di Stéfano was wearing the light blue and white bands of the Argentina jersey with distinction. The teenager who less than two years earlier was in the grandstands watching Brazil in the Campeonato Sudamericano in Buenos Aires, flattered to be asked if he might consider representing mid-table Huracán, was called up by his country for Argentina's defence of their continental title.

The tournament, staged in Ecuador, a lengthy, nervous long-haul flight away, had begun with some critical curiosity about how Di Stéfano might fit into an Argentina side confident of its systems of play, and of its position as favourites, having triumphed at the previous two editions of the Campeonato Sudamericano. Di Stéfano, despite being the league's leading marksman, could not expect to be first choice. The striker he edged to second place in the rankings for league goals that season, San Lorenzo's René Pontoni, seemed the preferred spearhead of Argentina's head coach Guillermo Stábile; Di Stéfano's old team-mate from Huracán, and future co-star in *Con los Mismos Colores*, Tucho Méndez, was also a regular up front for Argentina; Boca's Boyé had a place in the front five. Moreno, meanwhile, was back in the forward line following his stint away playing club football in Mexico, and, even at 31, the long nights of no last orders on the Malbec and dusk-till-dawn music had not eroded his capacity to swing a game. By the end of the Campeonato Sudamericano, Moreno would be named as the tournament's best individual.

Di Stéfano finished the tournament with six goals, a tally Méndez also reached. He had started it among Argentina's reserves. He came on as a substitute – they were allowed in this tournament – for the last half-hour of Argentina's second fixture, against Bolivia on a hot, sticky night in coastal Guayaquil when he registered his first competitive international goal, the sixth of seven Argentina scored that evening without reply.

He still had a case to make for himself, even after that happy debut. 'When Di Stéfano replaced Pontoni, there was a moment of uncertainty,' reported *El Gráfico*'s correspondent. 'The problem is not because Di Stéfano is not a magnificent player, but because we already had the forward line perfectly put together around Moreno. Now it will need a little time and practice for the Blond Arrow to adjust to it. He operates distinctly from Pontoni.' As with River's shift from the elaborate La Máquina system to one more tuned to the young Di Stéfano's perceived forte on the swift counter-attack, there was a hint that the newcomer's talents might intrude on a game plan built around finer principles.

It did not. Argentina had their tougher fixtures of the Copa America still ahead of them after the battering of Bolivia. Pontoni had already rattled in a hat-trick in the opening 6–0 win against Paraguay. Peru would present less flimsy opposition, and in a brutal encounter they finished the evening with nine men on the pitch, thanks to two dismissals. Di Stéfano started, and his goal ten minutes into the second half gave Argentina the lead they held onto for a 3–2 win. He would act decisively in another tight contest five days later in the round-robin format, as the scorer of Argentina's only goal in a 1–1 draw against Chile. That night, he showed he was not just about speed and icy finishing. There was the virtuoso moment when he dribbled past three Chileans on his way into their penalty area, and his shot bounced off one post, onto the back of the goalkeeper and then onto the other post until the lucky keeper gratefully smothered it.

From there on, until the top of the group became unassailable, Di Stéfano kept his place in the Argentina XI. 'Pontoni, whose value has long been established, has had to give up his spot to the biggest revelation of Argentinian football in 1947,' *El Gráfico* reported as Argentina comfortably held onto their position as the Campeonato Sudamericano's bosses, masters of their continent. 'The intelligence and quality of all the team, including The Blond Arrow, makes the adaptation easier.'

The squad returned to Buenos Aires in time for the New Year, and to a reception with the President of the Republic. General Perón, into his second year in office, recognised very well any vehicle for rallying patriotic support, and a triumph by sportsmen wearing the colours of the national flag was certainly one. What Perón probably did not foresee was that several of the footballers he was greeting and congratulating would soon be mobilising in the name of workers' rights – principles on which Perón had built so much of his popularity and power.

CHAPTER 5

REBELLION

The new idol of the Argentina national team, the blond bomber of River Plate began his run-in to the 1948 domestic season with a run-in with his bosses. It was not the first time, nor the last, that Di Stéfano would find himself at odds with the River Plate president, Antonio Liberti, over the terms of his employment with the then league champions. But he was not alone in his frustration with the modus operandi of Argentinian clubs.

To grow up with River Plate in the mid-1940s was not only to learn at the feet of renowned masters of attacking football, *vanguardistas* like Carlos Peucelle, the cerebral passer turned coach and strategist, or like Adolfo Pedernera, Juan Manuel Moreno and Ángel Labruna of La Máquina. It was also to gain an insight into the politics of the shop-floor. In the season Di Stéfano made his River Plate debut, 1944, the captain was not Pedernera, the tactical leader, but the goalkeeper José Eusebio Soriano, a Peruvian with an aura of authority, and the respect of the dressing-room. On the field, in his six-yard box, Soriano had 'a great positional sense', recalled Amadeo Carrizo, his junior understudy, 'and he was relatively unspectacular.' His tidy approach complemented the more extravagant football further up the pitch; and it reflected what Carrizo describes as Soriano's 'sober, serious' character. The skipper kept an eye out for his colleagues, looked after them, and not just those at his own club. The articulate Soriano was among the leaders of the movement Futbolistas Argentinos Agremiados, a nascent player's trade union with a long list of complaints about the treatment of members of their profession.

By the time General Juan Domingo Perón had risen to the office of state president, having generated a loyal constituency among the working class in his time in the Ministry of Labour, unions in Argentina had gained substantially in terms of rights and protections for workers. Footballers at the elite end of the game were scarcely a government priority, but many of them did have a raw enough deal to be entitled to envy men in other, less exciting jobs. The exploitation Di Stéfano had witnessed during his season on loan at Huracán, where scant salaries would go unpaid for months on end, was widespread at middle- and lower-ranking clubs and in the experience of players in the lower divisions. Clubs frequently behaved with an impunity the system made possible: they held a player's registration, and could thus prevent his going elsewhere even if his salary payments were in deep arrears. The player had few avenues of protest. And the power-holders in Argentinian club football were getting richer. In their home match against Boca Juniors in the 1947 campaign, River's directors had celebrated as, for the first time ever, a single match brought in over 100,000 pesos from ticket sales.

The following season, the players bit back. Taking a lead from their neighbours in Uruguay, who had organised a mass strike in the late 1930s, and emboldened by Perón's popular strategy of labour reform, the Argentina Players Union, with men like Soriano and the San Lorenzo defender Oscar Basso at its forefront, pushed for reform. Their organisation lobbied to be officially recognised by the Argentina Football Association, who reluctantly agreed to listen, and apprehensively tried to assess how sincere the players might be about the ultimate threat: to down tools entirely.

To what extent Di Stéfano regarded himself as a rabble-rouser for a broader cause when he took on Liberti and the River Plate directors in the close-season, the beginning of 1948, is probably open to argument, but in later years he would put his arguments about why he deserved a pay-rise in the context of the struggles of his fellow professionals. He had a keen idea of his own value, certainly; he had a prickly sensitivity to the idea of being ripped off. Yet there was, beyond that, something of the Robin Hood about his attitude towards directors and presidents, a combative 'us' and 'them'. He expressed it from an early age. It would live in him to the end of his playing days.

Even before his 21st birthday, Di Stéfano had become a feisty negotiator, snappy, stubborn, armed with his never-back-down principle, backed by his father in his pursuit of what he regarded as a fair deal. Having clearly become a much more valuable asset to River Plate in the previous 12 months, he could indulge in some brinkmanship. Not long after he had returned triumphant from one corner of South America, Ecuador, as Argentina's tyro champion, he flatly refused to go to another, as River's celebrated Blond Arrow.

The Argentinian champions had accepted an invitation to play a summer tournament in Chile. Di Stéfano said he wasn't going until an improved contract, which the club and the player had been in talks about, was settled. He played hardball, making it plain he was au fait with the various, higher salaries being paid to his team-mates. He stayed at home, but noted that the impasse in talks was suddenly broken when River, without Di Stéfano, were soundly beaten in the Chile tournament by Uruguayan champions Peñarol. They really did need their free-scoring centre-forward. The accord on a new deal, which included a component which Di Stéfano described as 'under the table' emoluments, might have ushered in a happy co-existence between employer and employee – however, the player almost immediately felt disgruntled again when, put on a flight to join the rest of the River squad in Chile, he became agitated by the small size of the plane and the alarming willingness of the pilot to provide too close a view, en route, of the peaks and valleys of the Andes. When he touched down, furthermore, nobody from River was there to meet him.

So far, so fussy prima donna. Except that this felt like yet another let-down in an ongoing, attritional struggle. Few footballers in Argentina would have resented a team-mate standing up to executive bullying or parsimony at that time. And this uncompromising negotiator in the boardroom was still the utterly committed spearhead of River Plate when he was on the pitch. River began the defence of their league title, in April, with four wins in their opening five fixtures. Di Stéfano was averaging a goal per game in that first month. Muñoz of La Máquina was back on the right wing after missing almost all the previous season, and with Moreno and Labruna as inside-forwards, Di Stéfano at number nine, and Loustau at outside-left all seemed good on matchdays, and reassuringly familiar for the supporters of River.

Argentinian football appeared to be cleaning up some of its problems, too. British referees had been imported wholesale for the 1948 season. Their interpretations and applications of the rules differed from time to time from those of the local officials the players were used to, and this change in standards may have partly explained the fresher look to the top of the division. By the time River hosted Platense in late June, coming off a series of three games without a victory, Platense had emerged as surprise pacemakers in the table. Goals from Di Stéfano and Labruna restored the old hierarchy in the match between the champions and the new pretenders.

Meanwhile their rivals, Boca Juniors, were struggling. When River went to Boca at the beginning of August, Di Stéfano had an extra motivation for a win. He had started putting small wagers on Boca–River derbies with a Boca supporter with whom he was spending more of his time. Her name was Sara Freites Varela, and she was four years younger than he. Her family were originally from Galicia. She lived in the Boedo district of Buenos Aires, which lies between Barracas, where Di Stéfano was born, and Flores, where he lived in the large house on Avenida Carabobo. They had met through mutual friends. A romance blossomed, and they had their private rituals: if Boca beat River, he would present Sara with a box of chocolates; when River beat Boca in the middle of 1948, the obligation would be hers. Her affections soon shifted to River, where she would watch her beau play and then join him for an evening in a restaurant or at the cinema.

In the early days of their courtship they did not talk a great deal about labour practices in Argentinian football. There was enough of that going on in the dressing-room. The players' union had taken their battle for recognition with the Argentinian FA to one of the government tribunals that had been encouraged and empowered under Perón's charge at the Ministry of Labour. They achieved something: clubs were ordered to pay outstanding debts to employees. But several did not meet the October deadline to do so, and the conflict came to a dramatic head in November, with six matches left of the season. The players staged a strike; the club executives responded angrily. They resolved to go ahead with scheduled fixtures using amateurs, most of them junior players, in place of the senior professionals – and there were many – who honoured the strike action.

As Di Stéfano remembered: 'There were resentments between those who chose to play and those who did not.' He and Pippo Rossi, allies in almost everything, stood among the most determined rebels. Di Stéfano could survive the months without pay, because of his savings and his family's comfortable circumstances. He recognised that continued industrial action would hurt others less privileged.

River won none of the half-dozen matches they played in the period without their senior professionals. Having suffered high-scoring defeats in the previous two games, they had already lost some of their initiative in the race for the title to Independiente. Di Stéfano remained River's leading goalscorer, and finished his curtailed campaign with 13 goals from 24 games. River ended the damaged season as vice-champions. And there was no imminent end in sight to the dispute.

Those on strike tried to be careful with how they managed their campaigning. The Argentinian press expressed some hostility to the strike action. So players made themselves available for fund-raising games, with proceeds given to good causes. River accepted the trip to Italy to help Torino, who had lost players and staff in the tragic air accident at Superga mountain. Di Stéfano bore the long flight, and impressed Italian audiences enough for Torino to make known to River their interest in signing him. But back home, the quarrelling between bosses and the blue-collar ranks continued, as did a need for wise public relations by those on strike. Fans needed persuading that the reason they were unable to watch football of a standard they were accustomed to was that those lucky enough to play it in front of audiences of tens of thousands felt they were subject, as

Minister of Finance Ramón Cereijo later sceptically put it, 'to what, according to them, is inhuman treatment'. Cereijo, a keen follower of, and administrator at, Racing Club de Avellanada, would acquire some notoriety for his treatment of Racing's players in the months ahead. One of them, the winger Ezra Sued, claimed he confiscated passports to prevent Racing footballers leaving the country. Some were considering turning their backs on the Argentinian game's feudal employment practices, and taking their skills elsewhere.

The possibility of a lucrative life abroad became a real temptation in 1949, thanks to events almost 3,000 miles away from Buenos Aires, in Colombia. Football there, underdeveloped and with no international reputation to speak of, was in a state of even greater civil conflict than it was in the Argentina of agitated players rubbing up rough against their bosses. A small group of ambitious club presidents in Colombia were launching a plan to raise standards, up the level of professionalism in the top division; they met resistance from the guardians of the amateur game, the Colombian Football Federation. It led to a split, and the emergence, at great pace and in a climate of edgy and violent political turbulence, of a glamorous, well-funded new league, one that, because it had pulled free of the moorings of the Federation and the wider umbrella of the sport's continental and world governing bodies, could break some rules.

One of the prime movers in Colombia's nascent professional football culture was Alfonso Senior Quevedo, president of a recently formed Bogotá club, modestly called Millonarios. He saw the player unrest in Argentina as serendipitous, coming at just the time he was reforming the top flight of Colombian football by boldly striking out in pursuit of his independent-spirited league, known as the División Mayor, or Dimayor for short. To make it take off, it needed some glamour. Senior hired an Argentinian coach, Carlos 'Cacho' Aldabe, and gave him a double role: he would manage the Millonarios team, and he would also recruit – and for that he needed to be discreet, to act like a secret agent. Aldabe's first big mission: to fly home to Buenos Aires, and see how bad attitudes were getting among the leading players there, and if their imbroglio might be exploited.

Senior wanted one man in particular, a player whose name was resonant across the continent: Adolfo 'El Maestro' Pedernera. Pedernera was no longer with River, but with Huracán, where his career was in limbo, even without the uncertainties of strike action. Pedernera found Senior a far easier man to negotiate with than the River directors he had clashed with in previous years, or than Huracán's president, Colonel Ducó, the military man who, rumour had it, had reached for his pistol during the negotiations over Di Stéfano's loan from River two years earlier. Pedernera asked for a down payment of $5,000 just to say yes to Millonarios, and a basic of $200 per month. In Argentinian terms, the suggestion was exorbitant. From Senior in Bogotá the answer, relayed via Aldabe, was simple: 'Si, Señor, and you can tell your friends there's more where that came from.'

While Pedernera was lining up his move to Colombia, the ornery contest between Argentinian players and owners dragged on. Strike action threatened the scheduled opening of the 1949 league season, and River Plate hired in players from the provinces to provide cover for those who were still in rebellion. There was brinkmanship on both sides, and Di Stéfano was by now clearly identified as a hardliner, along with his buddy Pippo Rossi. They were two of the last River Plate players finally persuaded to sign revised contracts shortly before midnight on 5 May, the deadline set after the first fixtures of the season had been played without those footballers still on strike.

As Di Stéfano understood it, if they did not sign, they would be prevented for playing at all for River, who would continue to hold onto their registrations. He had reason to believe the club were talking to Torino about transferring him there, but as he stated in an open letter to Argentinian newspapers, he felt corralled into putting his signature on what he said was a contract with River with certain figures left blank, yet to be filled in, because of the late hour.

The stand-off between the players' union and their antagonists, the club presidents, had been only partially broken. The union was now recognised by the Argentinian FA; but the clubs had set a salary cap, a maximum wage. In the minds of the principal activists for players' rights, little had been gained. 'No professional footballer has freely signed a contract in recent times,' wrote Di Stéfano and Rossi to the papers. 'Freedom of contract exists in Argentina for every human activity except professional football. The current regulations of the Argentinian FA have a set limit on remuneration, which effectively represents the best organised way of curtailing freedom of labour that could be conceived, because anybody who does not bend backwards to accept the despotic conditions fixed for them has no alternative but to abandon their means of earning a living, the profession they and their families depend on: football. Yet they are legally considered the property of the club, who can loan them, sell them and, if they rebel against the way they are treated, hang them out to dry.'

So it was not a contented Di Stéfano who took his place in the River Plate line-up three days after being, as he felt, coerced into agreeing a revised contract, one subject to an across-the-board wage cap. But he still scored in River's 7–0 thrashing of Atlanta.

He did so the following weekend too, in a 3–2 win at Banfield; and he scored again the next Sunday as River beat Huracán 3–0. By the beginning of August he had contributed nine goals to putting River, at the top of the league table, just ahead of Racing, the club with the allegedly iron grip on its players' passports.

At the beginning of August, Pedernera was in town, back from Bogotá, the Colombian capital, with stories he wanted to tell. The Colombian Dimayor league had taken off with startling, sudden success, in terms of its profile and attendances. Pedernera's lucrative deal had already made headlines in Argentina. Increased gate receipts at Millonarios's Campín stadium in anticipation of his arrival had reportedly covered his first year's salary before he even kicked a ball wearing Millonarios's blue strip. The likelihood of other stars of Argentinian football following him to Colombia was a common topic, and a talent-drain became a fear – but also the subject, in the grandstands of Argentina's first division, of some humour. Supporters at a match between Lanús and Platense, on seeing a linesman casually and rather skilfully playing keepy-uppies with the ball during an extended hold-up in play, began chorusing: 'Off you go, off you go, to Colombia.'

Di Stéfano would soon hear noises from a crowd he was used to hearing fete him that sounded a little ominous. Some River Plate supporters, suspicious their leading players had been approached by the Colombians, had taken umbrage. Di Stéfano, left out of the XI because of a muscle pull, was with Sara watching a River match against Lanús at the Monumental when a section of supporters celebrated a goal from Eliseo Prado, the striker who had taken his place in the line-up, by chanting: 'Di Stéfano, go! Go to Colombia and don't come back.' It hurt him, as did the realisation that River had come to the conclusion their best option in the circumstances of a fracturing relationship was to try to sell him to Torino.

By Di Stéfano's account, he overheard Liberti, the president, talking on the telephone about him, in Italian, to somebody from Torino. He then reacted angrily when Liberti apparently suggested he be left out of the line-up for an important fixture against Independiente. A delegation of players complained at the idea: Di Stéfano started the game, and struck the third River goal in a 3–2 away win. A week later, he provided solid evidence of commitment to the cause. In the derby against Boca Juniors, Carrizo, the River Plate goalkeeper, was knocked unconscious in a collision with Boca's Emilio Espinoza, and had to leave the field for what Di Stéfano reckoned was six minutes. Without substitutes to call on, an outfield player needed to volunteer to keep goal. Di Stéfano put his hand up. One photograph from the match shows him leaping high into a thicket of players and reaching bravely to paw away a cross. When Carrizo returned to consciousness and to the pitch, River's virgin scoreline had been preserved by the locum gloveman. River held on to the 1–0 advantage Labruna's goal, from a Di Stéfano pass, had given them. Di Stéfano would get his chocolates from Sara, and enjoy the fact that his professional career had included a stint in goal. 'When people said I could play in every position on the pitch, it was an exaggeration,' he later remarked, 'but the photo of that River–Boca game actually proves it.'

The day Di Stéfano donned the gloves turned out to be his penultimate in a River jersey. On 7 August 1949, he scored his last two goals for River Plate, in a 3–2 loss at San Lorenzo. During the match, one of his markers, his Argentina international team-mate Ángel Perucca muttered to him: 'Why are you running so much? You're on your way to Colombia.'

The same week, Pedernera visited the offices of *El Gráfico* magazine. He turned on the charm, explaining why he had chosen to take his brilliance, his aura away from his native country, and to the once obscure but now apparently dazzling Dimayor of Colombia. He knew his flight to a league in open rebellion with its own Federation, and therefore the wider game's establishment, had drawn some scathing criticism in Argentina. So he explained to journalists at *El Gráfico*, sceptical about the threat of the Colombian experiment, but sensitive to the deepening crisis in Argentina's own game, how moved he had been by the reception he got in Bogotá, and how conditions for footballers in Argentina had left him feeling he had no choice but to go. 'It was impossible, morally and materially, to accept offers from Buenos Aires,' he said.

Pedernera had not just flown home for his own image-making. While there, he persuaded Di Stéfano and Rossi, his old colleagues from River Plate, that Millonarios could more than compensate them for what they would lose by quitting their employer, and leaving their home. Di Stéfano calculated that the pay on offer in Bogotá in a year would be as much as he would earn in the next decade at River Plate. As for Torino, it seemed a great distance away from family and from Sara, and he admitted five years later that part of him was feeling so bloody-minded about River that he did not want the River board making money from Italy out of his sale. The antagonism with President Liberti and the months of industrial action had left wounds.

He spoke to Sara about their long-term future. If he chose Bogotá, he explained, they could be married when he was 23; if he went to Italy, he might be 25 by the time they could settle down together. He had plans to buy a ranch. A stint with Millonarios would finance it.

Rossi was equally enthusiastic, perhaps more so. He had fewer local ties to sever. So he and Di Stéfano informed River they intended to leave for Colombia, for Millonarios, in the middle of the season, and to bear the sanctions that FIFA, who had expelled Dimayor for its breach with the Colombian Federation, would likely impose on the players once River filed complaints against Millonarios for taking on players without the permission or authorisation of the club, River Plate, who held their registration. Colombian football's revolution was taking place in isolation, the Dimayor excluded from FIFA's structures. Rossi and Di Stéfano were heading off to a so-called 'pirate league'.

The official farewells were cold, the goodbyes to team-mates discreet, because they felt a little like fugitives; they knew they were a disappointment to River supporters, and were told they were also acting unpatriotically. *El Gráfico*, having listened to Pedernera's arguments, wrote wistfully of the caravan of leading Argentinian players to Colombia: 'It is a brilliant financial operation, the logical aspiration of every professional, and now the way has opened for two more notables, both from River Plate, Alfredo Di Stéfano and Néstor Rossi, to go. We're becoming used it, but that does not mean we have to give up regretting it as spectators, nor thinking about Argentinian football's situation internationally.'

CHAPTER 6
EL DORADO

On 9 August 1949, wrapped up against the winter cold, Di Stéfano was driven by his father to Morón airport in Buenos Aires to join Rossi on a Pacífico airlines flight out of the country, bound for Bogotá, the capital of Colombia and what was now being called a sporting 'El Dorado'. For Di Stéfano's family, the adventure seemed a fraught idea. While he always had the support of his father in standing up to River over his rights and terms, Di Stéfano's decision to pursue his career, however tempting the money, a long way away was a journey into the unknown. There was also the travel. 'He hated flying, and we all knew that, and that was what we thought when he said he was going to Colombia,' recalls Norma, who turned 18 just as she said goodbye to her eldest brother.

After the hugger-mugger, incognito trip to the airport, Di Stéfano's aviophobia was hardly soothed once he and Rossi embarked on the first leg of their long relay towards Bogotá. As the plane headed for the Andes, the pilot became aware of problems with one of the engines. The immediate destination was Santiago in Chile, from where, after refuelling, the pair of adventurers were scheduled to set off again in the direction of Colombia. With repairs now needed, they were told they should prepare to spend longer on the ground in the Chilean capital. That cloud at least had a silver lining. They agreed to try and catch up with an old friend. José Manuel Moreno had already seized the moment of industrial action and deadlock in Argentinian football to leave River for a second time and had signed a contract to provide Universidad Católica, a leading Chilean club, with a year, maybe more, of his unique, masterly form of on-field entertainment, and to give the night owls of Santiago a glimpse of his legendary social stamina.

Di Stéfano and Rossi decided to surprise him. Santiago is a big city, but the pair had every confidence that they would locate their old friend quickly enough. A simple instruction to a taxi-driver to find the finest restaurant in town would lead them, if not to the man, to someone who knew where Moreno might be. They found him; he was thrilled to see them, and by the time Di Stéfano and Rossi had to return to the airport for the onward flight, engines fixed, the old amigos from River were in high spirits and Moreno was joshing that he should come with them to their Colombian El Dorado. When they said their last, hugged farewells, on the tarmac, the trio were all singing one of the folk songs the River Plate players appropriated to celebrate victories, or gee themselves up on the road, and in the dressing-room. With Rossi's loud voice booming, they rattled through an upbeat rendering of 'A mí me gusta el vino' – 'I like wine' – enjoying its staccato chorus line: 'Piririn, pin, pin!'

Di Stéfano and Rossi did not sound, that August day, like men anxious about the Faustian pact they had made with their careers. The rebel pair headed for Bogotá, via further hop-scotching up through various South America airports – Lima, Peru; Guayaquil, Ecuador; and Cali, Colombia – fully aware they were joining what was now routinely scorned as a 'pirate' project, a league organised by a body, Dimayor, which had months earlier been expelled from the Colombian Football Federation, Adefútbol, and thus from the South American Confederation, CONMEBOL, and from FIFA. The money looked great, but the risk was of being marooned there and unable, because of a likely ban, to return to their profession anywhere other than Colombia; they were beholden to a circus whose marquee, so rapidly erected in a dangerous, unsettled place, had a fragile look.

Half a century after touching down in Colombia, Di Stéfano recalled that the El Dorado they came to glistened a little less brightly if you looked around. 'There was a sadness in the atmosphere in Bogotá,' he noted, 'people dressed in black, in mourning.' Many Colombians were in mourning for loved ones killed in politically motivated violence that would cost an estimated 200,000 lives in the decade up until 1958.

The catalyst for that violence, and to an extent for the peculiar sporting adventure that made Colombia the most lucrative and perhaps the most razzle-dazzle football culture in the world, had been an assassination. The charismatic leader of the Liberal Party and powerful candidate to win an imminent general election, Jorge Eliécer Gaitán, was shot in the street in April 1948. The next two days of rioting left 600 dead. Among the strategies taken up by the conservative Colombian government of the time had been to give administrative and financial support to professional football, hopeful it would act as an opiate to distract the population, particularly in Bogotá and other major cities.

There was certainly an appetite for elite football, which was why the men driving Dimayor, the professional league, had pursued their project so vigorously. At their head was Alfonso Senior Quevedo, president of Millonarios, the club he had helped found in 1946 and was in a hurry to build up. To do that he needed to sprinkle the club with glamour, and Pedernera, followed by Di Stéfano and Rossi, were going to provide it. The strike in Argentina ushered them towards him; a nervous Colombian government gave him state support to push his ambitions forward. The prize-money on offer for the 1949 championship, some 10,000 pesos, came directly from the state treasury. The local media, strictly monitored by government, promoted the sport enthusiastically.

When Di Stéfano and Rossi touched down in Cali, Senior was there to meet them and accompany them on the final leg of the trip. He was canny enough to know that disembarking with the two latest stars would associate him even closer with their bold capture, and the event had been meticulously choreographed. Some 30 buses had been leased by Millonarios to ferry supporters to Bogotá's Techo airport, and a reported 5,000 people were there to help roll out the red carpet for the two Argentinians. *El Tiempo*, the leading Colombian newspaper, had prepared its superlatives. Its evening edition told how 'today the fastest, speediest forward on the whole continent arrived. His movements towards the opposition goal are fantastic, and he has fully deserved his nickname "The Blond Arrow". His shooting has an uncanny precision and he has an extraordinary capacity to slip away from his markers.' Then they really went overboard: 'He can use both feet with the same power.' Yes, Di Stéfano had two good feet, but his right was always a more dextrous instrument than the other.

The hype had a jingoistic purpose, but readers and football followers in Colombia were not naïve. They were also growing quickly, in numbers and in expertise. Senior had noted that Argentina's *El Gráfico*, with its full-colour, soft-focus covers making matinee idols of footballers, its earnest and detailed analyses and its occasional breast-beating about standards and innovation in sport, was achieving significant sales in Colombia, where copies were flown in from Buenos Aires shortly after they came off the presses. Radio coverage was expanding. Tours by Millonarios to various South American cities, and by clubs from elsewhere in the continent to Bogotá in the three years preceding FIFA sanctions against the rebel league, had broadened the knowledge of fans, and helped establish 'Millos', as Senior's club would become known for short, as a significant name in the game.

Senior made sure Di Stéfano felt at home. Pedernera, among those greeting his two former River and national team colleagues, took them to their new residence, in the Teusaquillo district, not far from the Campín stadium, home of Millonarios. They were to be among various tenants from the growing expatriate football community in a large house, where the landladies, a widow and her sister, not only provided meals but, they were warned, maintained a certain vigilance over their guests' behaviour. Alerted to that when they arrived, Rossi and Di Stéfano became conspiratorial. Pedernera introduced the new arrivals, explaining they were well brought-up, civilised young men. Di Stéfano, upstairs, unpacking in his new quarters, suddenly heard Rossi's booming voice from below: 'Alfre,' he shouted, using the informal name by which he called his sidekick, 'Can you bring down our books, so we can do some studying?'

He was kidding. It did not take long for the celebrated Argentinians to win a reputation among the polyglot groups of players migrating to El Dorado that was neither scholarly nor ascetic.

What they conspicuously were was united. In the same house that Rossi and Di Stéfano called home, and later nicknamed, with a little boastfulness, 'La Pensión del Campeonato', the House of the Championship, were compatriots Óscar Corso, another Millonarios player, and two Argentinians, Luis López and Heraldo Ferriero, who were with Independiente Santa Fe, a club with whom, the newcomers learned, there was a significant city rivalry. Also billeted there was a coach at Santa Fe, one José Castillo, a character with interesting stories to tell to his younger housemates as they relaxed over games of cards and sociable dinners. Castillo was a Spaniard, who had represented Barcelona and the Spain national team as a midfield player in the 1930s. He had left the country because of the Spanish Civil War, during which his leftist sympathies had caused him to be arrested and detained. He began his exile coaching in France, and then settled in Colombia, where he remained until the end of his life.

Di Stéfano and Rossi had barely two days in which to meet those team-mates they had not known in Argentina, or to admire the Millonarios headquarters where they would travel to each day by bus for practice. They were both in the starting XI for Millonarios's next fixture, at home to Deportivo Barranquilla.

That Sunday, it poured. Senior and his staff at Millonarios had done everything to make the debut of Di Stéfano a headline event, to bring the city to a standstill for the first appearance of the idol in the blue jersey of Millonarios, but so hostile was the weather that the Campín, official capacity 23,500, was not even quite full. That would become less and less usual as the season went on.

Those who were there, soaked to the bones, having endured a 40-minute hold-up when the rain turned torrential, saw plenty of what all the fuss had been about. Di Stéfano played with authority and panache. He scored twice in a 5–0 win over the team from the coast. The triumph added impetus to the championship, in which Millonarios had started the day in third place. Their emphatic win moved them up to second, behind Deportivo Cali.

El Tiempo eulogised the trio of Argentinians, Pedernera and the pair of newcomers. 'They are three distinct types of player,' it observed, 'but united by one common denominator: class.'

Pedernera, the subject of a good deal of swooning already that year, had been the 'ultimate expression of football intelligence', and Rossi's debut had been authoritative: 'We would have to say Rossi dominates the pitch, and gives the impression that each of his feet possesses a magnet to draw the ball to him. He distributes the ball mathematically, and has a rarely seen efficiency and skill in breaking up opposition play. A complete midfielder,' the paper concluded, 'equally adept in helping in defence and in attack.'

Of Di Stéfano's debut the praise was a little more tempered, or at least did not match the flowery panegyrics applied to Pedernera and Rossi. On such a sodden, slow pitch he could not show his speed on the ball and on the chase as often as he would on a true, zippy surface. 'He kept something back,' *El Tiempo* thought, 'although his directness and movement make him extremely threatening.' The goal with which he opened the scoring was 'a sign of his capabilities. The nickname "Blond Arrow" is not just a slogan of journalistic propaganda, but a true reflection of what he is.'

Life at the forefront of this spectacle seemed good, even if the odd, unpredictable storm could hit Bogotá suddenly and brutally and required, as the gushing reporter from *El Tiempo* called it, some 'Olympian stoicism' from the 18,000 in the audience for the drumrolled debuts of El Dorado's latest glitterati. If Di Stéfano and Rossi had any doubts they had signed up to a club with soaring ambition and a sense that they belonged at the top of the sport in Colombia, they did not last long. Indeed, five-goal fiestas soon seemed routine. A week after the destruction of poor Deportivo Barranquilla, who later dropped out of the league entirely, Atlético Bucaramanga let in five Millonarios goals. Seven days after that, Di Stéfano, Pedernera, Rossi and company put another five past Deportivo Pereira.

So often would Millonarios score five goals in a game over what became a sustained period of dominance in Colombia that their loyalists came up with a phrase, 'Cinco y baile' – 'Five and then dancing'. Once the fifth goal had been scored the rhythm of matches would alter, and showmanship seemed to become more of a priority than adding to the scoreline, with players indulging in tricks and teasing, long sequences of passes as if to see how long they could maintain uninterrupted possession. In 10 of Millonarios's 26 matches in Di Stéfano's first season there – he had joined four months into it – they scored five goals; in another three they scored half a dozen. The last of those, a 6–3 win over Santa Fe in the derby, included a curious incident after the last Millonarios goal. Its scorer, the Peruvian midfielder Ismael Soria, appeared to be ticked off, not applauded, by some of his team-mates after he converted the goal, as if they had agreed to set their ceiling at five. Soria, it turned out, had been extra motivated because a local milliner's shop had offered a stylish hat to whoever scored the last goal of the game.

All too easy? The fixture list, with early matches against clubs who would finish well down the Dimayor that year, had been kind to Di Stéfano and Rossi. But they had also joined a Millonarios with ground to make up, notably on Deportivo Cali. The championship finished with a pleasing suspense for its promoters: Cali and Millonarios were tied on 44 points each after the 26 league matches. The tie-breaker would not be goal difference but a two-legged play-off. Pedernera scored the only goal in the away leg, from a penalty given to Millonarios for a foul on Di Stéfano. Millos won the home match 3–2, their first goal a strike from Di Stéfano from just inside the Cali penalty area. Pedernera, the pathfinder for the Millonarios mission, added the second. Mission accomplished.

The players sensed this was only the start. The allure of this Colombian adventure, for all the opprobrium and the bans that its recruits would have to bear, was contagious, and being communicated to footballers elsewhere, not just across South America. Other Dimayor clubs were busy looking for the calibre of footballer who might do for them what the celebrated Argentinians were doing for Millonarios. As the months rolled on, the competition Di Stéfano had joined seemed more and more genuinely elite, and although it was shunned by the game's establishment, resented in those countries whose leading players were being enticed away, and boycotted by FIFA, it quickly assumed more of an international flavour than he would have found in the Argentinian top division he had left.

There, there had been excellent footballers from Uruguay, Paraguay, and the odd Italian or Spaniard; in Colombia's El Dorado, there was a greater diversity, so much so that club contests assumed some of the characteristics of an international tournament. Di Stéfano recognised several of his opponents from the cast-list of the 1947 Campeonato Sudamericano in Ecuador, and saw that clubs were developing strategies of hiring groups of compatriots en masse. Deportivo Cali, well-funded and the pacesetters of the 1949 championship, set off on one scouting mission to Peru that ended up looking more like an air-lift: 14 Peruvian footballers came back on a single plane-load to strengthen the bid for the league title. Independiente of Medellín raided what was left of the Peru national squad. At Junior, a Barranquilla-based club, Portuguese became the lingua franca, so heavy were they with Brazilians. Pereira and Boca Juniors, a Cali club named after the Buenos Aires giants, peppered their line-ups with Paraguayans. Municipal, of Bogotá, had a weakness for Costa Ricans. Or, rather, good Costa Rican players had a weakness for the mammoth salaries they were offered to move from Central America.

By the time the pioneers Di Stéfano and Rossi had been in the country for 18 months, the net had spread still wider, so that among the nearly 450 footballers involved in the Dimayor, barely more than a third were native Colombians. There were England internationals, and players from Spain, Italy, Czechoslovakia, Romania, Yugoslavia and Austria sharing practice ground and playing field with the best from South America.

The Argentinians always had the most powerful aura, El Dorado's most radiant star status, and, from the outside, they could look like a clique. Di Stéfano would talk of a 'family'. He would say so not as the family's junior member, as he had been in the River Plate of his first two seasons there, but as one of the father figures. The charismatic Rossi would be another, tall, big-voiced, and as close a friend as Di Stéfano had known in his professional life.

Di Stéfano, Rossi and Corso would breakfast together in their digs, catch the bus together to training, and spend companionable hours at the club's headquarters, being well looked after, sampling Colombian dishes, enjoying the local beer, Bavaria, and appreciating the excellent coffee, from whose export the country's landed classes were enjoying considerable post-war economic benefits. Di Stéfano would become fussy about the quality of his coffee after his time in Bogotá.

They did not live like hermits. The heady mix of unprecedented wealth, indulgence by club directors and worship by supporters made for a lifestyle very distinct from that of the vast majority of Colombian citizens. One of the recruits at Santa Fe, the English winger Charlie Mitten, noted that after leaving Manchester United for Bogotá and the Dimayor: 'The country had a huge social divide. There was the huge mass of poor people and above them a tremendously wealthy millionaire elite, mostly descended from the Spanish conquistadors. We very quickly found that we were accepted into the inner circles of Colombian social life. As a professional footballer, I rubbed shoulders with oil barons, wealthy landowners and cattle ranchers and their cohorts. I lived like a millionaire.'

Like the Argentinian exiles from a national game wrought by conflicts between employer and indignant employee, El Dorado's small English contingent had moved there after becoming disgruntled by the perceived restrictions on footballers' earnings and freedom of movement in Britain. 'Here we were,' Mitten reflected in his authorised biography, *Bogotá Bandit*, 'English footballers, pioneers – that's how we regarded ourselves – the first rebels against a restrictive and archaic system which treated its principal characters as second-class citizens, mixing freely with this upper class. Soccer was regarded as a profession in Colombia, and we players were treated as heroes, like lord mayors!'

To many of the newcomers, this previously obscure corner of football culture seemed innovative, enterprising, full of razzmatazz. Players and spectators would hear the noise of aircraft above the Campín stadium, look up and see a plane trailing an advertisement for consumables from its tail fin. The same aircraft might also drop a parachutist onto the pitch at half-time, dressed up with publicity logos. Neil Franklin, the former England defender, who left Stoke City for Santa Fe, found Colombian football 'highly commercialised', and Bogotá 'the most cosmopolitan city I ever visited'.

As for the standard of the game, Franklin, who did not stay long in El Dorado, was less complimentary, although in this he was in a minority. To him, the attitude of some Argentinian players could seem a little spoiled, haughty, their approach to practice blasé.

He remembers that at Santa Fe, where Di Stéfano's house-mates and compatriots Ferriero and López, and later the distinguished Argentinian inside-forward Héctor Rial, all played, there was an imaginative approach to practice drills – 'they included a lot of other ball games, such as basketball, and made sure they were games played at speed, so that you had to keep agile, so your eye had to be good and your stamina had to be good' – but no great diligence. 'Training,' wrote Franklin, who had won caps for England, 'was not quite the strong point of the Argentinians. They were very good ball players, very good exhibitionists.'

In this sporting Babylon, some men lost their way. Most notorious was the unravelling of Heleno de Freitas, a Brazilian whose brilliance made him, in some eyes, a challenger to Pedernera or Moreno as the continent's finest footballer of the 1940s. But his eccentric behaviour and off-the-field habits had gained him a notoriety even before he joined the Dimayor's Brazilian diaspora at Atlético Junior in Barranquilla.

The Argentinians in Bogotá were intrigued by Heleno, and knew his reputation. He had briefly played for Boca Juniors in Buenos Aires, his idiosyncrasies making as much impact as his goals. Team-mates thought him an ego-maniac. He gambled. Gossip had even linked him romantically to Eva Perón. Eduardo Galeano, the Uruguayan writer and football essayist, described Heleno thus: 'He had the looks of Rudolph Valentino and the temper of a crazed dog.' When he reached coastal Colombia, the lifestyle paid for by his handsome Dimayor salary soon fuelled the rumours, and his fame as a womaniser spread about Barranquilla quickly. The Colombian novelist, Gabriel García Márquez, then working as a newspaper reporter in Barranquilla, concluded: 'As a striker, Heleno could be great, but he could be awful, and he was an invitation for other people to say bad things about him.' After less than a season Heleno left Colombia, having added ether, which he would snort from a soaked handkerchief, to his other addictions, and within three years was permanently resident in a Río de Janeiro psychiatric home.

Nothing quite as experimentally bohemian was going on in the football community of Bogotá, but there was a dandy life to be enjoyed for Colombia's young, feted, single elite. 'I was a household name within weeks,' recalled Mitten. 'I couldn't walk down the street without being stopped by well-wishers. All the shops would be trying to outdo each other in giving us discounts, and we got invited to every function going.' Though curfews would often operate across Bogotá, a city of deep political schism and dangerous social turmoil, the stars of El Dorado led a gilded existence. On weekday evenings, with matchday still at a distance, Di Stéfano and Rossi would go out, share a beer or an aperitif, then dinner. Home fixtures would be followed by grander soirées, of music and dancing at the club's headquarters.

Half a century later, Di Stéfano looked back on his first year in Colombia, and remembered the environment as one of 'a lot of carousing, a lot of "life" in that sense'. He had flowers sent to him by suitors at the house he shared with Rossi. He received more invitations to go out, to bars and restaurants, than he could say yes to. Di Stéfano very deliberately drew up some strict personal boundaries. He would socialise happily, and then firmly call last orders on himself, according to the proximity of matchday. He had cultivated the resolve and self-discipline that colleagues throughout his career would observe and describe: a Di Stéfano happy to keep the company of revellers, partial to a glass or more of wine and the odd whisky on the night after a game, and the night after that, yet rigorous in always hauling up the drawbridge when there was imminent work to be done.

In Bogotá, after a heady first four months, there seems to have been in him a moment of epiphany. He recalled in his memoir, *Gracias, Vieja*: 'I said to myself: "I am not going to get involved in bad things here."' He was liking El Dorado, but he was missing a loved one.

When Millonarios rewarded the Argentinians for their contributions to winning the 1949 Dimayor title with a ticket home for the Christmas holiday, he sent a telegram to Buenos Aires saying he would be home soon, and that Sara should prepare for a wedding in January. He also said, with apologies, that in place of an immediate honeymoon she would be flying back to Colombia with him, and to a large commune of a house, where Pedernera and his wife were installed, and Rossi, still single, still boyish, would have his room, too.

Marriage gave him an anchor. 'Alfredo needed someone like Sara,' remembers Norma Di Stéfano, smiling at the memory of the domestic shortcomings her oldest brother sometimes revealed. 'She took care of everything in the household.' By the end of 1952, that household had expanded. Nanette and Silvana, the first two Di Stéfano children, were born in Bogotá, where their father's reputation as the most commanding, complete footballer in South America was growing and growing.

CHAPTER 7

THE BLUE BALLET

Visitors to Colombia in the early 1950s had a keen sense of what was the national obsession, even when they arrived in the country's most remote nooks. In 1952 a pair of adventurous Argentinian doctors turned up in the country on a motorcycle, having set off from the lower tip of South America with the intention of discovering the continent, broadening their minds and offering medical assistance to needy communities. They recognised, to their delight, that the people of Colombia were captivated by football and thought Argentinians the game's experts.

The younger of the travellers was one Ernesto Guevara. He would become better known as just 'Che' Guevara, and, later, with his beard and beret, as an iconic face on posters adorning the walls of tens of thousands of undergraduate bedrooms. But he was not yet a famous revolutionary while he rode though Chile, Peru and Ecuador, and then, via an unintended diversion on a boat negotiating the Amazon, clocked up his 7,000 miles to reach the city of Leticia, where a drooping bulge of Colombian territory pushes into the borders of Brazil and Peru. Then, Guevara was merely an intellectually curious 24-year-old student of medicine and society, and a keen goalkeeper, a position he had chosen in his favourite sport because it best accommodated his tendency to asthma.

His companion on the trip through South America, Alberto Granado, was four years older, and fancied himself the artful inside-forward. Their nationality and skill at talking authoritatively about football helped them gain an unlikely gig, for which they were rewarded with hospitality and some much-needed pesos. In Leticia, the intrepid travellers were taken on to coach and play for a local works team.

Guevara recorded in his journal that Granado's 'accurate passes' led those who had gathered to watch a tournament played over the course of a day to nickname him 'Pedernerita', 'Little Pedernera', after the cerebral schemer Guevara and Granado knew from the great River Plate teams they had watched as boys and young men. Colombians knew him best as 'El Maestro' Pedernera who, as player, recruiter and now player-coach, had galvanised Millonarios, the club now standing at the summit of Colombia's El Dorado league. Granado felt thrilled to be compared. 'They never stopped honouring me with the nickname,' he wrote.

A few days later, he and Guevara reached Bogotá, where they made it a priority to meet up with some of their celebrated sporting compatriots, men who had stories to tell about rebelling against the establishment. Pedernera and the other former stars of Argentina's league, and indeed its national team, had been in their northern exile for three years by 1952. Guevara and Granado, the idealists and football fans, wanted to get to know them.

More important, they wanted to cadge some tickets to the biggest show in town. On 8 July, via one contact and then another, they met with 25-year-old Alfredo Di Stéfano, at the Embajadores restaurant. They described to him some of their adventures, heard from him about his, and, being fellow Argentinians and young men a long way from home, all three allowed themselves some nostalgia.

'We chatted about football, medicine and, as our final topic, the sierras of Córdoba,' recalled Granado. Di Stéfano had a gift to ease the homesickness of his two visitors, some Argentinian yerba mate tea, to fortify them for the next stage of their journey, and he gave them tickets for the next day's Millonarios fixture at the Campín.

Guevara, writing home to his mother, grumbled that their seats were 'in the cheapest part of the arena; our compatriots are harder to get anything out of than government ministers' – though Granado evidently enjoyed the spectacle. He wrote of 'a match well worth seeing, in fact one I'd put in any gallery of the great games I have seen in my life, which is more than few.' Millonarios had the virtues of South American elegance throughout their team, he reckoned, and he was surprised at the leap in quality shown by the Argentinian winger Reinaldo Mourín, who he remembered as no great virtuoso back home but saw elevated by the company he now kept. 'Rossi, Raul Pini – a Uruguayan – Antonio Báez and Julio Cozzi all set about their tasks very well,' wrote Granados, apparently emboldened by his brief stint as a paid football coach to cast an expert, pundit's eye over the game. 'And Di Stéfano was unbeatable.'

Di Stéfano frequently looked unbeatable at that stage in his career as Millonarios established themselves as the flag-bearers for Colombia's exciting new football experiment. Its rebel league had seen off some of its sceptics and short-term participants, and was setting high standards. Che Guevara and Alberto Granado watched Colombia's national reigning champions at their peak. Millonarios had regained the Dimayor title in 1951, mastering a league that was getting bigger, with more clubs keen to join the party. That year, the top division had 18 teams, up from 16.

Some would struggle to keep up. Huracán, a club with a name adopted from Argentinian football, finished a 34-game season with just nine points. They still kept sufficiently in tune with the freewheeling style that was associated with El Dorado to score at almost a goal per game.

So did the Dimayor's leading marksman. Di Stéfano had scored 31 goals towards Millonarios's 1951 title, and the club romped to an 11-point lead over the second-placed Cali club Boca Juniors, with the Uruguayan-stocked squad of Cúcuta in third place, 12 points beneath the Bogotá bigwigs. Millonarios's final record of 28 wins and just 2 losses from their matches might suggest their annexing of the main prize was a breeze; Di Stéfano's push to end up as leading scorer was not. The Paraguayan pair of strikers at Boca Juniors, Alejandrino Genes and Ángel Bermi, scored 54 times between them for what was the league's most potent attack; Deportivo Caldas's Julio 'Stuka' Avila – he took his nickname from the German bomber aircraft – maintained a vigorous chase at the top of the scoring ladder, ending the season just a goal short of Di Stéfano's total. His goals, 24 of them in a 30-match season, had been a principal reason for Caldas's interrupting Millonarios's sequence of championships in 1950.

Millonarios, faced with that setback and the increasingly competitive environment at the top of the Dimayor, had needed to strengthen even after the signings of Di Stéfano and Rossi. Pedernera's influence in the forward line was reducing with age, so he was doing more coaching and recruiting. But even when 'El Maestro' was absent from the pitch, Millonarios still had the most admired attack in the league. Di Stéfano's game had been evolving impressively and Millos now profited from the intelligent work at inside-forward of Antonio Báez, who had been an understudy at River Plate to La Máquina's fabled five. Millonarios, like the River of the 1930s and early 1940s, had earned their own sobriquet for the elegant football they practised. In their marine shirts, they became 'The Blue Ballet'.

The Colombian newspapers, who devoted plenty of space to analysis of the national obsession, liked the phrase. They felt the Millonarios of the early 1950s required new paradigms for the description of the sport, and styling it a form of art suited that notion. Reporting on Millonarios's brilliant start to the 1952 season, *El Espectador* concluded 'it is now antiquated to talk of a "classical" formation that has goalkeeper, then two defenders, three in midfield and five forwards'.

The architecture of the 2–3–5 formation, the convention for much of the early part of the century, had been outgrown. Of a derby against Santa Fe, the same newspaper was moved to observe that the flexible interpretation of positions by the senior players, their swapping of roles, was both a captivating sort of choreography and evidence they shared the same wavelength: 'They are men who understand one another and a lot of the time they don't need a single, specific plan.'

The Blue Ballet, by common consent, was at its most majestic in 1952, and by the time Di Stéfano hosted Guevara and Granado in Bogotá, he had plenty to tell them about an eventful championship so far. There had been further episodes in the fractious rivalry developing with Deportivo Cali; plus, a great deal had changed regarding Colombia's status vis-à-vis the rest of football, from which it was now far less isolated. He described a sporting culture that had matured. Even the less talented opposition Millonarios encountered on their way to the third league title of his time there 'played with courage', Di Stéfano would stress. They needed it, too.

The Blue Ballerinas, he said, 'had reached that ideal level, where every footballer in the side had a sense of responsibility, and the conviction we should provide the public with something to enjoy'.

Di Stéfano enjoyed himself from his first appearance in the championship that year. He had missed the opening match, an unusual absence with a fitness issue, and as *El Tiempo* reported, 'the team missed him'. He certainly made an impact in the second fixture, at home against Deportivo Manizales, a new club formed by the amalgam of Caldas and Once Deportivo, and still spearheaded by the formidable 'Stuka' Avila. The best divebomber of that afternoon, though, was Di Stéfano, who launched himself at a Báez cross that flew across the penalty area around chest height, well in front of Di Stéfano. He met it thanks to his powerful spring, connecting with his body almost parallel to the ground.

'Sensational,' noted *El Tiempo* of the goal, 'and one of his trademarks, a palomita.' A gloss here: derived from the Spanish word for a pigeon, a 'palomita' is a goal converted while the scorer is airborne. There would be plenty of them in the Di Stéfano portfolio over the years.

Millonarios beat Manizales 5–1 that day, and a sharp-eared reporter from *El Tiempo* jotted down the exasperated dialogue between a pair of Manizales defenders as they left the pitch at half-time. 'You're making the ball look so slippery you couldn't even pick it up with your hands,' one admonished the other. The reply: 'How can I get anywhere near it when Báez and Di Stéfano have it all the time?'

Di Stéfano accumulated goals of all sorts in Colombia. His career there coincided with his early to mid-twenties, the conventional peak for an attacking footballer, and for most athletes involved in explosive sports, and his speed was conspicuous when Millonarios increased the tempo of their ballet. They triumphed in what had looked like their most challenging fixture of the championship season, away at Boca Juniors – runners-up the previous year – thanks to the rapid breaking of Di Stéfano. Latching onto a long pass from Pippo Rossi, his housemate and now the most admired midfielder in the Dimayor, he won his one-on-one duel with the advancing goalkeeper.

Still more eye-catching would be Di Stéfano's acceleration over a longer distance to steer Millonarios to a 2–0 victory. He took possession of the ball just inside the Boca half and the whippet winger of his teenage years reappeared, turbo-charged. 'None of his opponents could catch him, so quickly did he sprint down the right flank,' *El Tiempo*'s correspondent wrote. 'His cross was impeccable for Mourín. Di Stéfano, studious, direct and athletic, was unstoppable throughout.'

The combination of speed to reach the penalty area and then sangfroid, facing off against a goalkeeper, had become his copyright. The Colombian press swooned, and reached for their measuring tools to depict a goal in the 3–0 Bogotá derby win over Universidad, a virtuoso run that began in his own half of the pitch, and 'at bullet pace, left markers trailing behind. The last of those was Martinez, over whom he opened up a lead of more than five metres.' The finish would be precise, from a sharp angle.

Millonarios's defence of the title included 11 victories by margins of three goals or more. Occasionally they played with a hint of smugness. At one point during a 4–0 mauling of Bucaramanga, Di Stéfano, having chased down a ball heading out of play, found himself beyond the goal-line. Play continued, the ball pinging around the

Bucamaranga goalmouth, their keeper moving this way and that, while Di Stéfano could apparently be seen grinning, amused at the way in which his colleagues toyed with the opposition.

The rivalries with more established clubs remained intense, fiercely contested. The preambles to Bogotá derbies against Santa Fe could be spiky. In the first round of matches, Millos had mauled their neighbours 6–0. Ahead of the second meeting, Santa Fe's head coach Alfredo Cuezzo corralled his squad in a military college, the better to concentrate their thoughts and keep secret their preparations, following strict disciplines. To which there came a derisive snort, through the pages of *El Tiempo*. 'I think we're a little bit too grown-up for barracks,' said the Millos goalkeeper, Julio Cozzi. 'We know how to look after ourselves, and we always produce on the pitch. The public know we don't need to go around with a rod to our backs. We put in the hours at the club, and then go home.'

Di Stéfano echoed that, with an implicit challenge to anybody suspecting the players at the top of the league table might be resting on their laurels, or becoming dissolute on account of their success and status. 'You see us as we are,' he said. 'We can go out for a beer, but we will always be ready, and in good shape and optimistic.' Pippo Rossi, who had by now assumed a coaching role as well as marshalling the midfield, likened his troupe to 'Dumas's musketeers, all for one. We are like a big family.' That was no lie. Rossi was by now an avuncular member of the uptown household of the Di Stéfanos: Alfredo, Sara, and the little girls Nanette and Silvana.

For a period of the 1952 championship, the Blue Ballet had to pirouette on without Rossi, the so-called 'Voice of America' – his shouts were audible even to those in the higher tiers of the Campín's bleachers – because of a lengthy suspension following a punch-up in a charged game against Deportivo Cali. Controversy stalked Cali versus Millonarios fixtures. When Millonarios beat Cali 2–1, an important win in the pursuit of the title, Di Stéfano tumbled in the penalty area, winning a spot-kick, which, after two retakes, the goalkeeper Julio Cozzi converted. Cali players grumbled afterwards about the way Di Stéfano had fallen, suggesting he had dived. 'Nobody touched him,' exclaimed the Cali goalkeeper Julio César Asciolo. Accused of this piece of cunning, Di Stéfano shrugged: 'Whether it was a penalty, or not, I can't say.'

Di Stéfano was never easy to referee, although his years of taking match officials on noisily were still ahead of him. The Dimayor was not much fun for many of them either. One, José Antonio Sundheim, was detained by police after a Cali–Millonarios game, having been found in possession of a knife. Bill Brewer, one of the clutch of English match officials imported to take charge of games – their foreignness deemed to establish their impartiality – reported he had a clod of earth thrown at him by a player disgruntled at a decision. Brewer very deliberately stooped to the ground, dug out a piece of turf himself and responded in kind, hurling it at the player. Tom Pounder, another British referee, told how on one occasion, immediately after the coin toss, one of the captains showed him the blade of a knife he had concealed up the sleeve of his jersey, muttering that arrangements should be made for his team to emerge as winners. Referees often had a line of police or army sentries to escort them on and off the field.

Football, and the Dimayor, was Colombia at play, and it had armed soldiers on touchlines; the Colombia of real life was politically edgy, and in an epoch known as 'La Violencia'. Life on its streets could seem menacing. Che Guevara thought so when he arrived at Bogotá and met Di Stéfano at the Embajadores restaurant. 'There is more repression of individual liberty than in any of the other countries we have been to,' Guevara wrote to his mother. 'It feels suffocating. The countryside is clearly in revolt and the army hasn't the power to suppress it. The atmosphere is tense and it appears there may be revolution ahead.'

Although the privileged guests in Colombia at that time were insulated from much of his, they sensed that the moneyed revolution of local football might nearly have run its course. Alfouso Senior, the enterprising president of Millonarios, the driver of the El Dorado epoch, had begun to lobby the government, who had been keen supporters of the project of professionalism once it appreciated it could captivate the public, saying that 'we need more money' in the early part of 1952. Although the fashionable clubs, led by Millonarios, still filled out stadiums regularly, there were symptoms of a waning appeal on the margins, or at least a diminishing bank of disposable income among the public. Only an estimated 2,000 people turned up for the Blue Ballet's thrashing of Bucaramanga on a cold, rainy Sunday in August 1952.

Crucially, something else had altered on the El Dorado landscape. If domestic football was losing some of its initial sheen, it was because international football was penetrating the calendar regularly. The isolation of the Colombian league, blackballed by the South American football associations because it had ridden roughshod over contracts that tied players to their previous clubs, then sanctioned by FIFA because of its contravention of its transfer regulations, had ended. The 'pirate' adventure had found a compromise with the leagues abroad whose booty it had absconded with.

In September 1951, football's governing confederation for South America, CONMEBOL, met in Lima, the capital of Peru, to address the issue of the rebel league, and what to do with its rebel footballers. A deal was reached in which the Dimayor and the Colombian FA, from which it had split, were brought together, and the prodigal league made answerable to its mother body again. There was also a compromise agreement over the renegade players. Colombian football could engage again with its South American neighbours, but with an important provision: come 1954, the footballers it had recruited without the correct, FIFA-endorsed transfer procedures and compensation agreements, would be obliged to return to their former employers. Clubs in Argentina would be exercising control again over their fugitives. Di Stéfano would be back under the authority of River Plate.

One side-effect of the lessening of sanctions and hostility from outside, thanks to the Lima Pact, was that his last two years in Colombia would be exceptionally busy. The Blue Ballet were allowed to play abroad and invite teams there, with FIFA's blessing. Millonarios, rising head and shoulders above domestic competition, would discover a new audience, and fresh sources of income, which Senior foresaw would be necessary after the portcullis came down on the big-spending, easy-hiring El Dorado era.

Indeed, international tours almost overshadowed the masterly march of Millonarios to their domestic title in 1952, and quite often sandwiched themselves awkwardly between domestic assignments. Di Stéfano, ever keeping tabs on how he was valued, had felt grumpy that the terms of his contract had not improved markedly when he signed a new deal with Millonarios at the end of 1951, having just contributed his 31 goals to the regaining of the Dimayor title. Though there would be extra bonuses for the players' appearances in tour matches, he could have been forgiven for feeling exhausted as Colombian football celebrated the end of its isolation with gusto.

By the end of the year they had played more fixtures against foreign clubs – 30 of them – than Dimayor matches.

After spending new year in Buenos Aires with Sara and five-month-old Nanette, Di Stéfano flew direct from there to Santiago to rejoin his team-mates for four matches against Chilean clubs and invitation teams. Audax Italiano were beaten in Santiago by a single goal, and by the time the Blue Ballet had taken the roadshow to Valparaíso and Viña del Mar, they were undefeated, having won three of the tour matches and drawn the other. They were the first Colombian team to have won a match in Chile.

Milestones like that kept being set. The previous December, Racing and San Lorenzo, both from Argentina, had been invited to Bogotá, and beaten 4–3 and 1–0 respectively. Technically, that was a maiden victory for any Colombian club over one from Argentina, but this was a Colombian club that spoke with the accent of the continent's south. The best Argentinians on the pitch in both games were those wearing the blue of Millos.

For Di Stéfano, Rossi and Báez, and for a Pedernera approaching the end of his days as a player and moving towards a career in coaching, the confrontations with clubs from their native country carried a special frisson. They had points to make, a determination to show Argentina that Colombian football provided them not with a luxurious form of semi-retirement, but an environment in which their competitive edge had been sharpened, their football made more expressive. Several years later, Di Stéfano spoke of 'showing the whole continent we weren't "over the hill"'. He was deliberately repeating a phrase which had been used by the Argentinian national coach of the time, Guillermo Stábile, when the mutineers had left in 1949, supposedly saying goodbye to their international careers to join the so-called 'pirate' league. The exiles also resented some of the scribes in the Argentinian press for the way they had sneered at those players who led the exodus north.

Against Racing, the champions of an Argentinian league weakened by the flight of talents to the Dimayor, the Colombian champions enjoyed themselves. At one stage, with a 2–0 lead, Báez and Rossi engaged in a prolonged bout of head tennis, passing the ball between one another, once, twice, three, four, five, six times off their foreheads, without it touching the ground. The Racing players, chasing the first couple of headers, then just stood back from the show-offs. The keep-ball continued, Millonarios spreading possession to as many players as possible without allowing Racing a touch, from midfield to left-back, up the left flank and then across the front players to the right, an extravagant display of pass-and-move authority punctuated with tricks and feints.

In the same match, Cozzi, Millonarios's Argentinian goalkeeper, drew a great 'Olé!' from the crowd when he took on, in his own penalty area, a pair of advancing strikers, and, dummying and trapping the ball, dribbled around them – a daredevil escapade, which may just have contributed, in later generations, to Colombia's reputation for goalkeeping showmanship.

But the moment Racing's staff would take back to Argentina as the most dazzling souvenir from their trip would be a brilliant Di Stéfano goal, one of the best, he reckoned, of his period in South America. With his back to goal, some 15 yards out, he received a pass struck powerfully and low at him by Julio César Ramírez, the Paraguayan defender who had become a mainstay of the Millos side. Di Stéfano took some of the sting off the ball with a cushioned touch on the toe of his boot. The ball spun up to the height of his chest, with which he pushed it lightly forward, while turning his head sharply left and right to gauge how tight his markers were.

They were too close, presenting too great a barrier for him to swivel his body around 90 degrees and attempt a shot on the half-volley. So instead he scissor-kicked, made a perfect contact to volley the ball back over his own head. His celebrating companions told him the Racing goalkeeper had hardly moved as the shot zipped passed him and rippled the net. 'One of those moments,' Di Stéfano called it, 'that come from luck or from intuition.'

For Millonarios, now a marquee opponent across the continent, Di Stéfano would have the opportunity to play against both his Argentinian clubs. Huracán, where he had spent a season on loan as a teenager, came to Bogotá and were thrashed 4–0. The Blue Ballet were also invited to take part in a tournament that would become a regular part of the South American calendar, in Venezuela, named the Little World Cup. River Plate were also involved.

Because of the Lima Pact, River regarded him as an asset who would be theirs again in two years' time. The players he knew from his seasons there embraced him warmly. Báez, who also had a past at River, enjoyed the reunions less. He was sent off 20 minutes into a draw between Millonarios and the Argentinian club. When they met for a second time in Caracas during the round robin, Millonarios won 5–1. Di Stéfano left the chastened River management with the firm impression that the Blond Arrow's powers had only grown in the three years he had been away from Buenos Aires.

In the two matches against River he scored three goals. His old club had seen, and suffered against, the matured, fully formed, all-terrain footballer who was now about a good deal more than fast running and cool shooting. He was becoming the giant Di Stéfano who would stimulate the likes of Eduardo Galeano, South America's most poetic writer on the game, to write: 'The entire playing field would fit into his boots, as if the pitch took seed and grew from his feet,' in *El Fútbol al Sol y Sombra* (Football in Sun and Shade). 'He ran the length of the field, from goal to goal, and then ran the distance again and again. He would shift from one flank to other and alter his rhythm on the ball from languid trot to unstoppable tornado; off the ball, he would lose his marker to gain free space, finding oxygen whenever a move was in danger of suffocating.

'He never stood still. Head up high, he could survey the whole pitch and cover all of it at a gallop, to tease open defences and launch attacks. He'd be found at the outset, in the middle and at the end of positive moves, and he scored goals of every variety.' He was, Galeano concluded, 'the engine behind teams that amazed the world'. He had emerged as the turbo-charged tyro at River Plate just after La Máquina; now he was the motor of Millonarios in Colombia.

The best of South America saw enough of him to verify that. In the year after the signing of the Lima Pact, Di Stéfano was reacquainted with the rough edges of football in Galeano's native Uruguay. Less than two years after the Uruguayan national team had won the World Cup, Millonarios played a series of matches against leading club sides there, found the standard high, and the refereeing taxing. They finished their narrow defeats by Nacional and Peñarol with nine men on the field, but managed a respectable draw against Montevideo's River. Brazilian clubs came to Bogotá, and in the case of Madureira brought the Colombian champions abruptly back down to earth, outclassed 5–2. The Colombian media, willing cheerleaders when the ballet looked thrilling, turned spiky, detecting some decadence among players who had been whistling around the continent honouring tour dates for much of the previous two months. The criticism hurt. Madureira stayed on for a second match in Bogotá. Millonarios set about repairing their pride efficiently. They won 3–0.

As the year went on, the games, in league, Colombian Cup and against foreign opposition, came with unprecedented frequency. On one single day in August, the club played two matches: a prestige fixture against Brazil's Botafogo, which they won 4–1, plus a league match, a 3–1 triumph against Sporting Barranquilla. Not every player was required to participate in both, but Millonarios's staff had come to expect that Di Stéfano would never run out of stamina. The busy 1952 schedule, including many stressful air journeys, detours to the Caribbean island of Curaçao and the jungles of Surinam, revealed not only Di Stéfano's gifts of speed, anticipation, creative vision, drive and leadership but his endurance and vitality.

And his hunger for prizes. To the very last day of the league campaign he kept up the chase for the accolade of again finishing as the Dimayor's leading marksman. He made it, his 19 goals for the league season one more than the tally of Carlos Alberto Gambina, a striker from Junior of Barranquilla. Nor did he ease up in the tour matches. He scored 17 times against foreign clubs.

After the Lima Pact, invitations for tour matches reached the offices of Millonarios from beyond South America. The Colombian paper *El Espectador* had boasted that Millonarios 'play a football Europe would envy'. So, bring on the envious. A Hungarian representative team, from a country making as heavy an impact on European football as Colombia was on South America, and building towards a silver medal at the 1954 World Cup, stopped off in Bogotá during a tour of the Americas; Rapid Vienna met Millonarios in Caracas.

But the event that would shape the life of Di Stéfano was an arrangement reached between Senior, the architect of the Colombian project, and a Spaniard he found to be like-minded, enterprising, rather patrician, a shrewd politician, and a sincere lover of football. He was Santiago Bernabéu, president of an aspirational but by no means soaringly successful Real Madrid. Bernabéu hit it off with his counterpart at Millonarios on first meeting. They became allies. The idea of mutual tours, Millonarios in Spain and Madrid in South America, excited them both. And when Real Madrid touched down in Bogotá in the middle of 1952, it excited Colombians.

Millonarios had taken command of the league by the end of June, and the championship took a pause, partly because Senior had lobbied the other clubs and stressed the benefit to the sport in general, and to the city, of a jamboree around the visit of Real Madrid. Di Stéfano recalled being struck by the royal treatment given to Real. The Madrid players and entourage would be greeted with full diplomatic pomp ahead of two scheduled Millos–Madrid fixtures at the Campín. Each match would be designated its own silverware: the City of Bogotá Cup, and the Chancellor of Spain Trophy. Bogotá's mayor had become a principal backer of Millos; the Spanish cabinet in Madrid was eager to extend its ties of friendship wherever it might. In the Americas, Spain often found more natural alliances than it did in Europe, where the governing regime of General Francisco Franco was regarded with hostility.

In mid-1952 Real Madrid were only the third best team in Spain, but in a Hispanic country like Colombia, they had a large constituency of enthusiasts. At Techo airport, a significant crowd assembled to welcome Madrid's players, bearing banners, waving scarves. And tickets were hard to come by in the immediate lead-up to the games. Which was another reason why the two travelling doctors and would-be revolutionaries who reached Bogotá in early July were delighted to find a contact who could put them in touch with the great Di Stéfano. And he got them tickets, even if Guevara felt miffed they offered anything but the best view from the stands.

Alberto Granado, Guevara's companion, wrote in his journal of 'a game where the attractive South American style came up against the battling qualities of European football, whose technique is not so crisp, but is effective'. He struggled to find much aesthetically pleasing about Madrid's approach, or their individuals, bar Luis Molowny and the impudent Pahiño, a striker who had outscored everybody in the previous Spanish league season and had an independent streak that might have appealed to Granado and Guevara. Pahiño was an avid reader of Russian literature, and rumoured in Spain to harbour anti-regime ideas. He was said to have upset the selection committee of the Spain national team when they spotted him grinning disrespectfully while the team were being addressed by one of Franco's generals ahead of a match in the late 1940s.

'I like the look of Molowny, a Canary islander,' wrote Granado, 'his skills are almost South American, and Pahiño was a real threat in the penalty area. He's from Galicia, and he has skill and a lot of courage.' Madrid, though, needed authoritative performances from their more combative footballers. 'I admired Joaquín Oliva,' Granado noted. 'He's a central midfielder who takes up a deep position, and steals the ball, and, with it, uses it well. The other defender who impressed me was Miguel Muñoz, a veteran of the Spain squad. The defence stood out and especially the goalkeeper Juanito Alonso. He doesn't look so elegant, but he's very effective. I reckon he prevented the Millonarios strikers scoring about five more goals.'

Madrid took a surprise lead, thanks to a goal after a quarter of an hour from their Argentinian, Roque Olsen. The tourists hung on to their advantage for 45 minutes. Di Stéfano was mastering Oliva and Muñoz, though, and he equalised on the hour. The winning goal, eight minutes from full-time, would be Pedernera's. 'El Maestro' was 33 by then, but this was not a fixture he was inclined to skip.

'Class overcomes strength,' concluded one of the headlines in the next morning's Colombian newspapers. Granado, the doctor who fancied himself the 'Pedernerita' of amateur pitches, enjoyed the manner in which the game had been decided. His companion, meanwhile, became irritated by a noisy man, supporting Madrid, in the crowd sitting behind them. Che Guevara, Granado reported, liked to watch live sport in silence, contemplative. When Millonarios's Báez teased his way past Madrid's Muñoz, and the excitable *madridista* at his back shouted, 'Just smash into him!', Guevara had heard enough. He turned round slowly and he growled: 'Hey, if you want blood, go and watch bullfighting.'

Alfredo Di Stéfano's River Plate junior membership card. He grew up as a supporter of the Buenos Aires club where he would later begin his professional career, and for whom his father had played a handful of matches from 1913.

In his first full season with River Plate in 1947, the 21-year-old Di Stéfano, nicknamed the 'Blond Arrow', finished with 24 goals from 30 league matches. River regained the championship.

Di Stéfano (centre) kept good company in River's forward line. José Manuel Moreno, pictured to his immediate right, Ángel Labruna (left) and Félix Loustau (far left) had formed part of the quintet of attackers known as 'La Máquina', The Machine.

River Plate's 1947 champions on the beach at Mar del Plata. From the left, the close friends Néstor 'Pippo' Rossi and Alfredo Di Stéfano, with Héctor Ferrari and Ricardo Vaghi.

Having turned their backs on River Plate, the ring-leaders of a bitter players' strike in Argentina, Di Stéfano and Néstor 'Pippo' Rossi, arrived in Bogotá in 1949 to join Millonarios.

© EL GRÁFICO

Di Stéfano preparing for the 1947 Campeonato Sudamericano in Ecuador, his first and last tournament for Argentina.

Real Madrid expanded their stadium's capacity to 125,000 in 1954, the year after Di Stéfano joined the club. By 1957 the European champions, with Di Stéfano and José María Zárraga pictured jumping to meet a cross in the Champions Cup quarter-final against Nice, expected to play to full houses.

In the course of the 1957/58 European Cup, Di Stéfano scored ten goals in seven matches. This photograph of him celebrating his hat-trick in the home leg of the semi-final against Vasas of Budapest inspired a sculpture at Real Madrid's training headquarters.

And then there were four. Real Madrid's players, with Di Stéfano far right, lift the 1959 European Cup in Stuttgart after their 2–0 victory over Stade de Reims. It was their fourth successive triumph in the competition, a sequence no other club matched in the first 60 years of the competition.

In the so-called Match of the Century, against Eintracht Frankfurt, Madrid recovered from 1–0 down. Eintracht goalkeeper Egon Loy – pictured imploring his defenders as Di Stéfano celebrates – then conceded six more times before Eintracht scored again.

Di Stéfano raising the 1960 European Cup to celebrate his fifth triumphant final of the competition in Glasgow with Canário, Rogelio Domínguez, Marquitos and captain José María Zárraga. He scored three goals in the 7–3 win over Eintracht Frankfurt.

ESTADIO SANTIAGO BERNABEU

Domingo, 4 de septiembre de 1960 • A las 8,30 de la tarde

FINAL I COPA INTERCONTINENTAL DE CLUBS CAMPEONES

C. A. PEÑAROL – R. MADRID
CAMPEON DE AMERICA   CAMPEON DE EUROPA

Precios de las localidades (incluidos todos los impuestos)

VENTA DE LOCALIDADES

World Champions. Real Madrid, as European Cup holders, contested the inaugural Intercontinental Cup title against South American champions Peñarol in 1960. Di Stéfano, pictured in the middle of the front row of the poster for the game, scored two goals in the Madrid leg, a 5–1 home win.

Di Stéfano with each of his five European Cups. He scored in every one of the victorious finals between 1956 and 1960.

CHAPTER 8

LOVE AT FIRST SCENT

By the end of July 1952, Millonarios and Real Madrid had become very well acquainted indeed, and there was something of the toreador and the bull about their relationship. On the field, they followed up their taut, compelling matches in Bogotá with further contests in Caracas, Venezuela, at the grandly named Little World Cup, a quadrangular event in which La Salle, a local club, and Brazil's Botafogo completed the cast-list. Off the pitch, a certain amount of jousting and complicated discussion was in progress between Madrid's directors and Alfonso Senior, the president of Millonarios, about the future of the Colombian club's excellent centre-forward.

The more Di Stéfano played against Madrid, the more he displayed of his portfolio of talents. In Caracas, a city he became fond of during the fortnight of the Little World Cup (but one which would, years later, spring a nasty surprise on him), Madrid upped their game against the South Americans. Their players had wised up after the two defeats in Bogotá, and perhaps felt bolder now they were not taking on Colombia's most popular club in that country's biggest city. On neutral territory, the ordered Madrid tamed the freewheeling Millonarios more effectively, and showed what they had as an attacking force, too. The matches were competitive and, at one point, so fierce that the Venezuelan referee Ruben Sainz was minded to send a player from each team off. The combatants? The leading goalscorer in the Colombian league that year, and the top marksman from Spain's leading division. Di Stéfano and Madrid's Pahiño had become entangled in a bout of fisticuffs. But both men could also hold their own in a verbal argument. They refused to leave the field; the referee backed down; the two number nines truced, and the match remained an 11-a-side engagement.

Pahiño scored half a dozen times over the course of the Little World Cup, but managed none in the two fixtures against Millonarios, both 1–1 draws. And if the Spaniard was not aware while in Bogotá and Caracas that his employers were eyeing up the possibility of Di Stéfano playing, one day in the future, in the position Pahiño had excelled in for Madrid, he must have been spending too much of his reading time on Dostoyevsky and Tolstoy, apparently his passions, and no time at all reading the press. The supposed interest of Madrid in Di Stéfano was widely reported from April 1952 onwards.

By the time Di Stéfano scored the first goal in the second of the two meetings between the clubs in Caracas, his personal register of success against Madrid was four goals in five matches. Millonarios had already been in Spain by then, the Madrid trips to Bogotá and Caracas a reciprocation of the tour arrangement hatched between Senior and his equivalent at Real, Santiago Bernabéu, once the Lima Pact of 1951 had opened up the possibility of Colombian clubs touring abroad free of FIFA sanctions.

Bernabéu had an important date on his agenda. In March 1952 his club were going to celebrate 50 years of existence. He wanted to put on a show. Indeed, he wanted his club to be putting on the best show. That was not something Real Madrid were regularly achieving in domestic football, even if Bernabéu had brought to the club a greater drive and ambition than had his predecessors as president.

Senior and Bernabéu shook hands on a deal that would celebrate Madrid's 'Bodas de Oro', or golden jubilee, by putting the Blue Ballet on stage in Spain in the early spring. Of all the expeditions Millonarios had scheduled in the year, the one to Europe, in which the Madrid anniversary celebrations would be the centrepiece, with matches in the Canary Islands and Valencia slotted around it, most enthused the players. Yes, it meant more time on aeroplanes, a discomfort for Di Stéfano, but the itinerary lined up looked exciting. They would go via Panama, Miami and New York, then to the Azores and on to the Spanish capital. 'We were thrilled,' Di Stéfano recalled at the time. 'We saw it as the highlight of that year. We had a spirit of adventure that made us impatient for it to start.'

While they were a cosmopolitan group, with the predominant Argentinians alongside footballers from Peru, Paraguay, Uruguay and Colombia, they were not so worldly that the idea of the USA did not leave them a little wide-eyed and, in some cases, mildly apprehensive. How would they order food, Rossi wondered, given that none of them had much of a command of English? Ismael Soria and Alfredo Mosquera, black Peruvians, felt concerned they would not be permitted to stay in the same hotel as their team-mates, having heard that in parts of the US there was racial segregation. They were relieved when they checked into the Hotel Bedford in Manhattan just as the same as their colleagues. But the players were disappointed to discover that because they only had transit visas they were officially restricted to the hotel premises, and police officers had been stationed at the front door.

With ingenuity, Di Stéfano and some of his colleagues escaped to explore Broadway, use the subway, visit the Empire State Building and duck in and out of bars and restaurants that looked just like those in the Hollywood movies they had seen at the picture-house in Bogotá. And they laughed when a barman slid their whisky glasses along the bar towards them, as it reminded them of the Billy Wilder film, *The Lost Weekend*. Welcome to the Big Apple.

If America, where they spent three days effectively as vacationers, having negotiated permission to leave the hotel to see the sights, seemed glamorous and exotic, Spain seemed a little grey. Di Stéfano arrived in Madrid for the first time when it was marking 13 years since Francoist armies had taken control of the capital, ushering in an end to the Civil War. Basic foodstuffs were still rationed, and the Millonarios tourists were told, by one hostel landlady who accommodated the squad, not to go out into the streets with too much cash on them, because of the risk of being robbed or scammed. Yet Spaniards were being regularly assured that the period of post-war austerity was coming to an end. Around Atocha station, where Di Stéfano and his colleagues were billeted in the Nacional hotel while they were in the capital, work had begun on expanding the access roads to the rail station. In the city's boutiques there were signs of a growing consumerism, and imported products were advertised in the newspapers. The Millonarios tourists found ways of spending their bonus money. Di Stéfano, who as a young man liked to look dapper, had himself fitted for a new overcoat.

They discovered a lively sporting culture. They attended a bullfight and a basketball match. They arrived to the headline news that, in a country that carefully regulated gambling, a butcher from Cantabria had scooped a record win on the Quiniela, the equivalent of the pools, predicting results of matches, of over one million pesetas.

The Millonarios players went to watch the reigning Spanish league champions, Atlético Madrid, suffer an unforeseen defeat against another heavyweight, Atlético Bilbao, as the Basque club were then known – the Francoist policy outlawing foreign names meant the club could only resume calling themselves Athletic Bilbao in the 1970s – at the Metropolitano stadium. The outcome, a Bilbao victory by 2–1, weakened further Atlético Madrid's defence of their league title, which Barcelona would take from them the following month.

For the curious outsider, the spectacle was instructive. On the Atlético Madrid bench was one of the era's more charismatic coaches, Helenio Herrera, a globetrotter of Argentinian origin whose life in football had taken him from Morocco to France and to various Spanish clubs. As his team went 2–0 down shortly after half-time, Herrera, never a self-effacing coach and a touchline gesticulator, would no doubt have been conspicuous. So, for a curious outsider watching his first Spanish league match, would have been the Atlético Madrid inside-forward, Larbi Ben Barek. The brilliant Moroccan, a distinguished international with France from the 1940s onwards, was a trailblazer not just for African sportsmen, but for a Spanish football beginning to show an appetite for importing high-class talent from abroad.

Millonarios's first opportunity to show themselves off to the Spanish public, ahead of the Real Madrid Bodas de Oro, would be an exhibition fixture in Valencia. It was Di Stéfano's maiden visit to a city he would later call home and develop a great affection for. He reached the coast, after a long bus journey, at precisely the time of year when Valencia is at its most vibrant, celebrating the festival known as Las Fallas, with its booming fireworks and street parades. Valencia versus Millos offered its audience something rather less pyrotechnic. The teams drew 0–0 in a contest the Millonarios players deemed badly refereed. Di Stéfano felt convinced he ought to have had a penalty awarded in his favour.

His first goal on Spanish territory would have to wait. The Millonarios itinerary next took the squad from the mainland back over the Atlantic to the Canary Islands. Unión Deportiva Las Palmas were struggling in the league table, but evidently motivated by keeping the company of these exotic guests. Thirty thousand islanders filled out the arena. The Canary Islands newspaper *La Provincia* thought they had not only been regally entertained by the distinguished guests but taught something, as well. 'Now we must hope these visiting aces have gained some imitators,' wrote the correspondent 'Juangol' – the nom de plume was then much in vogue on the sports pages – and he praised the calm teamwork of Millonarios. 'They play authentic football, delivering the ball to whoever is best placed to receive it, trapping it and slowing down the play when that's what needed and, rather than mad clearances, passes to colleagues in a position to continue the move.'

Meanwhile, *ABC*'s correspondent purred at the 'fine, dominating combination play' of the South Americans, but complimented the hosts on their rugged policing of the Millonarios strikers. The tourists felt a little unlucky in that Antonio Báez had a shot ricochet back off the post, and Adolfo Pedernera shaved the Las Palmas crossbar late in the game. A Di Stéfano header, meeting a Rossi free-kick, had been splendidly saved. A Di Stéfano goal, taking advantage of a defensive error, brought the scores level at 2–2. Las Palmas then achieved what few others would in the heyday of the Blue Ballet: they beat Millonarios – Di Stéfano, Rossi, Pedernera and all – thanks to a late winner. Di Stéfano put it down to complacency, to having gone into the game with too haughty an attitude towards a club close to the bottom of Spain's first division.

Back in Madrid, Millos would raise their game, sensing they were in prestigious company, part of a major event. Real Madrid's Bodas de Oro had the character of a grand production. A short film had been released in cinemas to commemorate the institution's half-century, directed by the renowned Rafael Gil; and a book on the club, the *Libro de Oro*, was published. A good deal of diplomatic pomp surrounded the occasion. 'You are the best possible emissaries of Colombia,' the Colombian ambassador to Madrid told the Millonarios squad, overlooking the fact that only one of the senior players in the regular starting XI, 'Cobo' Zuluaga, was actually a native Colombian.

ABC buffed up the social significance of the guest-list. At a time when strong international relationships were cherished by Spain in the face of its own austerity, as well as Cold War anxiety and isolation from European states hostile to the Franco regime, Colombia was a loyal friend, it said. 'Not only is there an explosion of enthusiasm to see what is plainly the best team currently in the Americas,' wrote Manuel Rosón, a journalist with strong ties to Real Madrid, 'but the visit marks the establishment of football relations with one of the countries of the purest, unbreakable españolismo.' His tribute then turned all colonial. 'Colombia: favourite daughter, loyal sister, whose heart beats in common with ours, who shares our glories and our misfortunes.'

Fact was that the same Colombia, loyal sibling, favoured offspring, had only just recently stopped being the expelled orphan of the football family. That was thanks to compromises reached with the South American Confederation and FIFA and spelled out in the Lima Pact of a few months earlier. Millonarios president Alfonso Senior would later thank his Real Madrid counterpart, the ambitious, well-connected Bernabéu, for having assisted in bringing together a frosty FIFA and a disgraced, 'pirate' league; and the reciprocal tours of 1952 between Madrid and Millonarios were appreciated by the Colombians as an endorsement of their mended status in the world game.

Madrid, for their part, needed the Millos stars, and the fact that this was the Blue Ballet's European premiere, to add lustre to their 50th birthday do. Bernabéu felt grateful that Senior had made his team available for the best part of a month in the middle of a busy year. For the Madrid public, however, though some football followers were aware of Millos's reputation, and familiar with descriptions of Di Stéfano's excellence, of Pedernera's vision, the name of a famous English or Italian club on the posters for the Bodas de Oro would have had more immediate resonance. But the league calendars in both those countries were too tight to guarantee their sending over a team in spring for a mini-tournament rather than a one-off exhibition match. So the third club on the bill would be Norrköping, of Sweden, serial champions of a nation of diplomatic bridge-builders, and happy to travel south as the representatives of northern Europe at Real's international celebration of their 50-year milestone.

A man can learn much about his host as a guest at that host's birthday, and Real Madrid's jubilee meant much reflecting on where the club had come from and where it might be going. The *Libro de Oro*, the 'golden book' brought out for the anniversary, emphasised a dramatic rise, particularly in the fourth decade of Real Madrid's existence, the decade in which Bernabéu, once a player with the club, and later a coach, and a servant in all sorts of administrative capacities, minor and major, had held the office of president.

At the time of his taking over, the club had recorded a tenth-place finish in the league, and had an average home gate of around 16,000. But Bernabéu had a dream, centred on a stadium that could house 100,000, where enthusiasts would stand outside the gates complaining that was not enough. Through ingenuity and a little help from his connections in the seats of power in the capital, he raised the money to purchase enough land in the Chamartín district and begin construction. By 1947, the outsized arena was Real Madrid's home.

It would later bear the name of President Bernabéu, a man who, the *Libro de Oro* informed a swelling fan-base and the distinguished visitors to the jubilee celebrations, was 'to Real Madrid as Philip II had been to Spain: the best of kings. His leadership of our club means knowing there will be no bad outcomes, that every hurdle will be surmounted. Under Bernabéu Real Madrid is in its golden age, at the forefront.' He brought to the task, this eulogy went on, 'a will of iron', 'a sharp vision', an 'unyielding belief in the greatest destiny'.

Shrewd businessman, warm in his friendships and sometimes fierce in his enmities, Bernabéu liked being flattered. He was at once a man of his times and sharp-eyed enough to see which way the future wind was blowing. He had seen action in the Civil War, volunteering to join Franco's army in his early forties. He would be awarded medals for his service to the cause once the conflict was over, and he emerged as an influential figure in the Madrid of the post-war recovery, as Spain crawled its way from austerity towards prosperity. In the *Libro de Oro*, the president's 'gravitas' and his 'parsimony' are emphasised. He was famous for personally wandering around his pride-and-joy stadium turning lights off when he left of an evening, and to players he always emphasised the need for 'humility'.

His ambitious stadium plans, when first unveiled, seemed wildly grandiose, a folly. And any reader of the *Libro de Oro* seeing the sentence 'Real Madrid now have as their watchword "Nobody is better than me", a watchword Bernabéu has gained for the club,' had better not have had a copy of the league table too close at hand, or indeed too many Liga tables of recent seasons. The capital's dominant club as Real Madrid reached the age of 50 were not Real but Atlético, the reigning champions. Atlético Madrid had won the league in 1950 as well.

Spain's best team in March 1952 was neither of the Madrids. It was Barcelona, poised to pick up their third championship in five years. Indeed, the 'golden age' of Bernabéu's Real Madrid presidency at that stage featured just one silver medal in the league, as runners-up to Barcelona. To find the last time Real had completed a season at the top of the hierarchy, you had go back to 1933.

What Real Madrid had cultivated, though, was a distinct image, or at least so visitors to the club in March 1952 would be assured. Among the long panegyrics devoted to the anniversary by *ABC*, the mainstream newspaper, was a piece by Domingo Fernández Barreira, doyen of the sports paper *Marca*, arguing that although Real Madrid might lag behind others in terms of trophies acquired, they stood at the vanguard of 'the sport of the masses'. 'Real Madrid is the antithesis of stagnation,' wrote Barreira. 'It represents, beyond doubt, the best instincts for development in Spanish football, as an institution and as a team. It always takes the first important steps forward, like making the Chamartín stadium a reality.'

The stadium's impressive dimensions would help Real Madrid's global profile. Di Stéfano had heard about its huge projected capacity on the radio in Argentina, though it took him a while to realise that the name he heard was not 'San Martín' but Chamartín, after the Madrid district where it stood.

Bernabéu encouraged cheerleaders in the local media. Barreira's anniversary tribute continued: 'More important than the current position in the league is how the team defines its unique style in modern football, a style and a school that never allows the brilliance of individuals to be suppressed, never lets itself become efficiently grey to the point of robotic. Real Madrid's is an artistic football, governed by inspiration, dramatic and handsome.' Quite a drumroll to usher in the festivities arranged around Real's Bodas de Oro.

Alas, higher forces conspired against the occasion. The rain bucketed down on day one of the triangular tournament. It was Norrköping versus Millonarios, Scandinavian rigour against the rococo of the Blue Ballet. At a quarter to five on 28 March, a sodden Di Stéfano, who wondered if it might even start to snow, so chilly was the air, kicked a ball in earnest for the first time at Chamartín. Within minutes he was aware that the Swedish team had dedicated two markers to him. The match finished in a 2–2 draw.

Expectations for the next fixture, Madrid versus Millonarios, would be framed in that context. Millos had played three matches on their Spanish tour, and not yet won. As Di Stéfano told the writer Rafa Lorente: 'The general opinion was that Madrid would beat us easily. They thought we were short of pace, played too many passes and dribbles.'

Two days later, Real Madrid were reminded of the importance of humility. It rained again, and the playing surface at Chamartín, churned up by the previous match and soaked further over the following two days and nights, appeared less than conducive to the sort of slick, passing game Millonarios favoured. When the defender Raúl Pini picked up an injury that inhibited his movements in the first half, Millos felt further compromised. There were no substitutes, but evidently no holding back on the severity of the challenges on that account. Di Stéfano finished the game with his ankle swollen to almost double its usual size. A press photographer took a picture of the enlarged, bruised joint after the final whistle. The damage had been done by the boot of Madrid's Gabriel Alonso.

But Di Stéfano had left a more lasting mark on the 70,000 in the arena, witnesses to the player's class. It had been glimpsed in flashes against Norrköping, and in Valencia and in the Canary Islands. It was now exhibited in the match that mattered most. Millonarios led 3–0 by half-time, two of the goals partly attributable to defensive errors, from José María Zárraga and Joaquín Navarro, but the superiority of the South Americans was plain. 'One extraordinary footballer soars above the rest,' observed *ABC*. 'Di Stéfano, strong and dynamic, quickly made spectators believe they were in the presence of an incredible player, with the gift of seeming ubiquitous, with the authority to provide the best opportunities for his team-mates.' A Di Stéfano pass, from deep, was at the origin of Pedernera's goal, Madrid's third after the winger Castillo had opened the scoring. In between, a fluid Blue Ballet move ended with a neat one-two between Di Stéfano and Báez and a thundering finish by Di Stéfano.

He put Millonarios 4–0 ahead just after half-time, meeting a cross from Castillo. 'Although they are a team with quality in all the positions,' *ABC*'s 'Juan Deportista' wrote, 'Di Stéfano is their impetus and the machine to create difficulties. His movement is exceptional, such that he appears in every position, including in defence when danger occurs there.' That protean responsibility would be needed in the later stages of the match, with Pini limping. An irritated crowd began to harangue the losing side, and Pahiño noisily appealed for penalties. By the end Madrid had pulled two goals back, Millonarios showing signs of fatigue.

The president of Real Madrid behaved magnanimously in defeat. In a Millonarios dressing-room filled with the bouquets of flowers each of the touring players had been presented with ahead of the kick-off, Bernabéu offered his congratulations to the victors. He made a point of seeking out Di Stéfano. The player was struck by the president's firm handshake, and a gesture that he would recognise over the next decade as a sign that the president's restless ambition was making him ruminative – Bernabéu was chewing on his cigar, moving his head in a slow nod.

He had a plan for Millonarios's Man of the Match. Would Alfredo come along with him, just down what is now the Castellana Avenue to the studios of Radio Nacional, and take part in a broadcast about the match, the tour, the Bodas de Oro? He wanted another voice, too, for the popular *Tablero Deportivo* show. The obvious one: the loudest voice in the Millonarios choir. Pippo Rossi had also made a strong impression on the Spanish public, and not just for his amplified bellowing. In the victory over Madrid, one newspaper noted, Rossi was 'ungainly, and pugnacious, capable of every irregularity the referee let pass – all of them – but a magnificent player and enormously active.'

Di Stéfano and his best friend Rossi happily agreed to join the chat show, under Bernabéu's watchful gaze. Towards the end of the programme, the Real Madrid president turned to one of the broadcasters present and, gesturing towards Di Stéfano, said: 'This guy just *smells* of football.'

By Bernabéu's own accounts, some of which are a little contradictory, conversations with Millonarios's directors had already begun in the VIP section of Chamartín about the possibility of his one day putting Di Stéfano in the centre-forward position then occupied by Pahiño. The Madrid president floated the idea of a $30,000 fee, to which the answer was not a firm 'No' but an indication that the situation was complicated, with Millonarios midway through the defence of their Colombian league title, and with a packed schedule of lucrative exhibition matches and tours ahead of them; they would get back to Bernabéu on the subject of the centre-forward. The conditions set by the Lima Pact, the compromise solution that FIFA and the South American Confederations had agreed the year before about the status of their pirate league and their stolen players, meant there was a fearsome tangle of vested interests to unthread.

Besides, Bernabéu was not the only powerful man seduced by the perfume of Di Stéfano's football. Nor was he the only one sheltering from the rain in Chamartín, admiring the Blond Arrow.

Josep Samitier, a former player of distinction for Barcelona and Spain, and Barcelona's coach until 1950, watched Madrid being outplayed by Millonarios in his capacity as a talent-spotter and recruiter for Barça. He liked the look of Di Stéfano, who remembered being first introduced to Samitier on that trip. Samitier backed his judgement by recommending to his club that they explore the possibility of bringing the player to Catalonia.

Samitier and Barça had spent much of the season already congratulating themselves on their excellent, resourceful acquisition policy, on their progressive instincts in looking abroad for players who would raise standards while also bringing something fresh and innovative to a sport on the rise in a country trying to escape austerity and insularity. Just as Atlético Madrid had benefited from enticing Ben Barek, the French-Moroccan who could curl a ball like a boomerang with the outside of his boot, Barcelona were making their way to the 1951–52 league championship in large part thanks to László Kubala, a striker who had come to be one of their own via a torturous and personally heroic route.

The son of a builder and a factory worker, with a family tree whose immediate branches were Slovak, Polish and Hungarian, Kubala was born in Budapest and grew up with a talent and love for football at an auspicious time to be a promising young footballer in his part of the world. His contemporaries would be the Magnificent

Magyars who reached final of the 1954 World Cup. But, for the young Kubala, it was definitely not an auspicious time to be an Eastern European. He had moved to Czechoslovakia as a teenager, according to some accounts to avoid Hungarian military service, and represented the Czech national team as a teenager, this after having scored goals prolifically for Ferencvaros in Hungary. He was back there, playing for Vasas Budapest, and indeed with the Hungary national team, shortly after Czechoslovakia's communist revolution of 1948. By the time Hungary's communists, taking their lead from the Soviet Union, took full power in that country, Kubala had left, seeking opportunities to earn his living away from the Eastern Bloc as a professional footballer.

Quite an adventure he would have. He disguised himself as a Russian soldier to reach the border with Austria, hiking over mountains to cross it, and made his way eventually to Italy, fearful all the while about the wellbeing of the wife and son he had left behind, and who were planning to swim across the Danube and meet him in Friuli in the north-east of Italy. They made it. So did he. He was offered a job playing at Pro Patria, a club then in the top division of Italian football. There the administrative problems began. Rather like Di Stéfano and most of the South Americans who had made their way to Colombia around the same time, Kubala was denounced to FIFA by his previous club, via the Hungarian Football Federation who identified him as a defector. Unlike Di Stéfano and the well-rewarded stars of the Colombian El Dorado, Kubala barely knew where to turn in his exile for money to put food on the table. Pro Patria let him go, because neither they nor any Italian club could see how he could be properly registered.

But he kept playing football in Italy, alongside fellow refugees from behind what was then known as the Iron Curtain. They formed a touring team called Hungaria, in which Kubala pulled most of the strings. He had enough talent around him for Hungaria to entertain, draw a curious audience and pick up money from clubs ready to host them. Kubala's brother-in-law, Ferdinand Daučík, was their coach. And in Spain they found some of their most important friends and allies.

Hungaria toured Iberia in the summer of 1950. Like Millonarios less than two years later, they played Real Madrid at Chamartín. Like Di Stéfano in 1952, Kubala scored two goals in the fixture. Bernabéu rather liked the look and the scent of this powerful, brave, skilled Eastern European striker at first glance too, but he found, as he later would with Di Stéfano, that his keen interest in recruiting him meant overcoming some unusually complicated bureaucracy.

Again, as with Di Stéfano, Barcelona were also in the bidding for Kubala. It reached a stage where both clubs offered the exiled Hungarian a contract, but Barcelona moved with greater stealth. The Spanish Federation supported their push to have him freed from the constraint of the FIFA ban that prevented him playing as a professional, and when they won the 1951–52 league championship, it was with Kubala as an official Spanish citizen, happy to broadcast his gratitude to a state that had released him and his family from the oppression of Stalinism. Kubala finished his first full season as a league champion and as Barça's leading scorer, his 27 goals just one shy of Pahiño's total for the campaign. His brother-in-law Daučík, meanwhile, was Barcelona's head coach.

In their boardroom, as the team closed on the league title, Samitier came to the directors with a plan to make Barcelona even stronger the following year. He suggested they should pair Kubala, the majestic Magyar, with the intriguingly fast, powerful master of Millonarios.

CHAPTER 9
TUG OF WAR

Leaving Madrid after the Bodas de Oro tournament was tough for some of the Millonarios players. They had been scheduled to fly down to Seville for the last match of their tour of Spain, but because of the inclement weather they ended up going by train. As the locomotive's wheels began to turn on the rails at Atocha station, the party were still three short. When the trio who had slept too late, partied too long or lingered while shopping finally boarded the train it was already in motion.

Di Stéfano had enjoyed Madrid, even if he reported that some of his lasting impressions had been of a Spainish capital still wrought by the effects of the Civil War, less sophisticated in many ways than his native Buenos Aires. He realised he had made a good impression on the sodden pitch of Chamartín, and would do so at Sevilla, despite being tightly marked. Once again he did not finish on the winning side. A missed penalty by Pippo Rossi could be blamed for the 1–1 draw in Andalucía. Di Stéfano could blame his friend personally, too. He had been about to take the spot-kick himself, not a duty he always sought, but Rossi was adamant that it should be he who struck it. He messed up, to Di Stéfano's surprise and to the delight of the goalkeeper, José María Busto, who saved it and received generous congratulations from Rossi for the speed and the stretch that allowed him to reach the shot. Soon afterwards, Di Stéfano showed how a dead ball should be struck. His goal came from a fierce direct free-kick.

By the time they set off back to Colombia, via Portugal, New York and Miami, each of the players clutching the hand-made Virgin de la Macarena statuettes they had been presented with as typical Andalusian keepsakes by their hosts in Seville, they felt tired. Several carried injuries that had prevented them playing the final match. They were now in a hurry to get home, Millos president Alfonso Senior having reluctantly had to decline the francs on offer for a supplementary match in France because the fixture list of the Dimayor could not been concertinaed any more to indulge its leading club's extra-curricular excursions. A gruelling calendar awaited them, and many miles on rickety aeroplanes. Just before they embarked on the transatlantic return, news reached them that the Norrköping squad, travelling home from Madrid's Bodas de Oro, had suffered an alarming emergency landing in France, en route to Sweden, their plane in trouble in stormy weather. There but for the grace of God go we, thought the Millonarios players, who had developed a refrain they spontaneously muttered together at the beginning of journeys by air. 'What pain we put ourselves through, all the way there, all the way back! All for the fatherland!'

Back in their adopted fatherland, Colombia, Millonarios's apotheosis year, the waltz through the 1952 championship, the tours, the VIP visits could not help but have a fin-de-siècle feeling. They knew the money would run out at some point for football's El Dorado experiment. Di Stéfano remembered a creeping awareness that trips to some of the clubs in the Colombian interior were not bringing in as many spectators as they had when the star-studded spectacle had been a novelty, and that Millonarios's own purse-strings were becoming stretched. He had agreed a new contract with them in February, but by the November was convinced they were in arrears with certain payments to him. On the field, though, there was little sign of disillusion: Di Stéfano's determination to finish as champions, beat all-comers and be the top scorer of the Dimayor again was as powerful as ever.

It was the terms of the Lima Pact, more than anything, that made the halcyon days of Colombian football feel finite. To fine-tune the deal, FIFA had delegated one of their éminences grises, the Italian Ottorino Barassi, a man so trusted by the game's governing body that during the Second World War he had been handed the World Cup trophy for safekeeping in case an invading army should remove it from the Rome bank safe where it had been stored. Barassi tinkered and talked with the leagues, clubs and federations who felt wounded by the El Dorado experiment, and with the Colombians, he came up with these key elements of the Pact, to resolve the issues of dozens of players who had moved clubs without registration of appropriate transfer fees:

The players of the División Mayor [Dimayor], who previously belonged to clubs from the national associations of Argentina, Bolivia, Brazil, Chile, Ecuador, Paraguay, Peru and Uruguay and have been transferred without the corresponding transfer certificate from their clubs of origin, are authorised to continue playing at their current clubs in the División Mayor until, at the latest, 15 October 1954. They are obliged immediately afterwards to return to their club of origin.

In short, time was being called on Colombia's party. Cinderella's glittering horse-drawn carriage would turn back into a pumpkin at midnight in the middle of October two years hence, and the founders and figureheads of El Dorado would have to plan for a heavy hangover after that. The Lima Pact also contained a warning:

> The Colombian Football Association [now with the Dimayor under its umbrella again] is not authorised to transfer a single one of these players to another national association, unless an agreement has previously been reached with the national association concerned.

Here was the clause that spelled out firmly than any club without a previous claim on any of the rebel players would be barking up the wrong tree if they started negotiating a transfer with a Dimayor employer.

Di Stéfano knew his situation was complicated, his future uncertain. In Madrid, on the March tour, he had heard that Bernabéu had made, or at least authorised, an enquiry to Millonarios about his availability. By the time Madrid arrived in Colombia in July for the reciprocal tour, the interest was an open secret. And once Madrid and Millonarios came together again for the Little World Cup in Caracas, and Barcelona's scout Josep Samitier was there to watch, Di Stéfano was well aware there were two important Spanish clubs monitoring both him and each other's moves, just as they had in the complex manoeuvring to capture Kubala over the course of three years of tug-of-war, and political machinations, with Barcelona seizing the initiative at the key moment and then celebrating the Hungarian's excellence weekend after weekend.

So much for the two parties from Iberia. Besides Madrid and Barcelona, there were two South American institutions with a hold on Di Stéfano: a temporary hold in the case of Millonarios, a longer-term one in the case of River Plate, to whom, under the terms of the Lima Pact, Di Stéfano would be contracted from the end of 1954. Then there were several other parties to whom the footballer was beholden. There was Sara, and there were Nanette and Silvana, both of whom had been born in Colombia and barely knew the Argentina of which they were both citizens.

There stirred in Di Stéfano, champion of the Dimayor, dandy of the El Dorado era, a sense of nostalgia as he entered his 27th year. He and his immediate, growing family now longed for home. While Bernabéu and his delegates were negotiating with Millonarios, and Samitier and senior members of the Barcelona board were making contact with River Plate, Di Stéfano was hatching a plan that, had any of the four clubs concerned with his future known about it, would have tested their patience. He wanted to step back from football, at least for a year or so, return to some of the satisfactions of the life he had known in Buenos Aires and indeed in the Argentinian countryside – be the apprentice agriculturist again. He wanted to be on a ranch, reading *Martín Fierro*, his favourite, formative epic poem with its memorable lines. Lines such as: 'With this I bid farewell, without saying until when; he who seeks security, chooses the softer path; I follow the hard way, and so that is how I will continue.'

After Christmas 1952, Di Stéfano gruffly turned his back on Millonarios. His wife and daughters had travelled to Buenos Aires for the holiday, and he joined them, skipping off from a post-season tour of Chile that had been added to the Bogotá club's criss-cross trajectory through the South American continent. He was adamant he would not be part of that tour and, furthermore, wished to extend his stay in Buenos Aires. He felt content being close to his parents and his siblings, settling into the house and garden he had bought in the district of Parque Chas out of his considerable earnings in Colombia. He could travel easily from there to a ranch at Navarro, west of the city, that he had also put money into and was now his father's chief farming interest. And he would not be flying in terrifying aircraft several times a month over the mountains and the Caribbean.

The notion that Di Stéfano might absorb himself in that bucolic life, at an age when he had reached his physical and athletic peak, and with nearly two years left until he was obliged, if they wanted him, to come under the orders of River Plate again, even now seems abrupt. To his colleagues, it can only have seemed odd, given his talent, his competitive drive and his love of his sport. In retrospect, given where football would later take him, it can also seem, as a Real Madrid director-general Inocencia Arias later put it, so improbable that it's 'like imagining Beethoven had given up music before he composed his fifth symphony, or most of his sonatas, in order to work as a butcher in Bonn'. But his appetite for a long break was genuine. He talked through his position with his sister Norma, among others, and she found him at ease with the idea of coming home.

His own account of that crossroads, unusually soul-searching, was set out to the writer Rafael Lorente in 1954. 'In me there are two characters,' Di Stéfano explained. 'There's the one that chases a dream, drives for adventure, to throw myself completely into something. The second one never admits the possibility of failure. With the dilemma of whether to set off for somewhere new or to stay in Buenos Aires, I heard two different voices. The first said: "I'll go, follow the adventure, however it ends up." The second said: "Don't worry, Alfredo. Everything will sort itself out, and you'll end up winning."'

The new adventure was Spain. Di Stéfano knew he was in demand. Both Barcelona and Real Madrid had talked to Alfonso

Senior, the president of Millonarios, about him. Senior then realised there was a problem with his superstar, his principal attraction, when Di Stéfano sent word he was not coming back to Bogotá for the 1953 Dimayor championship. Senior heard him explain that he'd had enough of the flying. Senior promptly wanted to know what Di Stéfano, if he was indeed bent on terminating his stay in Bogotá, was going to do about the $4,000 he had received from the club as an advance on the next season's salary. A dispute over the sum, which Di Stéfano maintained had been owed to him from the previous season, eroded their relationship.

Their relationship was not, though, at an end. For Millonarios, Di Stéfano would remain a going concern, a slice of asset, at least until the music stopped for the Colombian 'pirate league', in mid-October 1954.

River Plate, meanwhile, anticipated that, thanks to the terms of the Lima Pact, their interest in a player who had fled, along with several others, to Colombia in the previous four years would at least bring a dividend. The *froideur* between River and Di Stéfano had not thawed greatly since he left there in 1949, but the possibility of the former traitor playing for them again was there. River supporters had seen a stream of players leave, and standards drop as a result, although they had won the league again in 1952. A chief antagonist from the time of Di Stéfano's messy departure from the club was no longer at the helm. Antonio Liberti, the president he and Rossi had confronted at the beginning of the El Dorado exodus, had just been replaced by a new president, Enrique Pardo.

By the beginning of April 1953, still a year and half until Di Stéfano would be officially a River player again, and a full 12 months since the tour of Spain where Di Stéfano had met and been praised by Real Madrid's Santiago Bernabéu and Barcelona's

Josep Samitier, his pair of South American stakeholders were singing distinct tunes. Senior, at Millonarios, reported the absent player to FIFA for failure to honour his contractual obligations, which tied him to the Colombian club until 1954. There was both pique and pragmatism in the gesture. Senior had the power to complicate Di Stéfano's immediate future, and the complaint to the world governing body, which he could withdraw, acted as a reminder that for another 18 months Millonarios were still actors in what was becoming an intriguing drama.

In Buenos Aires, meanwhile, Di Stéfano was reportedly painting his dining-room when the phone rang and he was informed by his old co-tenant in Bogotá, the former Barcelona player José Castillo, of Senior's denouncing him to FIFA. Not far away, Pardo, addressing the subject of a player who had now effectively walked out on two clubs in the space of four years, was clarifying River's position. 'Essentially, Di Stéfano remains a River Plate player,' said the River president, in a teasing interview with the newspaper *Barcelona Deportiva*. 'Right now,' he added, 'it seems Barcelona Football Club are interested in his services. In that case, that club will have to ask our club, whether it's about a loan for one or two years or a permanent transfer. If we reach an agreement under the right economic conditions, there is nothing, as far as River Plate is concerned, to stand in the way of his joining and playing for Barcelona, once, of course, the player has no further commitment to Millonarios.' Pardo confirmed he had been in official contract with Barcelona.

At that stage Barcelona looked a step or two ahead of Real Madrid in the securing of Di Stéfano's future services. They had a supplementary motive, too, for acting urgently to bring in an established goalscorer, a footballer to excite their supporters.

Kubala had been taken ill, with what was diagnosed as tuberculosis, a condition that was then such a threat to public health in Spain that sinister songs were sung about it in school playgrounds – 'We are the tuberculosos, and we hurl and spit wherever we meet!' – and several different terms were in common use to refer to the disease. The story that Kubala was 'tísico', that he had contracted 'Koch's germ' (after the German scientist who identified the bacteria), made headlines, and the coverage of his battle against the infection would be on the news agenda throughout the winter of 1952–53.

Signing Kubala, guiding him to Spain and registering him as a Barcelona player despite all the hoopla that his ban and defection from Hungary entailed had been a coup for the Catalan club; Madrid had been outflanked on that piece of business, and then had to watch as Kubala led their rivals to the championship. Some Barcelona directors reckoned they could repeat the trick. The case of Di Stéfano clearly presented complications – his ban, and also his desertion of his current club, Millonarios – but, on the face it, signing him looked more straightforward than signing and importing Kubala. The Hungarian had the Red Army against him; Di Stéfano had merely gone AWOL from the Blue Ballet.

Besides, Barcelona's Samitier and the club's lawyers and treasurers were entitled to feel that having worked through the Kubala dossier, they really were the 007s of the increasingly complicated business of global recruitment in a sport of rebel leagues, independent-minded players, Iron Curtains and what was to become the most high-stakes club rivalry anywhere.

Samitier had charm and diplomatic skills, as well as a good eye for a footballer. He was a former player, now in middle age, and charming and paternal when he needed to be, even with egocentric players. In May 1953 the satirical magazine *El Once* had on its cover a cartoon showing Samitier as a nanny, recognisable by his face, slicked-back hair and cigar, but wearing a black dress and an apron. In each of his hands he has a squealing, fussy infant: the one on his right is Di Stéfano, his surname on his satchel, his shirt bearing the dark slash on white of River Plate, with a speech bubble above him that says: 'I don't want to go by aeroplane!' Clutched firmly in Samitier's left hand is Kubala, depicted as another belligerent child, in Barcelona kit.

Kubala had been demanding to recruit, not so much on the matter of wages but because he wanted his wife and child to be with him, and his brother-in-law, the coach Ferdinand Daučík, to have the lead coaching job. Madrid had baulked at that; Barcelona ceded. Now, in Buenos Aires, Barcelona's delegates set about persuading Di Stéfano, the inactive footballer, painting his dining-room, that a life on the Mediterranean would renew his enthusiasm for the game he excelled in. Barcelona sent their envoys to his house in Parque Chas; they reassured him that Sara, Nanette and Silvana would fall in love with the capital of Catalonia once they saw it; and they made a point of stressing that he need hardly ever use an aeroplane in Spain's Liga. Almost all the away trips around Iberia could be managed by bus or train.

Di Stéfano was coming round to the idea. His father, Alfredo senior, who once seemed so reluctant, when his eldest son was fascinated with, and fabulously gifted at, football, to indulge his aspirations to make it his work, now advised against the idea of his son's retreating from the game. Di Stéfano, now unmistakebly a man given to questioning the authority of employers, listened to his family. He heard Barcelona's entreaties. The voice inside him saying 'Follow the adventure' spoke loudest. He accepted the invitation to travel to Spain to meet the Barça president, get to know the city, but with no guarantees. 'Treat it like a holiday,' his father apparently suggested.

He, Sara, Nanette and Silvana touched down in Madrid on 23 May, two days before *El Once* depicted him as a fussy baby on the front of their magazine. Samitier met them at the airport and they set off by car for Barcelona, via Valencia, a journey long and stickily hot enough in the early Spanish summer for even the most fearful aviophobe to think twice about the alternatives to air travel, particularly with two young children stuck in the back seat gazing out of the windows at flat, parched sierra. The party stayed overnight in Valencia for a particular reason. Barça were playing there that night, in the Copa Generalísimo, as the Spanish Cup was then known. Barça were on their way to beating Valencia 6–1 on aggregate to reach the quarter-finals.

The scorer of the tie's first two goals? Kubala. So much for his debilitating tuberculosis. The ailment that doctors had earlier in the season reported made him 'unfit for sport' had proved an enemy no more daunting than crossing the Iron Curtain, or swerving past the best defenders of Spain's Primera División. Kubala's recuperation, up in the hills of Catalonia, had been remarkably swift given the extent to which the infection had initially affected his lungs. By the time the 1952–53 season was coming to its conclusion he was back in action and fighting fit. And, indeed, fighting. He had been sent off in a 1–0 Barcelona win against Real Madrid, a result that leapfrogged Barça over Real in the table, after an aggressive altercation with Joaquín Oliva, the Madrid defender.

Whether it was Kubala's recovery from TB, and the thought that, with the Hungarian healthy and the team triumphing, reinforcements were a luxury they might not require, or whether it was more sinister pressures, or a broad combination of factors, it appears that, even as Samitier checked Di Stéfano, Sara and the girls into a hotel while an apartment was arranged for them, Barcelona had started dragging their feet over aspects of the transfer.

A proposal from River Plate, direct from its president Pardo, had reached Catalonia just a few days before the Di Stéfanos did, offering two possibilities that would make Di Stéfano a Barcelona player from October 1954, when River were to assume his registration under the terms of the Lima Pact. Barça could have him on loan for two years, by paying River a million Argentinian pesos, or two million pesetas in Spanish currency, or buy him outright, for two and a half million Argentinian pesos, with the opportunity to stagger half the payments over two years. Pardo asked that, in either eventuality, the deal should be signed by the end of May. River received a prompt response, signed by the Barcelona president Enric Martí Carreto, offering less than Pardo's asking price, suggesting a one-year loan with an option to buy and proposing that Barça play a pair of friendly matches in Buenos Aires instead of a portion of the fee.

So far, so good, at least on the one front of what was a forked set of negotiations as far as Barcelona were concerned: their deal with River was one prong, the release from Millonarios the other. Readers of the daily press in Catalonia were still being presented with all the signals that Di Stéfano was the next big Barça star. He posed for staged photographs around the city, holding up Barcelona paraphernalia. He posed in the Barcelona jersey of the time, with its two broad vertical cherry bands on blue. He spent time socially with Kubala, with whom he struck up a warm friendship, one of very many that the genial, popular Kubala would establish well beyond the city he made his home. What they could not do was rehearse their dream partnership on the field. The Catalan Football

Federation, the body to whom Barcelona answered in terms of administrative rules, reminded the club that, because of the FIFA ban imposed on Di Stéfano because Millonarios had denounced him, he could not so much as play in a friendly for them.

By June, he had become frustrated and confused. Here he was, a footballer without access to his profession, living not on a ranch in Argentina but in a flat on Calle Balmes, one of the busiest streets of a city smug on the successes of a club he could not be a part of. That club seemed unable to explain what was happening and when the problems might be resolved to a young family who had just been getting used to the idea of a settled life in Buenos Aires. 'I got fed up,' he would say of that summer, one that seemed especially hot and humid to a newcomer to coastal Catalonia.

Come July, Barcelona promised Di Stéfano that a breakthrough was in sight. A deal had been reached with River Plate, a down-payment made to the Argentinian club. Barcelona's president now intended to tidy up negotiations with his Millonarios counterpart, Alfonso Senior, while Barça's squad were on a South American tour, an expedition similar to the one Real Madrid had made a year earlier. But, truth was, that prong of the transfer deal was turning blunt.

Barcelona had despatched a lawyer, Ramón Trias Fargas, to Bogotá to talk to Senior. The negotiations did not go well. The Millonarios president, already hostile to the player for having abandoned the club – owing them money, according to Senior – was also dealing with the effects of the Lima Pact on his and Colombia's extravagant football circus. A Millonarios without Di Stéfano was a harder sell for tour matches; a Millonarios without all its pirate stars would be a lesser brand still, come 1954. Barcelona found very little charity when they discussed the terms under which Millonarios would give up their remaining stake in the player.

To try to sweeten the fallout in Colombia from Di Stéfano's departure, Barcelona instigated a public relations campaign on behalf of the player. He put his name to a statement of contrition and affection for the country he had made his home for three years at Millonarios, and it was given to the Colombian magazine *Diario Gráfico*. 'If I made the decision not to return to Colombia it was because of the fear I experience having to make so many journeys in aeroplanes,' Di Stéfano explained. 'I will preserve the very best of memories of this country. My children were born there and my time with all of you will always have a place in my heart.'

The day that was published, Barcelona president Martí Carreto received a call from Trias Fargas, his emissary, telling him that Senior wanted $40,000 for what was effectively 14 months' worth of Di Stéfano. According to one meticulously researched chronicle of the affair, *El Caso Di Stéfano*, by Xavier G. Luque and Jordi Finestres, the Barcelona president was outraged, and set out his final offer very firmly: 'Ten thousand dollars and not a cent more.' Trias Fargas, tenacious through the whole saga, replied hopefully to Barcelona's president that he thought he could bring the price down from $40,000, and perhaps leaven it with an offer of some Barcelona exhibition matches in Bogotá, to be shoehorned into their current tour. He also raised an alarming spectre. He told Martí Carreto that people linked to Real Madrid had been talking to Senior.

Decades later, Di Stéfano, who spent the rest of his life being asked about the events of that summer, the long stay in Barcelona, the extended preamble to the transfer, would maintain he knew very little of what was going on in the offices of all four clubs concerned, or in transatlantic communications between Spain's two largest cities and Buenos Aires and Bogotá. He was certainly not alone in that. So secretive, and paranoid, did the toing and froing become that Barcelona's various executives and emissaries took to using code in telegrams about the transfer. A Trias Fargas message referred to 'Clínica Marly', or Marly Clinic, where he meant Millonarios; a Barcelona vice-president substituted the word 'Mora' for the Colombian club holding out for more money from Barça, while River Plate was 'Ricardo'. The diamond at the centre of all this, Di Stéfano, was codenamed variously 'Dulce', meaning sweet, or 'Roca', rock.

The rock concerned was gathering moss, his frustration hardening. The new Spanish season edged closer, the summer got hotter. Barcelona's Samitier sneaked him onto the pitch for some low-profile action, and gained a further insight into the competitive zeal released whenever Di Stéfano took to a football pitch, however lowly. Samitier arranged for a Barcelona reserve team to play at the Costa Brava town of Palafrugell one Sunday. Di Stéfano would guest for the home club. He scored, on a sandy pitch; he charmed. Offered the chance to take a Palafrugell penalty, he graciously insisted one of the regular members of the club do the honours. Then he growled. Samitier told him at half-time it would be best if, having had his run, and pleased the crowd and the holidaying *barcelonistas* who had come to watch, he gently retreated to watch the second half from the small stand, lest he be injured. 'When *I* put on a football kit, I play for 90 minutes,' came the sharp reply.

Over the next 12 years, Di Stéfano would go on to score more goals against Barcelona sides, and in much grander arenas than Palafrugell; and far, far more goals against Barça than any of the Barcelona executives who spent that summer exploring ways to complete his transfer would ever have imagined. Each one of them would be a painful reminder of how a deal with Millonarios never came to fruition and the agreement with River Plate would be rescinded.

Real Madrid were ready to play their hand.

Bernabéu, the president of Real, had put the details of the pursuit of Di Stéfano in the hands of a young, personable ally named Raimundo Saporta, 26 years old and soon to be named a director of the club. So young was he that Sara Di Stéfano apparently asked, when he introduced himself to her in Barcelona in the summer of 1953, whether he was the son of the Saporta with whom her husband had said he had an appointment. Di Stéfano had agreed to speak to him, but they did so as discreetly as possible. Saporta had, according to Di Stéfano's later recollection, a document to show him. It was a deal with Millonarios that he could go to Madrid, with their blessing, Madrid having agreed to compensate the Colombian club. The fee was $27,000, although for the time being both clubs would publicly state that Millonarios's yield from the deal was merely a commitment from Real Madrid to play some friendlies in Bogotá.

At first, Di Stéfano recognised the development as the obstacle it clearly represented: Madrid, with Millonarios in their camp, were pulling on one end of the Gordian knot that was stopping him playing football, while Barcelona, with River Plate their partners, tugged on the other, and the knot was tightening. There the stand-off might have remained except that both Spanish clubs had invested financially.

A further difficulty suddenly loomed for Di Stéfano, as for Barcelona, and for Madrid. The Spanish Federation announced that no foreign players could be registered by clubs for the forthcoming season after 24 August. They had been urged by the government to limit the number of non-Spaniards employed in the sport.

The timing suggests the unresolved Di Stéfano saga had a direct bearing on the edict. As the journalist and author Sid Lowe discovered, almost half a century after the imbroglio, in researching his book *Fear and Loathing in La Liga*, the president of the Spanish Football Federation, Sancho Dávila, had informed General José Moscardó, head of the Delegación Nacional de Deportes, effectively the sports ministry, that Di Stéfano had been the subject of 'an extraordinary fight, bigger still than over Kubala', and that because 'Millonarios cannot transfer him without agreement from River Plate, who won't give it, and River cannot sell him to Barcelona now... it is a mess.'

Moscardó's ministry then explained the reasons for capping the number of foreign players in Spain like this: 'Their participation benefits in no way the prestige of Spanish sport, and contracting them nonetheless involves a more and more considerable economic commitment.' Twin themes of early Francoist Spain, austerity and insularity, chimed through those words. The measure had its supporters within football. The former Spain national coach Eduardo Teus had campaigned prominently against too many foreign imports. The newspaper *La Vanguardia* approved: 'It should have happened earlier', it reckoned, and described the open-doors policy of Spanish professional football as creating 'a kingdom of opportunists, speculators and traffickers'. This in the same summer that Kubala, the asylum-seeker granted Spanish citizenship who had thrillingly put Barcelona at the summit of the league, made his debut for the Spain national team.

But it was not hard to depict Di Stéfano, caged in his flat on Calle Balmes, meeting Madrid's energetic emissary, Saporta, while trying to get answers out of Barcelona, as the sort of modern, itinerant opportunist that the more nationalistic protectors of Spain's most popular sport felt suspicious of. He had left two clubs, River Plate and Millonarios, in two different countries, Argentina and Colombia, on bad terms. He had spent the summer telling reporters from the Catalan media he was impatient to start representing Barcelona, while taking a different tone with others from the Madrid-leaning press. *El Once*, the magazine, satirised him in its edition of August 24, in a column written in verse, and including the line: 'Millonarios! Lovely name for a sporting organisation'. The ditty continued:

> I am a simple footballer,
> I've always felt the colours of a club,
> As I have said one thousand times.
> As I am a serious person
> And a respectful player
> I always offer my services
> To whoever is the highest bidder.
> Because the love of sport
> Burns in my heart
> And I think it's only wise
> To get something out of it.

But it was Barcelona, not Di Stéfano, who in another twist to the saga effectively suggested that the player should become even more promiscuous in his loyalties, let his head be turned in a completely new direction. Exasperated that Senior kept rebuffing them, and paranoid that the central government in Madrid was now set against Di Stéfano joining them, Barça came up with a new scheme to protect their investment and prevent his joining Real Madrid. They decided to explore the possibility of the rights for him they had bought from River Plate being transferred to Juventus, of Italy.

Juventus liked the idea, although there remained the problem that, without Millonarios's okay, the Italian club would not be able to field Di Stéfano until late 1954. And Millonarios's intentions were by now set on another course. Their president, Alfonso Senior, had been in Madrid in early August, where he'd had a fractious meeting with a Barcelona executive and had been wined and dined by Santiago Bernabéu and other Real Madrid power-brokers. Ominously for Barcelona, when Senior left the Spanish capital he did not fly back to Colombia but to Paris. There he had an appointment with FIFA, who held the key to making Di Stéfano available for action, once they were convinced Millonarios no longer had a complaint against him and that the terms of the Lima Pact had been honoured by the player, his Colombian club and his Argentinian former employers, River Plate.

Di Stéfano felt genuinely bewildered. The tale goes that at one of his meetings with a Barcelona vice-president he remarked that among the many films he'd seen in Barcelona that idle summer had been *The Third Man*. With only a thin smile, he said he felt just like Orson Welles's character Harry Lime: present but invisible; central to the script, but concealed in the shadows.

He had a growing sense of abandonment, too. It had emerged that his key point of contact with Barça since he touched down in Spain in May, the scout Samitier, would be leaving the club's employment. He felt doubts, well-founded, that Martí Carreto, the Barcelona president, was not as ardent in his desire to sign him as some of the other Barcelona executives. He became conscious that, without matches to keep him in shape, he was likely to seem a less attractive addition to a Barcelona squad that was already strong enough to have just won the league and the Cup, and indeed less alluring to a Juventus or a Real Madrid.

Saporta, Madrid's youthful emissary, had by the end of the summer cultivated a good relationship with Di Stéfano. They were contemporaries; Saporta was solicitous, helpful. He exuded a confidence that, in the confusing swirl of contradictory reports about where the saga was heading, could be interpreted positively. Madrid felt increasingly buoyant not only that they could block the possibility of the Blond Arrow ending up with Barcelona but that Di Stéfano would be theirs before he was Barça's.

Before the final finesse, the farce. FIFA, and specifically a former president of the Spanish Federation, Armando Muñoz Calero, who sat on the governing body's executive committee, proposed a solution. He had established that Millonarios's gripe with the player had been settled, that Madrid effectively had rights to the year that remained of his registration in Colombia; but Barcelona had paid River the first tranche of their piece of the player. So he suggested the two Spanish clubs share Di Stéfano, under certain conditions. The Argentinian would play for Barcelona in what remained of the 1953–54 season, for Madrid the next, for Barcelona after that, then Madrid, and so on until 1957.

A clue as to how quickly the document setting out these terms, sent at the same time to General Moscardó at the Spanish government's sports ministry, had been put together was that in the listing of the alternate seasons, 1955–56 had been left out entirely. A clerical error. Meanwhile no clues were needed as to quite what the implications were about the player's sense of loyalty: he would be required to learn quickly how to think and operate like the mercenary he had often been taken for. Not that he could say so out loud. Di Stéfano told the media he felt 'pleased how much effort had been made by the powers that be'. What he really thought, he kept to himself for a period, but in later years he was happy to share it with anybody who asked. 'How was I going to score goals for one of them one day and the other the next? It was an idea that came from people who knew nothing about football.'

Barcelona felt the more prejudiced by the solution, particularly as the clause that allowed the two Spanish clubs to override the timeshare agreement by transferring their slots of the Di Stéfano calendar specified that it could only be through a transfer to one another, and not to a third club such as Juventus. Meanwhile, the sports ministry had agreed that the ban on foreign players would be postponed, officially because, in Di Stéfano's case, negotiations to bring him to Spain had begun before the restriction was put in place. But Barça felt that the immediate beneficiaries of that were Real Madrid, now hurriedly readying themselves for Di Stéfano's debut.

It was the middle of September, the season had already begun, and in Calle Balmes, Sara began packing suitcases. In the Barcelona boardroom, Martí Carreto presided over a heated meeting of his directors. He explained that he felt he had no choice but to sign the compromise agreement with Madrid, a deal promoted by FIFA, the Spanish Federation and a government who had evidently become concerned that the issue might turn incendiary, as well as undignified. The sharing agreement obliged its signatories to make 'their maximum effort to consolidate the friendly sporting relations that exist between the two clubs'. For the Franco regime, anything that might stir up wider hostility between Catalonia and Castile was to be avoided.

Signing over half the rights of Di Stéfano was the last important thing Martí Carreto did as Barcelona president. Realising how humiliated Barça looked, having made the running in the transfer and lost, he resigned. Much later, in an altered, more open political climate, several people who had been close to Carreto at the time said he had felt pressured to retreat from the Di Stéfano deal, that specific threats had been made that his business interests, which involved commerce abroad, would come under government investigation if he pursued the transfer.

By the time a new president took over at a Barcelona still ambitious to build the biggest stadium in Iberia, Camp Nou, and to continue accumulating prizes, with Kubala as spearhead, the terms of Di Stéfano's future had been modified further. Barça had lost the battle, and the crumbs they were left with were deemed an expensive reminder of the defeat. In the middle of October, the interim Barcelona board signed a deal with Real Madrid that gave Madrid all the rights to the player that Barça held, effectively two future seasons, while in return Barça recouped the money they had committed to River Plate and their costs in bringing Di Stéfano to Spain and housing him and his family through that long, hot, confusing and highly charged Catalan summer.

CHAPTER 10

THE CHARMER OF CHAMARTÍN

The same day that the president of Barcelona cleared his desk, his resignation tendered because of the Di Stéfano affair, the man at the centre of the drawn-out dispute felt in a hurry. The league season had started, Real Madrid had agreed to pay their new centre-forward a starting salary of 600,000 pesetas and needed him to begin earning what was a considerable wage for his profession in austerity-era Spain. By the evening of 22 September 1953, the Di Stéfanos, Alfredo, Sara and the girls, were on board a sleeper train bound for the capital.

The schedule for the next 24 hours read like an assault course. 10.30am: Arrive Atocha station, brief chat with Real Madrid-friendly reporters. Noon: Medical at Chamartín, followed by lunch. 1pm: Drop off Sara and the girls at the Hotel Emperatriz. 3.30pm: Presentation to madridistas, supporters followed, at 5pm, by his first appearance in a Real Madrid jersey for what would be his first full match in front of a crowd for the best part of nine months. Nancy, the French club, had been invited to play the sort of friendly that often occupied Madrid in the middle of the week – events designed to keep the turnstiles revolving.

Di Stéfano knew he was not in the best shape well before the routine medical examination registered his weight at a shade under 79 kilos, a good 5 or 6 kilos above what he regarded as his optimum for a balance between agility and the muscular power he brought to bear on opponents. He could recite some of the names he was likely to be lining up with, having had plenty of time to follow the build-up to the 1953–54 season while underemployed in Barcelona, and from the several matches Millonarios had played against Madrid the previous year. But he was apprehensive at being pushed so suddenly into a match situation, one designed to invite supporters' judgement of his value. He was asked if the arrangement to debut, wave to supporters, introduce himself to the media all within a matter of hours suited him. 'Yes,' he replied to Madrid's chief liaison man, and now friend, Raimundo Saporta, and he said it without hesitation.

Madrid versus Nancy was not, by Di Stéfano's own admission, a lavish display of his varied repertoire, but he found he at least had plenty of stamina to leave a significant souvenir for a crowd swelled by his presence, some of whom missed the early moments because of hold-ups caused by a tram accident on one of the avenues leading to the stadium. He scored his first Madrid goal, with a header, in the 67th minute. Nancy were beating their hosts 4–1 at that stage, and Di Stéfano's goal would be the last of the evening.

For his league debut four days later he took his place at centre-forward in a stronger Madrid line-up. By now he had established his co-ordinates a little more in practice with the team, and learned a little of how the coach, a Uruguayan, Enrique Fernández, envisaged his role. His Argentinian compatriot, Roque Olsen, would play alongside him, at inside-forward; the skilful Luis Molowny would operate immediately to his left, while a young arrival from northern Spain, Paco Gento, had an opportunity to establish himself on the left wing. Di Stéfano's task, Fernández indicated, would be to play as a fairly orthodox number nine. Pahiño, the leading scorer in the league in 1951–52 and the player with whom Di Stéfano had been involved in a fracas in the Millonarios–Madrid game in Caracas, had moved to Deportivo La Coruña in the summer. It was Pahiño's position that Di Stéfano would be slipping into.

Saporta, meanwhile, had busied himself with helping to find a home for the family. They settled on a chalet in the El Viso district. Sara felt sceptical about the length of the contract Di Stéfano had signed, and thought two years rather than four might be the right length of stay in a place so far away from her and her husband's native Argentina, and, given Spain's post-war, internationally isolated situation, a country lacking some of the everyday comforts of Buenos Aires. Their new address was a good central one, in Calle Oría, less than a ten-minute walk from Di Stéfano's new place of work, a stadium under what seemed almost constant construction at the time, as it expanded. Its 80,000-odd capacity was greedily aspiring to accommodate another 20,000. Di Stéfano had an obligation to bring in the people to occupy those extra seats and standing places, and to elevate Real Madrid, the club whose supporters had gone a whole generation without a national championship to applaud.

On the morning of his competitive debut, Madrid were third in the Primera División. By the evening, *Carrusel Deportivo*, the popular new radio show that broadcast from around the country's arena, often via reporters resourcefully and rapidly making their way from a place in the crowd to a public telephone line, was excitedly broadcasting that Los Blancos, the team in all white, had moved to the top of the table after three matchdays, a tenth of the way through the campaign. Madrid had defeated Racing Santander 4–2. Di Stéfano marked the occasion with a goal. He had not, though, left a superstar impression on journalists. 'The 80,000 spectators who filled Chamartín felt a little let down,' reported *El Noticiero Universal*, 'because the phenomenon Di Stéfano did not show people the expected phenomenal things. He was obscured by two factors, close marking by Santander defenders and also the excessive weight he has accumulated.'

Di Stéfano's own initial impression was that, though Spanish football lacked some of the progressive thinking around the sport in South America, tactically and in terms of its openness to improvisation, nevertheless Real Madrid had good, professional habits in terms of physical conditioning. It took, by his reckoning, another three matches to feel he could belong, to sense he had lost the surplus kilos, recovered the physical and psychological match fitness that his long period of recess had blunted. However, if he was not meeting his own standards in his first month of action, then he kept it disguised behind some useful goalscoring statistics. In his second outing at Chamartín, he scored again, Madrid's second in a 2–1 win over Pahiño's Deportivo La Coruña.

In the next game, away at Sevilla, he ended the 90 minutes feeling in good shape, light on his feet, in tune with his colleagues, and sharp with his finishing. He had scored Madrid's only goal of that game, though it was not a good day for the team. They lost, dropping points for the first time, and fell off the top place in the table.

Was it to be the same old story for a club who had last won the league in 1933, a club whose reputation was for producing some attractive teams, nurturing some fine players, but who, even under the new leadership of an authoritative, ambitious and well-connected president, Santiago Bernabéu, usually flattered to deceive when it came to the business of clinching prizes? The loss at Sevilla might easily have been taken for a symptom of another year of Real

Madrid being their city's bridesmaid club. Madrid's next match, Di Stéfano's fifth as the footballer arousing the greatest curiosity at that stage of the Spanish season, would really examine how far they might have improved. It was at home to Barcelona, the champions.

In the timeline of Real Madrid's transformation in the Di Stéfano epoch, that October 1953 meeting between the Barcelona who less than two months earlier had a contract that said he would be their player, the Barça who had put him up in their city for a long period of the summer in the expectation it would be his home, and the Real Madrid who had then taken from Barcelona all their rights on him, is a D-Day, a Year Zero. The scoreline seemed emphatic even then. It finished Real Madrid five, Barcelona zero.

The man who had lingered around the capital of Catalonia, confused, frustrated and inert from May to September, took ten minutes to inflict the first of many damaging wounds on the prestige of Barcelona. Di Stéfano's goal, the opener, emboldened Madrid. By the 40th minute, they were 4–0 up against the club who had at centre-forward his predecessor as the league's most glamorous foreign player. László Kubala watched, impotent, as the amigo he had spent time with from April to August, the pal he had hoped to be exchanging passes with and probably to be taking out for the odd long night through various Ramblas and Avenidas, galvanised the opposition. Di Stéfano looked as if he could carry on galvanising Madrid long into that night. He scored their fifth goal with seven minutes of the match left.

The result was that the clubs swapped places at the summit of the league, Madrid leapfrogging Barcelona, who would have to wait until early February to topple Madrid from top place again, and then they looked down on them only for a single week. The individual joust for the best goalscorer that season would be a duel as enduring as the two clubs' race for the title; Kubala, like his club, finished second, behind Di Stéfano, whose 28 goals at a neat average of one per game made him the Pichichi, the top marksman, of the league, four goals ahead of Kubala's haul. Barça would have the satisfaction of inflicting on Madrid their heaviest defeat of the campaign when the teams met each other in Catalonia in the spring, but Di Stéfano left a calling card at Les Corts, Barcelona's home ground, too. The crowd there received him as expected, with hostility, mindful of recent history and of the menace he clearly posed to that club's sliding supremacy. He listened to seven minutes of jeering before scoring the first goal of the day. Barça then responded with five of their own.

It would not be enough to derail Madrid's momentum. The newcomer, the outsider, had rapidly become the figurehead of the team. He seemed ubiquitous. Di Stéfano looked for responsibilities on the field, to pop up in areas beyond those traditionally compartmentalised for the number nine. He was also pressed into tasks he did not push himself forward for. He became the designated penalty kicker, at least until, in later seasons, alternative specialists joined the squad. But if any of his first Madrid team-mates imagined his diffidence about taking spot-kicks came from a fear of the concentrated pressure around one man that penalty-taking means, that notion would be dispelled by Di Stéfano's sixth match for Madrid.

It was his first capital derby, away at Atlético's Metropolitano stadium and so robustly contested that it persuaded Di Stéfano that the most intense rivalry for the Real Madrid he had joined was not with Barcelona but the one shared with their nearest neighbours. It was certainly a handy fixture on which to make a decisive impact. Real Madrid were awarded a penalty in the first minute. Di Stéfano converted. They won another four minutes before half-time. Di Stéfano converted to equalise for 2–2. The leadership of the league wobbled again when Atlético went 3–2 up. Cue Di Stéfano. With his first hat-trick for Madrid, he brought the scores level. Olsen, with the last goal of a see-saw afternoon, ensured all the points went back across the city with the visitors.

Penalties had never been a key part of Di Stéfano's repertoire; nor would they have figured in any calculations he might have made privately about how likely he was to finish as the highest goalscorer in a single league campaign, an honour he had by the age of 28 achieved in Argentina, Colombia and now Spain. Di Stéfano did work, though, with characteristic determination, at taking direct free-kicks, his principal weapon the power and precision of his right foot. The architecture of the average defensive wall was, in the football of the 1950s, generally less sophisticated than it would become in the latter half of the twentieth century, but then the balls were heavier, so there was less possibility of elaborate bend and curl. There were also fewer free-kicks, as referees tended to be more forgiving of heavy challenges. But when Di Stéfano did have a dead ball in front of him, and the goal within 30 metres, it was a drumroll moment, a prospect to anticipate with breath held, and an expectation of the spectacular.

Madridistas thrilled to many unexpectedly spectacular moments from their new idol. Atlético ended up on the wrong side of another narrow defeat against Real in the derby at Chamartín, Di Stéfano scoring the two goals that answered Atletico's early lead and maintained his club's position at the top of the table. One of the goals was especially nifty and captured nicely by a cameraman behind the Atlético goal, for broadcast in cinemas for the so-called *No-Do* programme, an abbreviation for *Noticias y Documentales*, an important source of news for Spaniards, as well as a propaganda vehicle for the Spanish regime. Visitors to movie theatres watching the *No-Do* sports résumé at the end of February saw black-and-white pictures of an unusual goal. They could clearly make out Di Stéfano's joy as he turned his head around, back to goal, to confirm that the audacious backheeled flick he had attempted, blind to where the goalkeeper stood, had indeed bamboozled Luis Menéndez, the Atlético keeper.

Readers of *Marca*, meanwhile, had the image of what looked like a performing seal on their front page one late March morning in 1954. It was Di Stéfano, horizontal to the ground, his right knee bent so the lower half of his leg pointed to the sky. His heel had just connected with a ball some four foot off the ground, a ball coming at him fast, having skimmed off the head of Olsen who had leaped up to meet a corner. The acrobatic flip, resourceful, spontaneous but reminiscent of similar actions he had tried, with success, in South America, gave Madrid the lead in that match. Pity that it took place in low-key Valladolid. Several times in years ahead, Di Stéfano would find himself asked to re-enact the remarkable strike, in simulated conditions, for the camera.

These improvisations were instinctive; the readiness to try them took practice. Gento, a timid teenager who had arrived at Real Madrid from Cantabria a few weeks before Di Stéfano, looked on in some awe at the manoeuvres his worldly, weathered senior colleague would rehearse. 'In training, he never stopped inventing ways to shoot and dribble and it was like that for all the 11 years we were team-mates,' Gento recalled. In time Gento would become a footballer audiences looked to for his own unique tricks with the ball. Many of them he learned from Di Stéfano.

He got used to taking orders from him, too. Gento had been recruited by Bernabéu for his potential, and his searing pace. He arrived raw, and, by his own admission, naïve. Di Stéfano took the measure of the flying winger and deemed him to be at his best when he stuck to his flank. When Gento strayed into the inside-forward's territory, a barked instruction, delivered in a gravelly *bonaerense* accent, would correct him. 'Hey, Paquito! Get down that wing, and put in the cross as soon as you can. And sweat for it!'

Gento was not the last colleague to think that orders from the Blond Arrow sounded like barbs. Di Stéfano's notoriety as a gruff commanding officer was established early in his Real Madrid career. Younger players found it alarming, a jolt to their ears. Amancio Amaro, who also came to Real Madrid from the provinces – Galicia, in Amancio's case – and, like Gento, later rose to the top of the club's hierarchy and the affections of supporters, remembers that an apprenticeship served alongside Di Stéfano meant moments of real terror. 'If you didn't put together a move well, or it broke down because of you, you would hear about it,' Amancio testifies. 'Alfredo was a very strong character, a *cascarrabias*, a curmudgeon. You needed to realise you had to watch what he did more than listen to what he said to you. On the pitch, he would insult you.'

Amancio, talking about a Di Stéfano he remained close to for half a century, chuckles at how he used to be chided. 'He would insult me, using swearwords. Afterwards, with the match over, we'd be mates again. You started off respecting him so much, you wouldn't answer back, but in time you would say something in reply. What he wanted was to make things better, get you to improve. His words and his phrases were used as a stimulus, not as a censure.'

The words and phrases had an intended shock value, and to many Spanish colleagues, the oaths sounded novel. 'He had a vocabulary I hadn't come across before,' smiles Amancio. 'In La Coruña, if you did something bad, they'd call you a donkey. Here in Madrid it would be *puta madre*, son of a bitch, and stronger things I wasn't used to. With Alfredo's insults, there was never a double meaning! He had a vocabulary that came, shall we say, from the other side of the Atlantic.'

Di Stéfano also brought with him what would become a trademark, his earthy aphorisms from South American football. He spoke about the game like the graduate of River Plate's La Máquina he was, the man schooled under the machismo of Argentinians like José Manuel Moreno, the man who had been the bosom buddy of roaring Pippo Rossi. But he had first known them as an apprentice. He arrived in Madrid a grown-up, with attitude.

He kept the sage sayings of Carlos Peucelle, his influential coach and mentor in his early days at River, as touchstones. Madrid players came to know by heart Di Stéfano's parable, learned from Peucelle, of why football should never be a sport of long balls punted hopefully into the air.

'What's the ball made of?' he would ask.

The reply: 'It's made of leather.'

Next question: 'Where does leather come from?'

Correct response: 'It comes from cows.'

'And what do cows eat?'

'Why, grass of course.'

Ergo: 'Keep the ball on the grass, boys, that's where it has always been meant to go.'

At Madrid, Di Stéfano evolved his own ideas about where he was meant to be on the field. 'He revolutionised the concepts we had in Spain about the game,' according to Vicente Miera, a team-mate at Madrid and later coach of Spain's gold-medal winning

Olympic football team. 'We were used to football being thought of in distinct segments, defenders concerned with marking strikers, a midfield organiser without much right to get involved in creative play, a centre-forward waiting for the ball to come to him. Alfredo was all-terrain, with the capacity to finish as well. When he arrived it was as a number nine. We thought he was going to be always up front, expecting passes. No. We very soon saw he would be coming deep, exchanging passes, contributing to the organisation of the team, defending when the opposition had the ball. It was really striking the different things he did, the way he thought.'

Not even Madrid's goalkeepers could expect to be out of earshot of his commands, or allowed to play at their own tempo, when Di Stéfano deemed it necessary to act more urgently. The Spain international keeper Vicente Train remembers how moving to Real Madrid from Espanyol meant rethinking his own role, not simply as the last line of defence, but as an initiator of attack. 'In one of my first matches for Madrid, I was coming out to retrieve a ball more or less around the penalty spot,' Vicente told me. 'I jogged out to catch it and, all of sudden, from nowhere, there was Alfredo, getting to the ball before me, way back in my own penalty area, and bringing it under control. I was left there standing like a statue. And where was the ball? Before I knew it, it was up at the other end of the field, because he wanted to get the next attack going more quickly.

'That was how Alfredo was. He would impose himself everywhere. If there was a team-mate he felt was dozing off in the slightest, he'd be right up next to them: "Hey, wake up!" There was no permission in his team to be static, standing still. Whether you had the ball or not, you had to be on the move.'

Enrique Pérez Díaz, the long-serving defender known as Pachín, describes the role Di Stéfano defined for himself as 'like a postman.

He picked up the ball like a postman collects letters, then carries the letters, then delivers them. All at top speed. Alfredo would come back from the forward line or midfield to where you had the ball. When you gave to him you had done your job, you had to go back to where you were supposed to be for the next phase of play.'

Pachín, like the rest, remembers what might very well happen if you then put a foot wrong. 'Sometimes some shouting on the pitch is needed,' he shrugs. 'We knew that we, as Madrid players, were winning the things we won because of Alfredo. We admired him.'

Di Stéfano's authority was not all stick and no carrot. The goalkeeper Manuel Pazos, a team-mate for Di Stéfano's first season at Madrid, tells the story of the journey back from Valladolid on the day of the extraordinary acrobatic, backflipped, backheeled Di Stéfano goal, a day that ended badly for a team who at 3–1 up had sensed they were in touching distance of the first league title for the club in 21 years.

Poor Pazos then let in three Valladolid goals in four dispiriting minutes late in the second half. Fernández, the coach, spared Pazos any compassion when he spoke to reporters about the dramatic reverse afterwards. Di Stéfano, though, soothed him, making a point of sitting next to the suffering goalkeeper on the long bus journey back to the capital, and telling Pazos: 'For sure, they'll blame you. It really isn't your fault. We all lost, together, and when we win, we all win together.'

Pazos never played again for Madrid, but three weekends later, he could call himself a champion. Madrid recovered from the setback, and captured the league title with a match to spare. The club, the Madrid of Alfredo Di Stéfano, had finally broken through a glass ceiling that had held firm since 1933; and his hat-trick on the penultimate day, at home to Valencia, ensured he would finish as the league's leading scorer for a season he had started late, in a country he had lived in barely a year.

Spanish football had a new magician, a new monarch. To be the king of that domain was to rule over a growing constituency of supporters. The press and radio were devoting more time to it, making coverage a greater commercial priority. Spaniards whose Sundays were not diarised around watching live matches were taking more of an interest. Futbolín, or table football, with its figurine players lined up along four metal bars operated by handles, became a very popular diversion, with the devices appearing in bars and in children's gardens or garages through the 1950s. Manufacturers found an increasing demand to paint one of the teams in all white, to replicate Real Madrid.

Real-life stadiums were getting bigger, too. Barcelona had planned the Camp Nou, and there was good reason for Di Stéfano's impression that the stadium he had made his theatre was a permanent building site: the Madrid president wanted it bigger and bigger, to meet the demand for tickets. The year after the breakthrough league title, the Chamartín arena would bear Bernabéu's name, as it still does today. Santiago Bernabéu had seized his moment of triumph to gain approval from the club's board for the rechristening of the ground, as he accepted his members' congratulations for having thwarted Barcelona by making the footballer they thought they had acquired into Real Madrid's motor.

His brilliant first season meant Di Stéfano joined the sport's privileged class. His acting career, the sideline that put him on the big screen in the 1949 Argentinian film *Con los Mismos Colores*, resumed in Spain when he, along with his Madrid colleagues Miguel Muñoz and Luis Molowny, and the veteran Atlético Bilbao forward

Telmo Zarra, were invited to take cameo roles in *Once Pares de Botas* (Eleven Pairs of Boots), directed by Francisco Rovira Beleta. It told the story of a young aspiring footballer and his adventures, romances and perilous temptations on the way to the top of his profession. It came out in 1954. Within another two years, a similar storyline had inspired another film put on wide release in Spain. *La Saeta Rubia* (The Blond Arrow), directed by Javier Setó, starred Di Stéfano as, well ... as Di Stéfano, footballer and moral compass for a group of errant boys, who mend their scampish ways under the famous footballer's benign influence.

A Di Stéfano book was published in Madrid shortly after the league title win, based on a series of interviews with the player by the writer Rafael Lorente. Its tone was convivial, and its readers were guided very deliberately to understand that the 28-year-old subject of *Di Stéfano Cuenta Su Vida* (Di Stéfano Tells His Life Story) was a person of principles, that the various conflicts that had taken him away from River Plate, then away from Millonarios, then from Barcelona to Madrid, said more about iniquitous employment practices by the clubs or football cultures involved than about any recusant tendencies in the man himself; that this was no mercenary but a braveheart. The prologue to the slim volume was written by Armando Muñoz Calero, the FIFA executive who had acted as broker of the deal proposing that Barcelona and Real Madrid share Di Stéfano. His words extolled the virtues of the footballer and the man.

Fame in Spain brought the Di Stéfanos into contact with its high society. Madrid's league champions would be welcomed at the city's chic restaurants, eateries like Valentín, and to places like the art deco Bar Chicote, on Gran Vía, where on a lively night they would rub shoulders with actors and artists – on an especially lively, long night they might even order their cocktails while the Hollywood actress Ava Gardner sat perched on a barstool ordering her umpteenth. Di Stéfano was not the only celebrated entertainer from the Americas to make a new home in Madrid in the mid-1950s.

Nor was he the only footballer to move in glamorous circles. Spain was struggling economically, ruled by dictatorship, observantly Catholic, but in its cities there was an elite with money, and some entertainers and sportsmen were among those with pesetas to spend. They mixed socially, and in some cases, more intimately. In the small world of Madrid's privileged classes, tales travelled fast along the grapevine. Through the autumn of 1954, much chatter surrounded the developing friendship between Atlético's Gerardo Coque and actress and chanteuse Lola Flores, known as the queen of flamenco. She had previously been involved with a leading Barcelona player. The Coque romance was on, then it was off, and then on again. It was not a well-kept secret. Every underwhelming display by Coque for his team would be derided by Atlético fans, who attributed it to his late nights with Lola 'La Faraona' Flores. Coque's career ebbed; Lola Flores's soared.

La Faraona later became a friend to Alfredo and Sara Di Stéfano, whose arrival at the grand Flores house parties close to where they lived in El Viso would prompt a special ritual from the celebrated dancer and singer. 'Alfredo used to come to the door, and he and Sara would be shown in, and, when Lola knew they were there, she would come out to greet them, take Alfredo's coat and fold it very carefully in a special place. She would not do that for any of the other 80 or 100 guests.' The description comes from Lola Flores's nephew, Quique Sánchez Flores.

Quique witnessed his aunt's assiduous hospitality towards the Di Stéfanos as a young boy, and would hear much more about the earlier years of their friendship from his mother, the actress, dancer and singer, Carmen Flores, and from his father, Isidro Sánchez. Isidro was a Real Madrid player and a colleague of Di Stéfano. Isidro and Carmen Flores holidayed with the Di Stéfanos and were close enough for Alfredo Di Stéfano to be chosen as godfather to Quique, who grew up to become a distinguished footballer and a fine coach.

'The way my mother described my parents' social world to me was as part of quite a closed circle of people in Spain who mixed together because of their art,' Quique told me. 'That's whether their art was the performing arts or football. I can see why Alfredo fitted in. He was a great storyteller and had a good sense of humour when he was among his friends. He respected people with talent, and he admired them for it. And Sara was an amazing friend to us, she always knew everything that was going on. They were an interesting couple. She covered Alfredo's back when he needed it.'

Di Stéfano the admirer of people with talent was, in his professional circle, an admired spotter of talent as well. His employers cottoned on to that. The commander of Real Madrid's Spanish champions was, by the end of his first, glorious season, being consulted by President Bernabéu about future strategy, and specifically about possible recruits and probable discards to and from the title-winning squad. The forceful opinions he expressed, loudly and candidly and sometimes with alarming invective on the field were sought, in softer tones, in the boardroom.

Bernabéu felt eager to ensure the wait for the next league title would not be another two decades. He met with Di Stéfano, and the player gave him two pieces of valuable advice in the summer of 1954. The first was to think long and hard about giving up on the young Gento. Madridistas had not been won over by the winger, and some had made that known from the grandstands. Bernabéu explained to Di Stéfano that he had not been convinced through the course of Gento's first nine months in the white of Madrid that he belonged. Moreover, there was another player in his position, from the same part of the country, Francisco Espina, who might prove a better long-term prospect. Espina should be easy to part from his club, Racing Santander, added Bernabéu, if Gento could be sent back there as compensation.

Di Stéfano thought otherwise. For all the expletive, exasperated, cranky bellowing at Gento to stay in his left-wing channel, to time his runs better, that had peppered the season, Di Stéfano liked Gento's pace, and saw many potential goals from his crosses. He argued that the introvert Gento, just turned 20, would fulfil the talent Di Stéfano had seen in practice if Madrid gave him time and their patience. So Pacquito Gento did not leave. Indeed, he remained a Real Madrid player for a further 18 garlanded years.

For the next four of those years, he would benefit from the arrival of another footballer Di Stéfano recommended to Bernabéu in 1954 as part of the masterplan to keep Madrid at the summit of Spanish football. Héctor Rial was an inside-forward with a clever eye for a pass and a competitive steel forged, like Di Stéfano's, first in the Argentinian game of the late 1940s and then in the rebel Dimayor of Colombia, where he played for Santa Fe. Rial, born in Buenos Aires, had Spanish citizenship, through a parent's lineage, so there would be no red tape to cut through to register him as a foreign player.

Bernabéu put himself to work at negotiating Rial's move from his then club, Nacional of Uruguay, and later despatched his trusted aide, Saporta, to South America to resolve what turned out to be another tricky transatlantic transfer, though nowhere near as complicated as the previous summer's coup had been. Di Stéfano, in the meantime, contacted Rial and told him to write two letters, one to Real Madrid, expressing his pay expectations, another to Di Stéfano, saying, privately, how far he would lower them if push came to shove. Both letters should be addressed to Di Stéfano, he stressed.

In the official letter Rial asked for 200,000 pesetas. Seeing that, the rebel, the trade unionist, the Robin Hood in Di Stéfano was aroused. He searched out a pen with the same colour of ink as Rial had used and he tampered with the orginal letter, upping the demand to 250,000, before delivering it to Bernabéu's office. He had secured Rial a pay rise of 25 per cent without his compatriot asking, without the president knowing. Madrid, none the wiser, accepted the wage immediately.

Favour done, cunningly, Di Stéfano put his mind to imagining how effectively Rial's through balls would liberate Gento down Madrid's left flank. A forward line ready to mesmerise not just Spain but all of Europe was halfway to taking perfect shape.

CHAPTER 11
AMBASSADORS

José Mangriñán never supposed his surname might become a verb, find its way into common Spanish usage. He never imagined advertisers would seize upon his brief fame and turn him into a symbol. The truth, as he told his nearest and dearest, was that the task he was assigned one hot September day, the day that made of him a household phrase, took him by surprise and turned him somewhat apprehensive.

Mangriñán was an upright, quiet lad from a pueblo near Valencia and, at 25 years old, still an aspiring footballer rather than an established one. He had been on the margins of Valencia's first team during the 1953–54 season, when his club won the Copa del Generalísimo and finished in third place, behind Barcelona and Real Madrid, in the Spanish league. Their opening fixture for the next campaign was the toughest of all, a visit to the champions.

It already seemed a daunting expedition, and then before kick-off there were preambles to celebrate the home team's excellence, which put the away team's nerves further on extra edge. A short ceremony on the pitch honoured Madrid for their title; another, organised by the newspaper *Marca*, saw Alfredo Di Stéfano presented with his individual trophy for having scored more goals than anybody during the previous campaign. As Mangriñán watched all this he was digesting the instruction the new Valencia coach Carlos Iturraspe had given him during the tactical briefing. 'You, I want you to mark Di Stéfano. Follow him everywhere. Don't give him a glimpse of sunlight. Got it?'

Mangriñán got it alright, and by the end of the first Sunday of the 1954–55 Primera División, had got a lot more besides: A choice bruise or two, left by the boot of the most admired footballer in Spain; a brutal challenge in the eyes of the Valencia players and coaching staff, who deemed it worth a caution, at least, from referee José Mazagatos. Mangriñán had an expanded lexicon of oaths by the end of the day, too. Di Stéfano's reputation for industrial language on the pitch was not just reserved for erring team-mates. Mangriñán, by the account he later gave friends and family, heard himself called a number of names that afternoon, and heard them close up and personal.

The young *valenciano*, no giant at five foot nine, fresh-faced, benevolent looking, had obeyed his coach Iturraspe's orders to the letter. He followed Di Stéfano when Di Stéfano spearheaded the Madrid front line; he tracked Di Stéfano's runs into wide positions. He tailgated Di Stéfano the midfield forager, and, if you look carefully at one of the photographs from the game, you can see him surreptiously tugging at the left arm of Di Stéfano as he readied himself to head a cross.

Most of the time, Mangriñán played hard but clean. His dueller lost his temper. The win-at-all-costs animal in Di Stéfano emerged even before half-time. The sun beat down on Chamartín, and Di Stéfano moved to the touchline during a break in play to take a slug of water. Mangriñán, his shadow, stuck close. 'Hey kid, do you want a sip of water?' said the senior man. The kid said he did, gratefully took the bottle handed to him apparently in the spirit of sportsmanship by his opponent, and then the penny dropped: Di Stéfano had whizzed away from him, with the ball back in motion, having handed over the bottle in a sly effort to distract Mangriñán for a moment, to give his persistent marker the slip.

Valencia had ambushed the champions, 2–0 up within quarter of an hour. This at the home of Di Stéfano's Real Madrid, except as the reporter from *Carrusel Deportivo* told radio listeners, live, Di Stéfano had 'disappeared', was 'not himself', largely because of the limpet wearing the number four shirt for Valencia. At the interval an irate Madrid number nine found himself on the way to the dressing-rooms still stride for stride with Mangriñán. 'Kid,' he snapped, 'are you going to follow me all the way to my own dressing-room, too?'

Soon after the restart, Di Stéfano made his thumping, pugnacious late tackle on Mangriñán. In the outrage and indignation that followed there was a brawl, with players from both teams, including Di Stéfano, involved in the pushing and shoving, and referee Mazagatos had to call them to order. Di Stéfano, in a unique moment of liberation from his stalker, then thought he had scored; the effort was deemed offside. Madrid hit the Valencia post twice. Héctor Rial, the new signing, headed in his first league goal 11 minutes from full time, but that was just about Madrid's only crumb of comfort in a 2–1 defeat.

'Mangriñán was a lion,' beamed Valencia's Salvador Monzó to reporters as he left the pitch. 'Di Stéfano was a mouse in lion's claws,' added Vicente Seguí, scorer of his team's second goal, warming to the theme. Journalists sought out the valiant, unsung Valencia number four. 'I kept close to him, like I was told to by the coach, and Di Stéfano didn't take it too well,' Mangriñán told them. The next morning's edition of *El Alcázar* newspaper wrote of a marking job that 'could have dried out the Pacific Ocean'. The paper had a sermon for the best player in Spain: 'Di Stéfano would do well to complain less about the work of his opponents and try to play the football he is capable of.'

Neither of the combatants forgot that day in a hurry. Mangriñán never played a more famous 90 minutes than when he stifled and suffocated the great Alfredo Di Stéfano, but would again and again be reminded in all sorts of unanticipated ways that he had tamed the untameable. A stationery shop in Valencia started promoting its deluxe blotting paper as 'Papel Mangriñán' – 'It soaks up every drop of ink, never leaving a smudge.'

Di Stéfano, once his radioactive period of irritation at, first, Madrid's defeat and, second, his own impotence, had cooled, would acknowledge that a fair and skilled marshalling job had been accomplished. He may even have been mildly amused that his duel with the little-known Mangriñán coined the word *mangriñánear*. Spanish football followers began casually using the verb to describe the close attention of a defender to a striker. Then Spaniards with only passing interest in the sport made it a metaphor: a possessive spouse might *mangriñánea* her husband, a jealous boyfriend *mangriñánea* his lover.

The word stuck because few defenders managed a Mangriñán on Di Stéfano, especially in his season defending Madrid's historic league title of 1954, and through his long pre-eminence as the most effective match-winner in the Spanish league. Mangriñán had not revolutionised the league. By the third week in November, Real Madrid were top again, a position they would not relinquish until the campaign's end; Di Stéfano had already scored 9 of his 25 goals for the season, including one at Barcelona, in a 3–0 win there. Little good the Catalan club gained from a detailed tactical analysis on how to stymie Di Stéfano laid out on the pages of *Vida Deportiva* magazine, with its nod to the effective patrolling work of the mighty Mangriñán, by the journalist Carlos Pardo in the lead-up to Madrid's visit to Barcelona.

Pardo, a well-connected Catalan, was soon busy with another story. He worked as the Spanish correspondent for the French sports newspaper *L'Équipe*, and they asked Pardo to help with a big idea: an annual competition that brought together the leading clubs from across the European continent in tournament conditions, on a far grander scale than been attempted ever before. There had been events like the Copa Latina, in which Madrid had thrived in the early 1950s, that acted as a slightly haphazard championship of southern European clubs. A 1954 contest between Honved, of Hungary, and Wolverhampton Wanderers, England's champions, had recently been billed as the match to decide the top club in the world. *L'Équipe*'s editors proposed something more definitive, a knockout competition with a broader base and a longer gestation between first round and final.

Pardo put in a call to Barcelona's executives, who agreed, half-heartedly, to a meeting where they promptly brushed off the idea as a 'utopia'. In hindsight, their indifference looks small-minded. But in 1954, Barcelona's executives had any number of reasons for thinking the notion of a long-running pan-European club football tournament too complicated, both practically and politically.

Spain's international relations were at a crux at the time, and volatile. Governments to its east were suspicious or openly hostile to the Franco dictatorship; there was an ongoing quarrel with Great Britain over the sovereignty of Gibraltar; and there were the hangovers of the Civil War, in which citizens of many European countries had fought against Franco's Nationalists, armed with munitions supplied from other European states.

Yet, at the same time, a new era of prosperity and partnership was detectable. Coincidentally, in the same week in September 1953 in which Alfredo Di Stéfano, sporting superstar of South America, had taken up his long-term residence in Madrid, the superpower that was the United States of America, under the presidency of Dwight D. Eisenhower, had signed an accord with Spain that, in return for the use of its territory for military bases, would provide significant economic aid and support. It meant the Franco regime was less of an anathema to the rest of the world. It had gained, in the USA, the most politically muscular Western nation as an ally, and the dollars and the imported goods reaching Spanish citizens would give a very powerful impression of progress, that the country had taken a long stride on its march away from austerity.

That changing climate had only a distant bearing on attitudes to a nascent European Champions Cup, but the journalist Pardo, *L'Équipe*'s delegated pathfinder for Spanish interest in the project, certainly found more positive attitudes in Madrid, seat of government, than in the boardroom of FC Barcelona. He contacted Real Madrid to see what they thought of the idea. Raimundo Saporta, vice-president of the club, invited him to come the next day to the capital, where a chauffeur picked him up at the airport.

Saporta then relayed his enthusiasm to President Bernabéu. The ball was rolling. The Spanish Football Federation approved, Bernabéu took up a senior place on the prospective organising committee, alongside Gusztáv Sebes, from the Hungarian Football Association. Here, for anybody who cared to see it, was a happy penetration of the Iron Curtain in the name of sport: communist, Soviet-bloc Hungary seated around a table with a representative of Franco's neo-fascist Spain.

UEFA, the body formed in 1954 to run European football, took up the baton offered by *L'Équipe*, and made the idea their event. FIFA looked on with mixed feelings. It had already launched something called the European Fairs Cup, a competition contested by cities, rather than clubs. The new alternative looked far more logical, and by the time Madrid had retained their domestic league title, finishing four points ahead of Barcelona, a list of competitors for a 1955 launch had grown to respectable size, illustrious enough for the tournament to call itself the European Champions Cup – with a small degree of flexibility. Some entrants to the first edition were not national champions; some major football countries, like England, did not enter a club at all.

For Real Madrid's players, it represented an opportunity. For their aviophobic star, however, there was one obvious drawback. Di Stéfano looked at the possible schedule for the first European Cup, to be played through 1955–56 on selected midweek dates as a home-and-away knockout, with a final in Paris, and saw there might be some flights to obscure airports. But this was also the Di Stéfano who, as the radio commentator Matías Prats put it, regarded every frontier as a challenge, something negotiable.

'We Spaniards had limited ourselves to think about prestige within our own terms,' Prats said of the coming of the European Cup. 'But Di Stéfano had put into view different signposts. He revolutionised the frontiers of how the game could be played. He replaced static ideas with something more dynamic, with his highly personal system of interpreting his role.' A man who could think outside traditional lines of coaching orthodoxy ought to be the ideal pioneer for a sport breaking down borders.

The Champions Cup whetted executive appetites. Bernabéu, relishing the idea of playing host to international guests at the biggest stadium in Spain that now bore his own name, reminded his players from the very outset of their European Cup odyssey that they should regard themselves as ambassadors. 'For Bernabéu,' recalls Enrique Pérez Díaz, alias Pachín, who joined Madrid in the late 1950s, 'you as a player had to be a madridista from dawn until dusk, behave accordingly, carry yourself with dignity.' Real Madrid's pathfinders in the European Cup had to be standard-bearers not just for the white jersey of Madrid, but for Spain, still a country of infamy for many of its fellow Europeans, a curiously backward place for others, and, as the players discovered, the object of a great deal of heartfelt homesickness for a significant diaspora. There were tens of thousands of Spaniards who had emigrated across Europe in search of work, or had been in exile since the war, who now, with the coming of the European Cup, welcomed a Spanish club playing in the cities they had moved to, and felt delighted if that club triumphed there.

'Don Santiago Bernabéu used to say to us, "You have to win this for the Spaniards out there in the crowd,"' remembered Ignacio Zoco, who captained Madrid on a number of European Cup expeditions, when I spoke with him before his death in 2015. '"They have spent their wages on watching you." There were many, many immigrants from Spain in a lot of the countries we used to go to play in, Switzerland, France, Germany. And that had an impact. They were very grateful to us if we won.'

For their debut match in the intriguing new competition Real's pioneers went to Switzerland, drawn to play Servette. As it happened, there were Spanish exiles living locally, in Lausanne, although these were not all labourers or fruit-pickers. Among them was the king-in-waiting, Juan de Borbón, who had an awkward, exiled status as the theoretical monarch of a Spain whose dictatorship felt uncomfortable about an alternative claimant as head of state living on its territory. Bernabéu arranged for the squad to meet the royal family, fully knowing that the Spanish press would be unable to report or print photographs of the meeting because of censorship. What Bernabéu did not plan was his star player behaving towards one of the royals with a startling lack of etiquette.

Servette proved no pushovers. They had a Mangriñán of a defender in the hefty Rudolph Gyger and a compact back line. Madrid made the running for the opening half but reached the break with no goals. Di Stéfano felt an additional agitation in that, in the heat of early September, his hands had swelled up, so he went into the dressing-room and half-time and immediately ran cold water from a tap over his palms and forearms.

While doing so, he heard a voice at his back. 'Saeta,' it said, addressing him as 'Arrow', his nickname from way back. 'It's not going too well, is it? You know the Spaniards out there are expecting a Madrid win.'

Di Stéfano turned round to see a teenager, smartly dressed. 'And who are you, kid?' he barked at him. 'Get the hell out of here!' The kid he was talking was Prince Juan Carlos, heir to the throne, and, some 20 years later, King of Spain once its monarchy was restored to Madrid. It seems Di Stéfano genuinely did not recognise the young man he had met at the previous day's function with the exiled royals; even if he had, the prince had crossed a line Di Stéfano regarded as far more important than any defined by the privilege of birth. He had come into the players' dressing-room and he had started airing his views.

The solicitous Raimundo Saporta, Bernabéu's right-hand man, smoothed over any offence taken. The second half also cheered up the watching Spaniards, high-born or not. Goals by Miguel

Muñoz, the Madrid captain, and Rial ensured a winning start to the European Cup adventure. Back in Chamartín, Madrid overwhelmed the Swiss 5–0 in the second leg, Rial with another goal and Di Stéfano with two.

So far, so good. The European Cup, even in its inaugural format, meant no journey was much like the last. Madrid's quarter-final took them beyond the Iron Curtain, to a place not of refugee royals but a socialist supremo. Madrid versus Partizan Belgrade would be an away tie where nobody worried about their hands or arms swelling up in the heat. The Army stadium in the capital of Marshall Tito's Yugoslavia, Paco Gento found, 'was like an ice rink, and our feet froze'. The winger Gento, reckoned Di Stéfano, was the lucky one. On the flanks of the pitch snow that had fallen heavily during the January night before the game seemed less compacted, less slippery than in the middle of the field. Di Stéfano lost his footing early in the game; the Partizan players ran with a surer balance. They had splashed kerosene on their boots to resist the snow clinging to the studs and soles. When a Partizan shot struck goalkeeper Juanito Alonso's crossbar, chunks of snow dropped down on him. When a snowball flung from the crowd thumped into the chest of the Madrid coach, Pepe Villalonga, a former military man, he saw it had a stone inside it.

That was not the only aspect of the away leg that unnerved the visitors; Partizan won 3–0 in Yugoslavia, which meant Madrid left Belgrade grateful indeed for Di Stéfano's goal in the first leg, played at the Bernabéu on Christmas Day, almost a month earlier. His was Madrid's fourth, in a 4–0 win, a brilliantly engineered effort, backheeling a pass from Rial to himself, with just enough cushion and angle that he could tee himself up to strike from close to the penalty spot with his right foot.

That goal turned out to be the one that carried Madrid through the so-called 'Snow Battle of Belgrade' that followed. But they rode their luck. Two Partizan goals had been ruled out in the Madrid leg, for doubtful offside calls. Rial, for his part, fluffed a penalty in Yugoslavia, slipping as he approached the spot-kick, and skewing the shot wildly off target. Rising to his feet, he heard a dry, caustic remark from his compatriot. 'What were you trying to do?' Di Stéfano asked him. 'Hit that soldier over there behind the goal-line?' Rial had argued to take the penalty ahead of Di Stéfano, a challenge to the hierarchy that took some daring, even if the penalty-kicking role was not something about which Di Stéfano felt especially territorial.

Trips behind the Iron Curtain, to the Soviet-sympathetic East, tended to put Real Madrid on edge, even when they had started to master the European Cup. They lived in a country where the government and its information ministry demonised communism; the journeys were long, the languages incomprehensible, and the scenes from the windows of their buses often puzzling. In Belgrade they saw women shovelling snow from the tramlines, a task that struck players who had grown up in 1940s, conservative Spain as being men's work.

Some years later, away to Dinamo Bucharest, they met women who they suspected had been employed for a very different purpose. 'That was certainly a surprise,' remembered Zoco, of the December afternoon when they checked into their Romanian hotel. 'We had our rooms, which we tended to share, two in each, all on separate floors.' When the players gathered for dinner, they reported a coincidence. 'One would say, "Hey, there's a lovely girl in the room next to mine," then the next guy would say, "Me too, and she wasn't wearing much." So we knew the intention, which was to distract us before the game.'

Di Stéfano and the senior players laid down the law: 'We're here to play football. After the match, anybody who wants to go out, do their own thing, fine. But before, focus on the game.' Zoco, one of the scorers in a 5–3 win, recalled that, 'afterwards, the coach said, "Okay, you have permission to go out." And, guess what? Suddenly a lot of the players, on a rare chance of a night out, start saying: "No, we'll go back to the hotel." Of course, when they got there, the girls had all gone.'

By the time of that episode, Real Madrid had become the continent's most seasoned European Cup travellers. In the maiden voyage of the competition, they reached the semi-finals via Servette and Belgrade. To make the final they had to overcome a more enduring member of the sport's elite. Real Madrid versus AC Milan would forever be a match-up sprinkled with stardust. In 1956, it put in opposition clubs with conspicuously internationalist tendencies. Madrid had their Argentinians, Di Stéfano, Rial and Roque Olsen; Milan had their Swedes, Nils Liedholm and Gunnar Nordahl, and a member of Uruguay's 1950 World Cup-winning side, Juan Alberto Schiaffino. The first leg, in the capital of Spain, was decided not by Spaniards or Italians, but by goals from Rial, Olsen and Di Stéfano, in a 4–2 Madrid win.

It would be enough, just, to shepherd Madrid's cosmopolitans to the first European Cup final. But the San Siro leg, a 2–1 defeat, gave Di Stéfano much to think about. Milan's Franco Pedroni, a defender, would be detailed to *mangriñánear* Madrid's most influential footballer, and the Madrid coach pre-empted that likelihood by designating Di Stéfano a position in central midfield. 'He had another excellent game,' Gento attested, 'covering practically the whole pitch.' Madrid finished the afternoon both anxious and indignant at the Austrian referee, Erich Stiener, who had awarded a pair of Milan penalties in the last half-hour.

Nine months in, the European Cup was already a resounding success. It had thrilled its inventors. It had stimulated the Real Madrid president and the club's players. But, at home, Madrid had relinquished their status as Spain's most effective team. By the time they took on Milan, their defence of the 1955 league title had long run out of steam. The would-be rulers of Europe had been found wanting in Spain, where they finished third in the league behind champions Atlético Bilbao and Barcelona and lost to Bilbao in the semi-finals of the Copa del Generalísimo. Their most significant yield of domestic silverware was another Pichichi trophy for Di Stéfano, the league's leading scorer for the second time in three seasons, with 24 goals.

He was now Europe's leading man, too. On 14 June 1956, *France-Soir* reported that the outcome of the inaugural European Champions Cup final between Stade de Reims and Real Madrid at the Parc des Princes had been shaped largely by one individual. 'The main reason for the Madrid victory is called Di Stéfano, who pulled apart Reims's defensive system.' In *Le Monde*, a similar verdict: 'Real Madrid fully deserved their win. They have a pearl in Alfredo Di Stéfano, the director of the brilliant white form of the game.'

It had been quite a final. The French club had partisan, patriotic support in France's capital city, although as Matías Prats, broadcasting on Spanish radio, noted, 'thousands of Spanish emigrants, workers from Germany, Belgium, Switzerland and France, added some passion to the Madrid support'. They watched the pride of Spain go 2–0 down after ten minutes and then the Reims head coach, Albert Batteux, fall into a trap that madridistas had begun to recognise. He delegated his midfield player, Michel Leblond, who had scored the opening goal, to apply his best efforts to adhesively marking Di Stéfano, to be his Mangriñán. It worked only partially. The Blond

Arrow, with a burst of acceleration at the end of a careful measured run, slipped away from his patroller to meet Miguel Muñoz's pass and begin the comeback. A Rial header made it 2–2; a third Reims goal demanded Madrid come back again. They did, through the defender Marquitos, on an unlikely safari upfield from central defence, and added a fourth goal from Rial.

Seven goals, the lead switched this way and that: a gripping final for the nascent competition, a fitting coronation for the maiden European Cup's outstanding player.

The showdown in Paris had been anticipated, particularly in France, as a duel between the two number nines, Di Stéfano and Reims's French international Raymond Kopa. Kopa was second best on the night but already knew that if he finished on the losing side, he would probably be playing in the next edition of the European Cup. Santiago Bernabéu had taken a shine to Kopa, and he was central to the Madrid board's plan to strengthen their position in Europe and restore their status, above the likes of Bilbao and Barcelona, in Spain. At the post-match banquet in Paris, Kopa's future colleagues, with Di Stéfano to the fore, made a point of getting to know the France star.

The signing of Kopa, like that of Di Stéfano three summers earlier, had its complications, not least the bar on foreign players imposed by the Spanish Federation. Kopa had to wait for Di Stéfano to be granted Spanish citizenship, for which he was eligible by residency, so the Frenchman could fill what was now a quota of one foreign player per team. But he found himself kept busy even before he could make his official league debut in October. 'There were so many friendlies taking place all the time,' Kopa recalled, 'and compared with Reims, Real Madrid was a big club, like a major industrial company, which had to make sure its investment on buying and paying its players was being matched by income.' Di Stéfano recognised that phenomenon, and had taken to calling his workplace *La Fábrica*, the factory. If midweek days were not taken up with European Cup matches, Madrid would be retailing their renown to all-comers. The players enjoyed the bonuses for their one-off exhibition matches, and Bernabéu enjoyed the fact that Madrid were becoming the most sought-after guests and opponents in the sport.

Spanish embassies across Europe noticed that. They began handling more and more money, as they were often the deposit-point for fees advanced by clubs and cities who wanted to host Real Madrid. Embassy staff abroad reported to the Ministry of Foreign Affairs that a visit by Real Madrid seemed to achieve moments of diplomatic thaw that high-level talking between men in suits could not. For many Spanish ambassadors, representing Franco's Spain in democratic Europe meant knocking on a lot of closed doors. Yet an invitation to a reception to meet Di Stéfano, Rial, Kopa and Gento could suddenly make an ambassador a good deal more popular. Fernando María Castiella, Spain's foreign minister in 1957, called Real Madrid 'the best embassy we have. They carry the name of Spain with prestige, and bring pride to our country.'

A certain diplomacy, Kopa noted, was also necessary if you were an outsider coming into this proud institution. When he told a French journalist he thought the quality of Spanish meat was poor, the complaint was relayed back to Spain's dailies and led to some rather hysterical, wounded headlines.

Kopa learned to tread carefully, especially around the self-styled minister in chief of the Real Madrid dressing-room. An intelligent man whose grandparents had been Polish immigrants to France – he was born Raymond Kopaszewski – and worked as miners, Kopa had come to Real Madrid as a number nine, the best in France and with a reputation there for standing up for himself. The question of how he and Di Stéfano would co-exist in the front five in Madrid's nominal 3–2–5 scheme was the elephant in the dressing-room at the outset of the 1956–57 season. To some, given Di Stéfano's diverse abilities, the idea that Kopa would ease into the central striker's role, with the Argentinian an inside-forward, seemed workable. But when Kopa turned up for practice he seldom had the impression that this was an arrangement Di Stéfano would welcome discussing.

Reflecting on his early months at Madrid, Kopa later referred to a 'tension, a pressure, a seriousness which stopped anybody there being completely serene or relaxed. There was permanent competition, rivalries everywhere, with yourself, with other players, and a public that was unforgiving.'

He struck up a warm relationship with Rial, who spoke a little French. He found Di Stéfano unpredictable, moody. 'He was a special case,' Kopa wrote in his 2006 memoir. 'A formidable player, a superstar and very conscious of his worth, he blew hot and cold. As much as he could be warm, lovable and a great joker, he could also behave like an arrogant despot, especially with people of lower social ranking than his. He'd greet you one day, ignore you the next. If you were a guest at his house, you'd have a fantastic evening. But he could equally come into the dressing-room without saying a word, or hello to anybody, and sit down in his corner.'

Kopa found Di Stéfano unpredictable, even perplexing: 'If it had been a bad day, and there was an edgy atmosphere, all of a sudden he would chuck his socks at another player and then burst out laughing, mess around like a little kid, and start giving you great big pats on the back.'

If there was a contest for the number nine position, Di Stéfano won it. Kopa played a handful of matches as Madrid's centre-forward, but Di Stéfano played many, many more there, while Kopa settled into a role on the right wing. The Frenchman made an excellent job of interpreting the position, tailoring it to his strengths. He learned to live with the quixotic ogre that his most admired colleague could turn into, the Di Stéfano who 'in the middle of a game could plant himself directly in front of a player and insult him in the crudest terms'. He appreciated that the same man would, 'in every match, bring talent, bravery and determination'.

Di Stéfano helped bring Kopa the European Cup gold medal he had denied him in the Parc des Princes. The Bernabéu stadium hosted the 1957 final, which Madrid reached having found that the growing popularity of the tournament was making it tougher. Rapid Vienna had been beaten only after a replay, which Madrid's canny executives, Bernabéu and Saporta, managed to persuade the Austrian club should be staged in Madrid. Not all of it was pretty; each team had a player sent off as the 270 minutes of tight cup-tie neared an end, with Madrid 2–0 up. The first two legs had produced a 5–5 aggregate result, Di Stéfano scoring three times.

The next round was more comfortable, 6–2 against Nice, and in the semi-final Madrid took on English football's first entrants to the European Cup, Manchester United, alias the Busby Babes, an exciting side regarded with some trepidation by Madrid because of the way they had disposed of Atlético Bilbao in the quarter-finals and for the ways they conformed to certain stereotypes of British football. Their centre-forward Tommy Taylor, at over six foot tall, intimidated; Duncan Edwards, a prodigy, had improbable vats of stamina. And Madrid's biggest threat was no Babe at all by now. But at 30 years old, Di Stéfano had the running in him to keep up with Edwards and could use his strength at centre-forward quite as effectively as the towering Taylor – as Harry Gregg, who kept goal for United against Madrid a number of times, recalled: 'I remember Di Stéfano charging into me once in a way continental strikers didn't often do with keepers. I was still shuddering from it an hour after the match.' Indeed, Gregg was still vividly remembering the force of the collision when he was 83 years old.

Di Stéfano scored in the 3–1 win against United in Madrid, and set up Kopa's goal in the 2–2 draw at Old Trafford. Come the final, in front of 120,000, at the Bernabéu, Italy's Fiorentina resisted stubbornly until the last 20 minutes. A Di Stéfano penalty then gave Real the lead and, from a Kopa pass, Gento secured a 2–0 victory to seal their successful defence of the European Cup. General Franco handed over the trophy.

Madrid had recaptured the Spanish league title as well, in 1956–57, Di Stéfano picking up another Pichichi prize for his 31 league goals. It was also the year he first collected a new decoration. The Ballon d'Or, awarded to the European Footballer of the Year, came into being at the same time as the European Champions Cup, another initiative from French sports journalism.

Its first winner, in 1955–56, had been Stanley Matthews, English and a fabulous dribbler; his successor was altogether a different, more protean sort of athlete. 'In the right winger Stanley Matthews,' wrote Gabriel Hanot in *France Football*, sponsors of the Ballon d'Or, 'there is something of Charles Chaplin; in Alfredo Di Stéfano, we celebrate a great knight, who brings together courage and invincibility. Stanley Matthews is light humour. Di Stéfano is an epic.' There was no intention to denigrate the popular Matthews, nor did Matthews begrudge handing over the title to a player he respected. Matthews knew Di Stéfano, and found him to be a man who 'radiated character and intelligence', who 'could size up any situation in a flash', whose 'mastery of the ball was complete'.

By the end of 1958, Di Stéfano had won his second Ballon d'Or, his reign as Europe's finest interrupted by Kopa, the 1957 winner – a system was then in place that prevented the same man being voted European Footballer of the Year in successive years. So Madrid had two Ballons d'Ors, Di Stéfano and Kopa, a pair of names in a forward line that was beginning to trip off the tongue as mnemonically as the famous five of River Plate's La Máquina – Muñoz, Moreno, Pedernera, Labruna, Loustau – did with Argentinians in the 1940s. Madrid had Kopa. They had Di Stéfano. They had Rial. They had Gento. And soon there would be another name as evocative as almost any of those four: Ferenc Puskás.

But the next international doyen brought into the club by Santiago Bernabéu would be a Uruguayan defender, José 'Pepe' Santamaría, as shrewd a choice for his virtues of reading a game, his steel, and as valuable a recruit as Rial and Kopa had been in making Madrid a more potent attacking unit. Santamaría struck up a firm and lasting friendship with his fellow *rioplatense*, Di Stéfano, and if there was one man who could outshout Di Stéfano with his ticking-offs to team-mates, it was Santamaría. 'Those two became real chiefs,' recalls Amancio Amaro, whose career developed alongside both.

In Santamaría's first season, 1957–58, the league title was retained with a significantly meaner defensive record than in the preceding three domestic triumphs. Di Stéfano's 19 goals meant he shared the Pichichi award at the end of a season where Madrid finished three points above Atlético Madrid, and had an opportunity to remind Europe why they were its number one club while also flexing their muscles over the rest of Spain. Sevilla had qualified for the Champions Cup as second-place finishers in the league, because Madrid's status as holders enabled them to defend the prize automatically, with the runners-up in their own country taking their place as Spain's official entrants. Sevilla felt grateful – or they did until they had to play Madrid in the quarter-finals. At the Bernabéu, they lost 8–0, Di Stéfano scoring half the goals that afternoon.

In Budapest, where Madrid met Vasas in the semi-final, Madrid's players appreciated that, Iron Curtain or not, they had become true global stars. Forty thousand Hungarians came to watch the team training ahead of the second leg. The first leg had produced a moment to burnish Di Stéfano's fame, too. Celebrating his hat-trick in the 4–0 win over Vasas, Di Stéfano leaped high in the air, arms extended outwards and upwards, knees bent, hair slicked back by the heavy rain. Augustin Vega, a photographer tight to the goal-line, clicked his shutter at the perfect second to capture the player several feet off the ground, evidently ecstatic. The photograph would later inspire a statue, erected near the Alfredo Di Stéfano stadium on the outskirts of Madrid.

He scored and roared about more goals than anybody in the European Cup in 1957–58, though it was perhaps one of the hardest Champions Cup final yet for Madrid to win. Milan waited for them in the Brussels final, and Cesare Maldini, the accomplished Italy defender, kept close track of Di Stéfano. Milan scored first, with just over half an hour to play.

Now Madrid really needed their pair of Ballons d'Or: Kopa crossed, Di Stéfano equalised. Milan scored a second, Rial responded immediately. For the first time in a European Cup final, extra time was required. A moment of Di Stéfano resourcefulness broke the impasse: taking a cross on his chest, he braced his torso so the ball bounced off it gently into the path of Gento, running from deep, who struck, in off the post, for 3–2.

Three European Cups out of three; four Spanish league titles out of a possible five; four times the Pichichi, twice European Footballer of the Year. Di Stéfano's stay in Spain, the one that started with his being contracted to flit from Madrid to Barcelona each summer, the residence that his wife Sara had thought might last two years at the most, had yielded quite a stack of achievements. There were two more Di Stéfanos in the home, too. Alfredito, Alfredo and Sara's first son, had been born in 1955, and Elena, their third daughter, three years later.

Into his professional life, there now came another superstar, one with whom he would rub along fairly well. Puskás, like Raymond Kopa, had the sort of résumé Di Stéfano might, in a green-eyed mood, have found threatening. A Hungarian, he had played in the 1954 World Cup Final, part of what was perhaps the most admired European national team of the post-war era. And he had one physical asset which Di Stéfano would be obliged to envy: his left foot, a tool of power, of precision; a magic wand.

Puskás had quite a backstory. He had been reported, mistakenly, to have been killed during the Hungarian uprising of 1956, and the fallout from that political upheaval meant there were complications around his signature by Madrid, in the summer of 1958. Like Barcelona's László Kubala before him, he had fled a volatile situation, cutting his ties with Hungary suddenly, for which he had been sanctioned by the Hungarian Football Association.

He was not young either. Puskás was 31 years old when Bernabéu introduced him to a sceptical coaching staff as the striker who could give something fresh to the game's most feted forward line, and some superstar glitter to Real Madrid's travelling show. He arrived looking overweight and out of practice, although Spanish audiences and his team-mates would appreciate fairly rapidly that the slight bulge around the midriff that Puskás tended to carry was no reliable indicator of waning acceleration.

Like Kopa, he was sage enough to recognise he needed to tread carefully around Di Stéfano. 'I studied Di Stéfano intensely,' Puskás would recall. 'He could be a little unpredictable. But what dominated his life was simply the huge desire to win, to be the best, at any cost. Threaten that, and he could be as pig-headed and ruthless as a little child. The standards by which he judged himself were very high, and if his own form did not meet them, he would put in even more effort, more energy. He could be suspicious of strangers, but charming and hospitable to friends.'

Puskás became one. They overcame a language barrier over games of cards – Puskás later joked about the notoriously thrifty gambling stakes Di Stéfano laid down – and developed a benevolent attitude to his colleague's dark moods. 'He'd grumble, he'd have a list of mistakes made at the end of a match: "Somebody hadn't moved into space quickly enough", or "Why hadn't somebody seen his run and passed to him". He had a right to grumble. I never minded.'

Puskás modestly ventured in his autobiography that he thought he 'made a small contribution to Di Stéfano's game'. In time, they developed a sort of telepathy, most notable in their return passes, their one-two's. Opponents, once bamboozled by the swift exchange of possession between the Blond Arrow and the so-called Galloping Major, would gather that Puskás had learned some words from Di Stéfano. 'You camel son of a bitch,' the Hungarian would mutter to the beaten defender.

In the short-term Puskás learned that Di Stéfano was often shadowed so closely, so regularly, by opposing defenders who hoped to snuff out his influence in the way young José Mangriñán once had, that the remaining members of the front five would be granted extra space and opportunity. On their first European Cup outing together, Puskás saw how frustrating it could be for Di Stéfano as Real Madrid's most marked man. Madrid began their third defence of the title against Beşiktaş of Istanbul. At home, Madrid struggled, Kopa's goal, the team's second, six minutes from full-time providing some relief after a stodgy, ill-tempered game. Late on, Di Stéfano was sent off, as was one of his Turkish opponents, Münir Altay. Madrid, without their suspended number nine, drew the away leg.

Di Stéfano made amends with four goals in the thrashing of Wiener Sportklub in the next round, though the goalless away leg in Vienna had been far tougher than the 7–0 at the Bernabéu. Puskás's European Cup adventure with Madrid had not got off to a great start, either. In Vienna, it was his turn to be dismissed, when the referee judged him to have reacted violently to being fouled.

Next, a local tussle. Madrid's trickiest knockout tie yet in their European odyssey would be the one that took them closest to home. Atlético versus Real in the 1959 semi-final went the way of the home side, by a single goal, in each leg. That required a replay, and the two teams from the capital set off to Zaragoza, four hours away by bus, to contest a place in the final, where Stade de Reims would be waiting. It would be Puskás who pushed Real Madrid there. Having taken over from Di Stéfano the duty of penalty-kicks, he had scored the one that gave Real their 2–1 win in the home leg. Finishing off a counter-attack, Puskás then scored the last of the three goals in Real's 2–1 win in the tie-breaker.

Another year, another gold medal. The fourth European Cup out of four came home to Madrid from Stuttgart in early June, after the least entertaining of the competition's finals so far, a rematch

201

against Stade de Reims. Puskás, injured, sat it out. Kopa limped through most of what would be his last match in Madrid's white after being fouled early in the game. Madrid led Reims from the second minute, and then waited for another 45 for what had turned into one of sport's absolute certainties: that if Alfredo Di Stéfano is playing in a European Cup final, he will score. From the edge of the D, at the second attempt, after his first shot had been blocked, he made sure he maintained his habit.

The global game. From left to right: Spaniard Paco Gento, Hungarian Ferenc Puskás, Uruguayan Pepe Santamaría and Argentina-born Di Stéfano in Scotland ahead of Real Madrid's victory in the 1960 European Cup final.

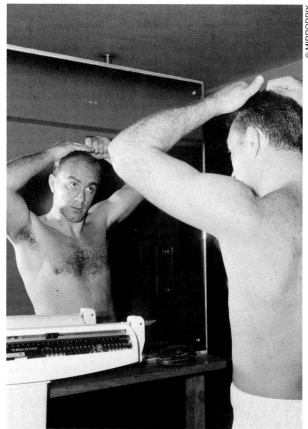

'Madrid's players are true ambassadors for Spain,' said the country's minister for foreign affairs, Fernando María Castiella. Di Stéfano, pictured while on international duty for Spain in England in 1960, prepares to look his best for his adopted nation.

The complete player. Di Stéfano demonstrates his skills at practice with Real Madrid, 1960.

The twentieth-century celebrity. Alfredo Di Stéfano during filming for one of the five feature films he took leading roles in during the 1950s and 1960s.

At home in El Viso, Madrid, with Alfredito and Elena, 1962.

Alfredo and Sara Di Stéfano with their first four children in Madrid in 1963, the year Di Stéfano was kidnapped in Venezuela. From left to right: Silvana, Nanette, Alfredo junior and Elena.

The calm before the storm. Di Stéfano, 38, with Paco Gento (right) in the Real Madrid dressing room three days before the 1964 European Cup final against Internazionale. The defeat against Inter turned out to be his last competitive match for Madrid.

Back to Barcelona. Eleven years after almost joining the city's principal club, Barcelona, Di Stéfano signed for Espanyol, their local rivals. He stayed for two years until he was nearly 40.

Old ties. Di Stéfano greets Ferenc Puskás ahead of his league debut for Espanyol, which, as fate would have it, was played at home against his former club, Real Madrid.

Di Stéfano ahead of his first appearance for Espanyol. 'It was really odd to see him in the blue and white striped jersey, a good friend but no longer a team-mate,' recalled Ignacio Zoco, his Madrid colleague.

Di Stéfano as Valencia CF manager lifts the European Cup Winners' Cup after victory over Arsenal, 1980.

The mentor. Di Stéfano at practice with Real Madrid players during 1983, when he oversaw a group of young players, such as Emilio Butragueño (second from the right), who would go on to dominate Spanish football into the 1990s.

As head coach for Real Madrid, his team were tantalisingly close to winning five trophies in a single season, but finished runners-up in each of them.

A hard act to follow. Di Stéfano, honorary president of Real Madrid and the club's most admired player of the twentieth century, at the 2003 presentation of David Beckham (left) – one of a number of superstars who came to Madrid at the beginning of the twenty-first century.

Only Cristiano Ronaldo, who joined Real Madrid in 2009, achieved a standard of individual success as a goalscorer to rival Di Stéfano's in the 1950s.

The Blue Ballerina. Di Stéfano, 86, is honoured by the Colombian Embassy in Madrid for his contribution to Colombian football in the 1940s and 1950s, when he played for Millonarios of Bogotá, the so-called 'Blue Ballet'.

National mourning. Spain's King Felipe VI signs the condolence book for Di Stéfano at the Bernabéu stadium after his death on 7 July 2014.

CHAPTER 12

THE MATCH OF THE CENTURY

By the turn of the decade, Real Madrid held fewer secrets for their opponents but could command an ever greater audience, attracted by their mystique. Televised games and more available news footage shown in cinemas meant that more of Europe could watch them, albeit in grainy monochrome. Their business patterns and strategies to consolidate their status had also become familiar. Madrid's model was bold: each summer they would bring in a high-profile, often exotic new recruit to strengthen the team.

Di Stéfano would usually put in a word to his president, Santiago Bernabéu, about who might suit: his old friend from the Colombian league, Héctor Rial, had arrived on his recommendation in 1954. Raymond Kopa had written his own slick brochure by guiding Stade de Reims to the maiden European Cup final, against Madrid, joining them shortly afterwards, and then discovering that in a joust for the position in the centre of the attack, he would come off second-best to Di Stéfano. Santamaría gave nous and some Uruguayan iron to the defence from 1957, and would become a closer friend to his fellow South American, Di Stéfano, than Kopa had been. Puskás was 1958's gift to the Spanish public, and to the Champions Cup, and quickly became part of a fertile pairing and friendship with Di Stéfano.

Puskás understood Di Stéfano, on the pitch and off it. Di Stéfano called him 'Pancho', and the nickname stuck. Besides scoring the winning goal against Atlético Madrid in the play-off of the semi-final of the 1959 European Cup, Puskás had scored 21 goals in his debut league season in Spain. That was two shy of Di Stéfano's tally, and Emil Östreicher, an adviser to Bernabéu who helped bring Puskás to Madrid, would recount a story about the duel between the two forwards to end up as the season's best marksman. 'It was one of the last matches of Puskás's first season, and he and Di Stéfano were one goal apart, with Di Stéfano ahead, on the number of goals in the league, both at the top of the division's scorers,' Östreicher told Puskás's biographer, Tibor Hámori. 'We were playing Sevilla, and, in a Madrid attack, Puskás had the ball at his feet, the goal at his mercy. He laid it off to Di Stéfano, to let him score.'

According to Puskás, the gesture had been made not just out of comradeship, but for the sake of peace. 'I thought,' Puskás later revealed, '"If I score here, he'll never speak to me again." It was the best way. We became firm friends.' Di Stéfano converted his 23rd goal of the season from Puskás's pass, and finished once again the leading marksman in Spain's domestic football, with two more than Puskás.

But Madrid did not finish at the top of the most important table; they were caught up and overtaken late in the campaign by Barcelona. That did not sit happily with the club president. It was Barça's first title since the transfer coup that had brought Di Stéfano to Madrid. Barcelona had also won the 1959 Copa del Generalísimo, and would be taking a certain swagger into the next season's Champions Cup. Bernabéu wanted antidotes to the Catalan revival. He did not want Barcelona intruding on the Madrid monopoly of the European Cup.

In his planning for the 1959–60 season, the Madrid president took heed of Di Stéfano's advice on one count, above all, with the signing of Enrique Pérez Díaz Pachín, a 21-year-old from Osasuna. A complication with Pachín's registration, dating from a previous, disputed change of club in his career, meant he would only be eligible for European and exhibition games. But he was a fine defender, and pacy, as Di Stéfano had noted during a match against Osasuna in 1958–59, when Pachín marked him in the second half. As Pachín remembers: 'Alfredo's speed suited me because that was what I was good at, and I had a strong half marking him. According to him, I didn't even give him a kick the whole time, either. And as we left the field heading towards the dressing-rooms, he called from behind me, "Hey, kid, listen. Would you like to play for Madrid?" I thought he was joking but said, "Yes, of course I would."'

Pachín would soon gather that Di Stéfano had considerable influence, and was serious. 'About two months later, Madrid called me, and they had spoken to the Osasuna directors and wanted to come and sign me.' He smiles at the recollection of the day that changed his career. 'In the first half of that game against Madrid, I had actually been given the job of monitoring Puskás, with instructions just to cover his left foot, because he was very left-footed. But that was impossible, he was so good at shielding the ball. We were losing 1–0 by half-time and I said to our coach, "I can't deal with Puskás." So he said, "Okay, we'll change the markers."' And so, marshalling the European Footballer of the Year, rather than being mastered by the Galloping Major, as Puskás was known, Pachín made his lasting, life-changing impression.

There were other newcomers. A Paraguayan, Manuel Fleitas Solich, was appointed as head coach, on the basis of his experience in South America and particularly in Brazil, where he had worked at the leading club, Flamengo. Brazilian football had cachet, thanks partly to the 1958 World Cup, where Brazil won their first of many, and partly because of the Brazilian players in the Spanish top division. Barcelona had just won the league with 21 of their goals scored by Evaristo, a Brazilian striker who Bernabéu had already started to covet; Atlético Madrid's Vava had troubled Real in the previous European Cup semi-final. So Real Madrid's two major rivals had tapped into a resource that Real had not. Bernabéu responded as Bernabéu would: by signing not one but two Brazilians in the summer of 1959.

The first, Darcy Silveira, far better known as Canário, filled an obvious vacancy. Kopa had returned to France, and Stade de Reims, so there was a potential space on the right wing. Canário offered guile and a certain worldliness. He had not quite made Brazil's 1958 World Cup squad – it was his bad luck to play in a position belonging at the time to Garrincha – but had been on the initial short-list, and Fleitas Solich was an admirer of his dribbling and his crossing.

And then there was the glittering new arrival, the player to dazzle Spain, and indeed a Europe already in awe of the serial holders of the Champions Cup. He had not only been part of Brazil's brilliant World Cup triumph in Sweden, he had been among the most feted stars of that tournament. He had a beguiling gimmick: he seemed to be able to put unique forms of torque and backspin on a ball. He carried himself with a captivating elegance. He was born Waldyr Pereira in Río de Janeiro; but everybody knew him as Didí. He was, wrote Eduardo Galeano, the praise-singer laureate of South American sportswriting, 'the hub of the Brazilian team. Lean body, long neck, poised statue of himself, Didí looked like an African icon standing at the centre of the field, monarch and master, firing off his poisoned arrows.'

Word had it that quite soon after Didí's arrival in Spain, aged 30, amid high expectations and fanfare, the Blond Arrow already had doubts about the value of this Brazilian and his poisoned arrows, the passes distributed over long range, with their distinct, dipping parabolas. Di Stéfano would look back on Didí's brief role in the rise of Madrid, and his membership of the grand cast of greats who played for Europe's most domineering club side, as little more than a footnote. But he also found himself obliged until long after his retirement to address the suggestion that he took Didí's renown as a personal challenge, that he regarded the newcomer with a suspicion born of territorial jealousy.

Pachín, who was close to both players, believes the truth was a little more nuanced. The Didí of Madrid was never the great Didí of Brazil for many reasons, he believes. Arriving new to the Real Madrid of the late 1950s could seem intimidating. 'I can tell you one thing,' said Pachín, 'to play in that Madrid team, you didn't need so much to play football very well as you needed to have a very strong character on the field. That was vital. I have seen players who were very talented just eaten up, by 90,000 to 100,000 people. You look up at that crowd and when you see what they're doing when you make a mistake . . . well, you have to have character to withstand that.'

Pachín and Didí formed a bond, as fellow freshmen, distinct though their backgrounds were, the one from provincial Pamplona, the other a World Cup holder from Río de Janeiro. 'We had a real friendship,' Pachín recalls. 'He used to like coming very early to practice and we would go out onto the field with some balls and he would show me the way he addressed the ball, and how it was different in Brazil. He said that the balls he grew up with were a bit smaller and absorbed moisture in a particular way. He reckoned you get more of an effect on them.' The effects this sage achieved were, to Pachín and many of the Madrid squad, fascinating, his free-kicks especially. His brilliance with backspin had a special name. The behaviour of the ball after the clever caress of Didí's right foot was likened to a falling leaf, caught in a gentle breeze: it was, in Portuguese, a '*folha seca*', a dry leaf.

'He would line up the balls, and I would stand behind where he was shooting them,' recalls Pachín. 'They'd look as if they were going to go out of play, but then they would slow up inside the goal-line.'

It looked like the perfect trick for a Madrid side deft on the counter-attack, studied users of the long, accurate pass; for a side with a centre-forward, Di Stéfano, who even with his broad, all-terrain tendencies, and even in his 33rd year, still had the burst of acceleration to win chases against defenders; Puskás ought to benefit, too, assuming Didí could land his dry leaves onto Pancho's left instep. And Didí at inside-forward, issuing his diagonal passes to Gento at outside-left, ought to be an opposing full-back's nightmare. For Canário, his compatriot, seeking to claim the regular spot on the right wing, Didí's special skill with the longer, feathery ball was also welcome. 'I had speed and a lot of running in me,' Canário recalled when we met in 2015 in Zaragoza, his home for the best part of half a century, 'and we worked out where I should start from when Didí hit those spinning passes.'

All these were potential partnerships that made Didí seem, in theory, a fine addition to the Madrid medley. But then there was Didí's other partnership. There was Guiomar Batista, Didí's other half, his lover who had become his second wife. By the end of his only season in Spain, plenty had been heard from her.

Guiomar was a singer who had a certain fame in Brazil well before she and her husband moved to Spain. Her relationship with the footballer, who had left his first wife for Guiomar, attracted a good deal of public interest, and there would be reports about how ardently he missed her when he was holed up in the national team hotel. Brazil's popular press printed stories about how close and in love they were. Sometimes, they reported stormy moments in the marriage.

Didí's move to Spain was big news in Brazil, and it would be bigger still once Guiomar took to regularly briefing friends at Brazilian newspapers, particularly Ronaldo Boscoli, of the Río daily *Última Hora*, with her forthright, regular opinions from the Spanish capital. Guiomar's range of interests, given a wide platform back home, would set off a few fires in her new home. They included politics, and Franco's running of the country: 'An elitist dictator,' she was quoted as saying, 'manipulating and cheating the poor'. Guiomar may not have been wrong, but her contributions to the Brazilian media at a time when Didí was still trying to establish himself in Spain were not always welcomed by his team-mates; nor, in time, by his employers. As Canário remembers with a shake of his head: 'She didn't exactly help. No, she didn't do him any favours at all.'

Canário, a warm and benevolent man, takes a pause. 'She wasn't somebody who adapted to his needs. She was...well, she was a stereotype of someone brash, with lots of jewellery and because she was married to a world champion, she had a few airs and graces. She was a bit impetuous. I even heard a story, and I don't know if it's true or a lie, that some while later, when Didí was off playing with Brazil, he came home and she was waiting for him with a pistol at the door.'

When the starter's gun was fired on Didí's Madrid career, there were promising signs that the fanfare around his arrival was justified.

The story then was Didí, not Didí and Guiomar. Madrid took part in the summer Trofeo Carranza tournament in Cádiz, a prestigious curtain-raiser, consisting of a series of exhibition matches with handsome win-bonuses on offer to sharpen the players' efforts. Madrid played AC Milan and lined up a gala front five, with Canário and Didí at outside- and inside-right, and Di Stéfano, Puskás and Gento in their customary positions. A Cesare Maldini own goal gave Madrid a first-minute lead, and Madrid went on to win 6–3. Two goals came from Di Stéfano, three from Didí.

The debutant would learn to treasure that day. By the beginning of autumn, with the league season under way, new coach Fleitas Solich was already briefing reporters sceptical about Didí's consistency and his familiarisation process, to 'remember the Carranza', to accept as evidence of his class his day in the sun against Milan. By September his impact had already begun to fade, his visibility on the pitch to diminish. *Marca*, the sports newspaper, noted as early as his league debut that 'Didí was unrecognisable and lacked rhythm'. Madrid lacked something else that day too: they were without Di Stéfano, injured. 'Di Stéfano is impossible to replace', *Marca* decided. This, in reporting a 7–1 home win against Real Betis.

Madrid lost their next match, at Valencia, and Didí came in for more criticism from the local press. The die had not exactly been cast, but the best that can be said of the 19 matches the Brazilian played for Madrid, all of them in domestic competition, is that he had his cameo moments and, occasionally, he did put the '*folha seca*' to effective work, with the odd free-kick. But he was still not the team's best user of a dead ball. Indeed, there was very little he could do to push Di Stéfano off any pedestal.

Perhaps this was a condition of what Di Stéfano's Real Madrid had become. Kopa, back at Stade de Reims, and back playing at centre-forward there, reflected on the case of Didí, alluding, in the pages of *Marca*, to his own challenges adapting to a Madrid where the leading man took on so many diverse parts – spearhead attacker, galvaniser, retriever of lost causes, midfield creator, barker of orders, issuer of tickings-off. Kopa told the newspaper he was happy, in 1959, to be back playing in his preferred position at Reims, rather than on the right flank, where he had been obliged to operate for most of his career at Madrid. 'I get to direct the play more now,' reflected Kopa after half a season back in France. He felt Madrid had not had the opportunity to see the best of him in the middle of the forward line. 'I think I played only three times with the number nine on my back, and scored four goals in those games.'

But Kopa would always be second choice, at best, at number nine, Ballon d'Or winner or not. 'The fact is,' he said, 'that, as Real Madrid's game centres around Di Stéfano, the shortcomings of others are more noticeable than they would be under normal circumstances.' Kopa felt at pains to add: 'I am the first to say Di Stéfano is the best footballer in the world.'

Guiomar's accounts of her own and her husband's experiences in Spain had a different emphasis. By the turn of the year, papers back in Río de Janeiro were publishing a stream of candid and explosive claims by Didí's wife. She referred to the 'white mafia' of Real Madrid; claimed in the pages of *Última Hora* that the Brazilian player's low standard of performance was because Di Stéfano had led a boycott against him by the majority of the squad; that a Spanish press campaign to denigrate him was being directly sponsored, even funded by Di Stéfano.

The perceived villain in this conspiracy would protest that, on the contrary, he and Sara had gone out of their way to help Didí and Guiomar settle in the city, advised them where to live, shown the understanding they naturally had, from their own experiences, of the challenges of moving from South America to Spain. But, on the field, it was certainly true that Di Stéfano was unimpressed by Didí, by his work-rate, by his failure to adjust to the tempo of Madrid's game. The 'dry leaf' free-kicks and passes were all very well, but he wanted to see the newcomer pulling up trees, especially in a league season that saw Real engaged in a fierce battle with a competitive Barcelona at the top of the table.

Poor Didí. He became more and more withdrawn. 'He was quiet, introverted,' recalls Pachín. Canário, Didí's compatriot, saw a man bewildered, and, as the nights grew shorter and the temperatures dropped, less and less comfortable. 'The climate really affected him, and the cold,' said Canário. 'There was one match when I really felt for him. It was snowing and at half-time he ran to the basin and started to drink from the hot water tap. The coaching staff told him off. He would cover his hands in vaseline to try to keep the cold out. He would take off his boots at the end of the game and his feet would be white with cold. He was a great player but never showed it here in Spain. And he was a lovely man. But he simply didn't adapt.'

Puskás, like Di Stéfano, diagnosed Didí's problem as a matter of speed. 'A slow player had no chance in that team,' Puskás said, and believed the Brazilian put on weight. 'He was skinny and slight when he arrived and then became fatter and slower.' For Pachín, personal affections aside, Didí was a square peg in a round hole. 'Technically, he was exceptional,' recalls Pachín, 'but he thought about the game in a languid way. He needed to be able to strike the ball with the outside of his foot, look for the long pass that held up. It didn't work for us. We wanted to play at one hundred miles an hour.'

And any period of indulgence was necessarily brief. Di Stéfano made it so. 'After a while, I think Alfredo was uncomfortable with him,' acknowledges Pachín. He suspects there may have been an element of envy. 'Uncomfortable, because of Didí's football and, well, secondly because he arrived with so much attention on him. What happened with Didí was a little like what had happened with Kopa. Kopa was a centre-forward and had to play on the wing at Madrid. Kopa made a success of it. Didí became more and more demoralised.'

Santiago Bernabéu was at first disappointed with his marquee recruit, Didí, and then alarmed. He detected an atmosphere in the dressing-room he sensed was volatile, unhealthy. On 25 March 1960, he wrote to his vice-president, Antonio Santos Peralba, articulating his concerns about the large shadow cast over the club by his principal superstar, Di Stéfano, and the embarrassment being caused by Didí and Guiomar. Di Stéfano, wrote Bernabéu, had such 'colossal status as a footballer, as a man, as the mainstay of so many triumphs, that it is natural he has his enemies, jealous of what he has acquired'. As for Didí, he had not turned out to be, as Bernabéu said had been intended, a team-mate who could serve 'to share the responsibilities', and make Di Stéfano's life easier.

What was more, the voice of Guiomar was being heard shrill from across the Atlantic, as her words to the Brazilian media found their way back to Spain. 'We know for sure she has been sending back articles to Río newspapers saying certain Madrid players are paying journalists here,' wrote Bernabéu. 'Our players know about all this, and it's created a bad atmosphere around Didí. Di Stéfano does not like him.' The story goes that that when Bernabéu confronted Didí with a copy of a paper reporting some of the claims sourced from the garrulous Guiomar, the president was shaking with anger.

Bernabéu's anxieties went beyond Didí. He wondered about the endurance of Madrid's squad. As the new decade began, his beloved club was at a crossroads. The 1960s had started with rivals Barcelona often playing the most captivating football in Spain and issuing some warning signals for Madrid that their hold on the European Cup was as loose as it had been at any time in the past four and a half years. Not only had Didí not raised standards in the way other foreign recruits like Rial, Kopa, Santamaría or Puskás had done, but the change of coach had not given the president great assurances, either. Bernabéu harboured doubts about Fleitas Solich.

The title race was distilling into a cliffhanger between Madrid and Barcelona, and when Madrid were drawn against Nice in the quarter-finals of the Champions Cup they suffered a shock. In the first leg on the Côte d'Azur they sped to a 2–0 lead, but found their French opponents unwilling to bow to the champions. Nice scored three times without reply in the second half.

This setback could not be blamed on Didí. He was on the margins, not involved in any of Madrid's European matches. The defeat in France, could, according to Puskás, rather be attributed to another absentee. 'Alfredo Di Stéfano wasn't there in Nice and his absence really showed,' Puskás later reported. 'It usually did. It hardly needs repeating that what Alfredo meant to Madrid was so important.' Di Stéfano was back in the line-up for the second leg, and on the scoresheet with Madrid's third goal in a 4–0 victory. For the fifth year on the trot, they had made the semi-finals of the Champions Cup. Only now they were not the clear favourites, not when Barcelona had also made it, having beaten the English champions Wolverhampton Wanderers 9–2 on aggregate.

Neither Spanish club wanted to meet the other in the last four. But that's what happened. Once again, UEFA's draw process meant there could be no all-Spanish final. Real Madrid, who had taken three games to reach the 1959 final at the expense of Atlético, would again play compatriots in the semis a year later, facing off against the same Barcelona with whom they were swapping first and second position in Spain's Primera División through the spring of 1960.

Before the collision could take place, Fleitas Solich terminated his stint as head coach. Madrid looked unstable, Bernabéu almost desperate. He called on Miguel Muñoz, once a team-mate of Di Stéfano, to come in as head coach. He made a mid-season signing which would prove far shrewder than the hiring of Didí: Luis Del Sol, an inside-forward from Real Betis, joined, to the approval of the Madrid players who knew him as a hard-working footballer and intelligent user of the ball.

If Didí and Madrid had been the mismatch of the decade, the club now prepared, under a novice coach, Muñoz, for what was being dubbed The Match of the Century. Or, rather, two of them: Real Madrid versus Barcelona for a place in the Champions Cup final, first leg at Chamartín, second leg in Catalonia a week later. Still more dramatically, the last weekend of the league programme would fall four days before the first European meeting.

Di Stéfano's view at the time was that Barcelona had the stronger team in terms of individual talents, in spite of the presence of Puskás and Gento in the Madrid front five, but he told Bernabéu he believed Madrid had the gumption and knowhow to overcome Barça in a two-legged European tie. He had also told an intrepid reporter from the British newspaper the *People* how good he thought Barcelona were, ahead of the Catalan club's tie with Wolves. When his analyses were reported back in Catalonia, he was criticised there for having effectively briefed the British club on how to beat Barça.

So barcelonistas had a new insult to add to the other resentments they held against the player who, seven years earlier, had nearly joined them: they labelled Di Stéfano a 'spy'.

Madrid bore one more wound by the time a buoyant Barcelona came to the Bernabéu arena on 21 April. They had finished second in the league by almost the narrowest possible margin. Equal on points with Barcelona after the last of the 30 matches, Madrid finished beneath them only by dint of the goal-average system used as the tie-breaker. Barcelona had scored fewer goals overall than Di Stéfano's team, but Barça's defence had been meaner than Madrid's. That made Barcelona champions. And they were most people's favourites coming into the European Cup semi-final.

Bernabéu visited the players on the morning of the first leg at their hotel in El Escorial, and made a short speech about the prestige of the club. His new coach, Muñoz, would be up against Helenio Herrera, the experienced, loquacious coach of the Spanish champions. Madrid's senior players knew that all their leadership nous would be required. As Puskás recalled: 'Our intention was to stop Barcelona's attacking game. We knew they would not come to just try and contain us. They played very technically, artistically. Up against that, we had our quality, our speed, plus our courage.'

They had their totem, too. Di Stéfano felt fired up and, once again, he was decisive. Barcelona had assigned Enrique Gensana as his marker. Di Stéfano had the better of that duel. Eighteen minutes in, he met a cross from Gento with a fierce header for the game's opening goal. A photograph taken immediately afterwards appeared in the newspapers the next morning, an evocative portrait of how the goal had roused both player and crowd. He stands on the goal-line on tiptoe, his arms swung up above his head as if to amplify further the noise made by the spectators he is facing, his mouth a rounded 'O'. The goal did rouse Madrid. Gento's confidence was up, and he supplied the cross for a second goal, finished from close range by Puskás. Less than half an hour had been played.

What followed was gripping. A drop in the tempo of Madrid's football reminded President Bernabéu of his concerns about the stamina of his team. Eulogio Martínez, who having an excellent season at centre-forward for Barça, pulled a goal back ten minutes before half-time, apparently from an offside position, though the luck would even out as Ramón Villaverde, Barcelona's left-winger and the leading light of the quarter-final victory against Wolves, pulled a muscle. Madrid had been visibly tiring. But they found a reserve tank of energy for the last five minutes. A Madrid corner was partially cleared, Di Stéfano was first to the loose ball and, shooting across the Barcelona goal, registered his second goal of the game: 3–1 after 90 minutes.

Herrera, the Barcelona coach, stridently predicted that a two-goal advantage would be insufficient come the next leg in a Camp Nou now justifying its ambitious construction with high attendances. The noise that greeted Madrid struck even those players accustomed to a raucous Barcelona crowd as several decibels louder than anything they had previously experienced in league meetings at the same venue. There was the noise of horns, too. 'The whistles when we came out onto the pitch were provocative,' recalled Puskás, 'but they got us going.' They got Puskás going, especially. Madrid had weathered some Barcelona pressure in the first 25 minutes; then the Galloping Major, hitherto low-key in the game, sprang into action, faced up to Antoni Ramallets, the Barcelona goalkeeper, and cool in the furnace, put Madrid 4–1 up on aggregate.

Madrid were on the march now, and when, 15 minutes from full-time, Puskás added his second goal, Gento had already scored. The tie was 6–1 to Madrid. The noise continued, though not so loudly that Di Stéfano, with three minutes remaining, could not make himself heard to Muñoz when he picked up the ball to take a throw-in near to the Madrid coach's bench. He asked him, 'Don't this lot ever tire of whistling? And who's blowing those damned trumpets?' To which Muñoz replied: 'The ones who are losing.'

So to Glasgow, for the first European Cup final of the Swinging Sixties, the fifth on the trot for the greatest club team of the 1950s. Hampden Park set a new record for attendance in the competition, with some 135,000 tickets sold, the priciest at 50 shillings, the cheapest for 5. There had been some expectation a local club might be involved, until Glasgow Rangers had been comfortably beaten by Eintracht Frankfurt, 12–4 on aggregate, in the other semi-final.

Madrid's players had seen footage of that match and of other Eintracht games. Canário remembers that the dozen goals the German club had scored against Rangers were foremost in their thoughts. 'We knew this was a strong team, that we needed to start well. We told ourselves that if they score three, we can score four. We would win whatever it took. We'd play it like a life or death game. Keep in mind this was the Madrid who had already won four European Cups. We were focused, we felt we had studied how the Germans played.'

Television made that study more possible than it had been even five years earlier. Broadcast technology had advanced rapidly, so much so that Madrid's quarter-final tie against Nice had been shown live in several countries outside Spain. Canário was struck not only by the huge gathering of spectators inside Hampden, but by the number of cameras around the touchlines. '"Madre mia!" I thought to myself seeing that big open field, and all the television crews and cameras, and beyond them all those people.' Eurovision, the mechanism for international live broadcasting, would take pictures to a dozen countries.

Hampden had a reputation for strong, gusting winds, and an irregular surface. Madrid's players were preoccupied with neither, although they would start the match facing the breeze. For the second half, happily for the 135,000 anticipating a show from the holders of the trophy, they would feel the wind very powerfully in their sails.

To a degree the most exhilarating European Cup final of the era of black-and-white broadcasting is remembered as Puskás's final. It is still very often known, and not just in Madrid, but across Europe, as 'The Match of the Century'. Ten goals were scored over its 90 minutes. There were two individual hat-tricks. In a contest full of enterprise from both teams, it flowed: the first offside was not called until well after the 70th minute. There would be much to appreciate for young impressionable Glaswegians present at Hampden, among them Alex Ferguson, who grew up to be a footballer and coach and would later manage clubs in European finals, including one against a Madrid coached by Di Stéfano. He craned his neck that night just to glimpse the lionised figures from Madrid in their long-sleeved white jerseys. It was a final to gladden the UEFA executives in the VIP seats, seeing their Champions Cup project reach its fifth birthday with a match widely celebrated as the pinnacle of how entertaining their sport could be.

It was Puskás's final in that he scored four of Madrid's seven goals. Almost from kick-off, Madrid sought to launch Canário down the right, via a sharp, brisk feed from Puskás that ran just a little ahead of the winger. Madrid intended urgency, and Del Sol, the player who had come to the club only months earlier, his arrival pushing Didí still further from first-team consideration, would have an excellent, busy evening.

It was Puskás's final for his impact on the scoreline, but it was Di Stéfano's for how he regulated the ebb and flow, and carried Madrid from an early setback to their swaggering best. When Eintracht took the lead, by no means against the run of play, having signalled they had width and pace on both flanks, Di Stéfano galvanised the response. He had marked out his territory according to Madrid's needs, calculating the strengths of Eintracht, and spent much of the first hour in a deep, playmaking position, collecting the ball in midfield, often facing his own goal, certain of his deft ability to revolve his body through 90 degrees, away from his marker, and always with his head up, knowing his next pass in advance, or whether he should drive forward with the ball himself.

The Hampden crowd would see quite a bit of the Di Stéfano repertoire in the course of their stadium's Match of the Century. His first significant move would be a turn to gain a yard on Hans Weilbächer. He gave immediate notice to Richard Kress, an evident threat on the wing for Eintracht and the scorer of the game's opening goal, of his effectiveness as a harasser, Kress the recipient of a firm challenge. A Di Stéfano stepover gained him the space to initiate the passage of passes that led to Madrid's first menacing shot at Egon Loy's goal. Del Sol ferried the ball on from Di Stéfano to Gento, whose low shot whizzed past the goalkeeper's left-hand post.

BBC Television, the host broadcaster, had a clear notion of Madrid's hierarchy. The commentator Kenneth Wolstenholme called Di Stéfano the 'great general of the Real Madrid side', noting how deep in midfield he chose to operate in the early stages of the game. Even with the limited camera capacity of the time, there were half a dozen occasions on which Di Stéfano was in frame delivering an angry word or a withering look to a team-mate. Early on, Canário was upbraided for a misplaced cross.

The players would say later they felt unconcerned by Eintracht's lead. But it worried watching madridistas. The Spanish radio commentator, Matías Prats, spoke of 'the spectre of fatigue', echoing the lingering concerns felt by President Bernabéu that the best men in the Madrid team were the wrong side of 30 years old, vulnerable to declining stamina.

'Eintracht made a better start than we did,' Puskás later recalled, 'and they were a goal ahead before we had properly opened our eyes. It was Di Stéfano who woke up first.' Wolstenholme's 'great general', upping the tempo of Madrid's approach play, combined with Del Sol to set up Puskás's first, venomous left-foot shot.

Di Stéfano had just given Gento a telling-off for the poor service the winger was providing into the penalty area, when he received a centre, from the other wing, which he could make use of. Canário, holding off a challenge skilfully, passed low and hard across the penalty area to where Di Stéfano had made a run towards the far post. He had to adjust his stride quickly, and was already losing his balance when he connected, firmly, from close to the edge of the six-yard box. With that, Madrid had drawn level, and Di Stéfano had completed an extraordinary collection. He had scored goals in all five Champions Cup finals ever staged.

Now he needed to ensure that all those goals would continue to be in a winning cause. It took about three minutes to turn Madrid's recovery into total authority over the contest. Deep in his own half, in a position towards the left of midfield, Di Stéfano passed short to Gento and then ran some 15 metres parallel to Gento, who advanced with the ball. Gento duly returned it, as Di Stéfano instructed. He sought out Del Sol, who called for a ball over the top of the Eintracht defence wide on the left wing, but Di Stéfano misjudged the strength of the breeze, the pass fell short, and was intercepted.

His reaction was to regain possession immediately, pouncing on the Eintracht clearance, driving towards the centre of the pitch, and, with a double stepover, taunting, daring opponents to come at him and commit themselves or to stand off him. Di Stéfano had glimpsed Gento and Puskás to his left, and fed the ball in that direction, anticipating that he would meet the cross one of them would then put into the penalty area. When Puskás instead elected to shoot, unsuccessfully, from a tight angle, Di Stéfano's anger was undisguised. After Loy turned Puskás's shot away for a corner, the Hungarian turned around to hear his team-mate scolding him, gesticulating with both arms.

Thankfully for the chastened Puskás, within a few seconds they would be embracing. From the same corner, at which Di Stéfano was closely marshalled, Gento crossed, received the ball again after it was partially cleared and looped in another centre which found its way to Canário to shoot. Loy saved, but could not hold the ball. Before the goalkeeper could retrieve it, Di Stéfano had popped it past him for his, and Madrid's, second goal.

Just before half-time they had their third, and the vast audience had been supplied by then with some choice skills to savour. Gento made a short pass to Di Stéfano delivered via a 'rabona'. There followed a contagion of tricks, including a 'blind' pass from Di Stéfano to Del Sol, passer's eyes fixed in one direction and, with his first touch, sending the ball, inch-perfect, completely the opposite way. 'I heard this Hampden surface was too rough to play football on,' Wolstenholme purred to his British viewers. 'What are these boys playing, then?'

Madrid were in their 'Olé!' mode, though not to the point of recklessness. Eintracht's Dieter Lindner realised as much when he found the ball whipped off his toes as he threatened the Madrid goal. His combatant, inside Madrid's own penalty area? Di Stéfano, back forming the last line of defence. At the other end, Di Stéfano won a header that allowed José María Vidal an opportunity for a volleyed attempt at goal, deflected onto the Eintracht post. Just before half-time, Puskás put his first stamp on proceedings, a swift counter-attack instigated by Del Sol and finished off with the power of Puskás's lethal left foot.

Soon it was 4–1. A penalty provided Puskás with his second goal, ten minutes after the interval. Madrid had their cushion, although with Di Stéfano so incorrigibly, instinctively martial, it never felt like much of a cushion. He even snarled at his captain, José María Zárraga, for a stray pass that allowed Eintracht to interrupt Madrid's higher and higher share of possession. The captain and the general would smile about the altercation soon afterwards. Zárraga fondly pinched Di Stéfano on the cheek as they joined one another with play momentarily paused so an injury to Vidal could be assessed and treated.

Puskás reached his hat-trick on the hour, the climax of another swift break, Del Sol a principal cog in the mechanics of the move, Gento's acceleration the key. The forward line from that stage onwards had a conspicuous addition. Di Stéfano, having done what *The Times*'s Geoffrey Green called 'most of the spade work', felt sufficiently liberated to leave the midfield patrolling to Zárraga and Vidal. He became the centre-forward again, though not quite an orthodox one, and certainly no goal-hanger. He continued to retrieve the ball from deep positions, wanting a broad field of vision in front of him. He had a good view of Puskás's fourth goal – the Hungarian's nimble turn and the rocket of a shot propelled into Loy's top corner.

Hampden hardly had time to catch its breath between goals after that. Erwin Stein had scored Eintracht's second goal a minute after Puskás put Madrid 6–1 in front. From the restart, Di Stéfano acted to stifle any ambitions the Germans might nourish about an extraordinary comeback. He received the ball direct from the kick-off, advanced with it into the Eintracht half of the field, played it short to Gento, indicating the winger should return it briskly, at which point Di Stéfano headed straight for goal, ball at his feet, through the middle of the pitch, and from close to the edge of the penalty area arrowed a low drive into the bottom corner. Di Stéfano had completed his own hat-trick, a dozen minutes after Puskás had reached his.

Stein had his second goal very soon after that; Di Stéfano chased his fourth. There were phases of the last quarter of an hour where Madrid freewheeled for a crowd noisily expressing their appreciation of the elements of showmanship in their game: the dummies, the feints, Di Stéfano's high-knee stepovers, Gento's backheels. 'Alfredo and I sometimes did play "keep-ball" in a match we knew we had won,' recalled Puskás, 'and in the last moments of that final, we passed the ball back and forth to one another.'

But there was purpose about Di Stéfano, too, and the crowd responded to it. They roared as he dispossessed, with a gentle shoulder barge, his own team-mate, Zárraga, in the centre-circle, his intention being to inject some speed into the pursuit of another goal. He attempted an overhead volley to meet a cross: spectacular in intention, messy in execution. Very close to full-time, he thought he had equalled Puskás's tally of goals for the evening. It was a move that recalled the younger days of the Blond Arrow, Di Stéfano zipping between two defenders, chasing a pass aimed over the top of them. He timed his run nicely, and felt so sure the light scoop he put on his volley had been perfectly measured that he was already raising both arms in celebration when the ball bounced back off Loy's left-hand post. Another inch or two and the Match of the Century would have had a pair of four-goal heroes, Puskás and Di Stéfano, and it would have ended up 8–3, not 7–3, to Madrid.

Puskás picked up the ball as soon as Scottish referee Jack Mowat blew for full-time. He had deliberately contrived to be close to it when he reckoned time was up. 'Alfredo and I had this game to see who could grab the ball at the end of matches,' Puskás explained, 'and I was counting the last minute in my mind. Alfredo had his hat-trick and I knew he would seize it if he could.'

But somebody else, not Di Stéfano, also wanted the ball as a souvenir. Stein, of Eintracht, scorer of both their second-half goals, marched up to Puskás and asked if he could have it. Initially Puskás said no, rather firmly. Stein persisted. Being Puskás, owner of a charmed left foot and a heart of gold, he eventually let the bold German take the ball away with him. 'This guy's lost the match,' Puskás reasoned. 'It's the least I can do.'

CHAPTER 13

FLAGS OF INCONVENIENCE

The praise showered on Real Madrid, five-term kings of Europe, victors in the Match of the Century, would not fade gently into a close-season lull. Several senior players, with Di Stéfano, the Argentinian now in possession of a Spanish passport and several caps for Spain, at their head, had another important date lined up just 11 days after the Hampden Park highlight. It was anticipated as an even greater endorsement of Spanish supremacy. The lords of the Champions Cup were presenting very favourable credentials to be masters of a new competition, this time for national teams, one which, like the pan-European club tournament, had been promoted by the eager internationalists of French football, and viewed favourably by UEFA.

The European Nations Cup, precursor of the quadrennial European Championship, had its first edition in 1960. The venue would be France, where the semi-finalists were due to gather in July. The qualifying competition had begun 15 months earlier and by the autumn of 1959, when home and away ties whittled down the contenders to eight countries, it had traction among supporters and indeed players from Oporto to Petrograd. Not all the federations and associations invited had said yes, so the starting line-up excluded Italy, and the 1954 World Cup winners, West Germany. England's shy trepidation at the sight of any new, innovative competition – which had led them to shun the first three World Cup tournaments meant they also said no to the new Nations Cup.

But there was strength and fascination across the cast. There was a France side with Raymond Kopa, late of Madrid, and Just Fontaine, the Moroccan-born centre-forward who had struck 13 goals in the course of the 1958 World Cup; a Portugal team whose football had been enriched by the contributions of players born in its African colonies, like the striker Matateu and the midfielder Mário Coluna. Hungary signed up, a talented squad even without their Magyar manqués, like Kubala or Puskás, who had emigrated. The competition had an enthusiastic take-up from the Eastern Bloc. The Soviet Union were in, their goal protected by the redoubtable Lev Yashin; Czechoslovakia had Josef Masopust, then in his prime, organising their midfield, and had been flexing their muscles in the last-eight eliminating round, to beat Denmark 7–3 on aggregate.

But anybody picking a favourite in the summer of 1960 was obliged to think long and hard if they did not name Spain. First, because of the serial European club champions from Real Madrid they could call on: Marquitos, hero of the 1956 Champions Cup final; Pachín, dynamo of the left side of defence; Luis Del Sol, clever and combative; Paco Gento, the whippet on the wing. And that was barely half of it. Less than a week before Real Madrid had won their fifth European Cup on the trot in Glasgow, Barcelona had lifted the European Fairs Cup, an ungainly, rather less glamorous international club competition that started life as a city versus city tournament. Barcelona had defeated Birmingham City 4–1 on aggregate in the two-legged final.

That was the Barcelona who had finished ahead of Real Madrid in the league, by the narrowest of margins, the Barcelona coached until the tail-end of their season by Helenio Herrera, who also had the job of selecting and coaching the Spain national team through the inaugural European Nations Cup. Barça, inevitably, supplied several players to the national squad, including Antoni Ramallets, the goalkeeper; most of the midfield; and, further forward, Luis Suárez, the Galician with guile and goals in him. Suárez would be named European Footballer of the Year for 1960.

Which meant Spain, organised by the self-styled best coach in the sport, Herrera, or HH as he was known and would refer to himself on occasion, had an attack spearheaded by the future holder of the Ballon d'Or and the man who had owned it for the previous two seasons. Di Stéfano, the boy from Barracas, Buenos Aires, was by the turn of the 1960s not only Europe's leading footballer, and La Liga's most celebrated player. He was Di Stéfano the adopted Spaniard, standard-bearer and leader of the national team of a country he had moved to seven years earlier, playing under the yellow-and-red flag of a nation that felt increasingly confident about itself, accepted, and liked.

In the summer of 1960, more tourists than ever prepared to make their way to the coastal playas and the urban plazas of Franco's Spain. It was still a dictatorship, but it now seemed a more congenial, acceptable place, at least if you looked at the holiday snaps folk brought home from its beaches. Peerless football was a good advertisement, too. A visitor planning to pass through Madrid on 9 June could have arranged to watch Di Stéfano, Suárez, Gento and company play the deciding leg of the European Nations Cup quarter-final at Chamartín, and, besides appreciating the quality of the individuals on show, might have sensed that rivalries based on club affiliation, of Barcelona versus Madrid, or Atlético versus Real, or on region, Catalonia against Castile, Basque Country against the capital, would not hamper the team. Herrera, a coach with a worldly background, had made a point of cultivating a collegiate atmosphere in the national squad. He claimed to have coined the slogan 'Club España' to nourish the idea among cliques of players who spent their weekends in fierce competition with one another that, with togetherness, they could be made unbeatable.

Being Herrera, he transmitted a conviction that they *were* unbeatable. Being Herrera, he was also canny enough to know that pride in representing the flag of Spain would not be second nature to some of his players: not to those who had grown up in families affected adversely by the Civil War; nor to any whose families felt their regions had been disadvantaged under the Franco regime. Nor, indeed, to any players who viewed the coach, HH, as a barcelonista.

Herrera's relationship with Di Stéfano had some shades of grey. Di Stéfano's interactions with many of his coaches, or anybody in authority, tended to. HH had an authoritarianism about him that had led to conflict with prominent players including, in 1960, Kubala, the Barcelona man Di Stéfano liked and admired most. In his memoir, *Yo Memorias*, Herrera recalled that his appointment as coach of Spain, made while he was on the bench at Barcelona, set some awkward challenges. 'Not all my experiences at the head of the Spain selección, the national team, were pleasant,' Herrera wrote in 1962. 'I remember the day when I was introduced to the Spain players, Di Stéfano and Gento did not offer me a handshake. I understood that to have come from a misunderstanding, and let it go.'

HH's affiliation to Barcelona, where he had spoken with bombastic confidence before and after some matches against Real Madrid, seemed to be the cause of suspicion. 'Alfredo Di Stéfano and his Madrid colleagues had let themselves be influenced by some quotes the newspapers had attributed to me,' believed Herrera. 'But they did not take long to realise that I knew my job and I wasn't some charlatan.' Herrera, whose public persona was never of a man who depended on flattery from others – he seemed abundantly capable of blowing his own trumpet – nonetheless acknowledged he was pleased to hear Di Stéfano say, after working with HH: 'I understand now that Herrera's fame as a coach is justified.'

Friction would resurface between a man regarded as the best player in the world – Herrera himself referred to Di Stéfano thus in the early 1960s – and perhaps the sport's highest-profile coach of that decade, but in the lead-up to the maiden European Nations Cup, Di Stéfano counted as probably HH's greatest ally on the field. Di Stéfano was not exactly a reluctant Spaniard, but it was the case he had become the figurehead of the Spain national team via a path that had not been mapped out with a European Nations Cup in mind. He gained citizenship primarily because Real Madrid had pushed for it, to facilitate the signing of Kopa, the Frenchman, in 1957—one of the limited number of places for foreign players permitted in their squad needed to be made available.

Di Stéfano obtained his Spanish passport in October 1956. So he no longer counted as an Argentinian taking up a place in the quota of foreign players at Madrid. He made his first appearance for Spain, aged 30, the following January, almost a decade after his last match in the jersey of Argentina. It went rather well. Spain beat Holland 5–1. The debutant scored a hat-trick, two of his goals coming from headers. That was a friendly, a fund-raiser at Madrid's home, and it looked like an auspicious pointer to prospects for the 1958 World Cup. Spain had quite a forward line. Suárez had come into the national side at the same time; Kubala was, like Di Stéfano, a Spanish international now rather than the Hungarian or Czechoslovakian of some years earlier (FIFA's regulations on switching national jerseys would become less flexible in the later part of the twentieth century).

Yet for all the talent they could call on in attack, Spain found the qualifying process for the 1958 World Cup, due to be staged in Sweden, arduous and frustrating. They needed to top a group that included Scotland and Switzerland. The matches against the Scots would produce plenty of goals: in Madrid it was 4–1 in Spain's favour, at Hampden Park 4–2 to Scotland. But by then, Spain were already playing catch-up, thanks to squandered opportunities against the Swiss in the opening match of the campaign, Di Stéfano's competitive bow in the red shirt of his adopted country. Spain had a 2–1 lead when Kubala fluffed a straightforward chance. Switzerland capitalised on their few chances. They ended up sharing the points in a 2–2 draw at Chamartín. Scotland had done better against the Swiss, and although Spain thrashed the Swiss in the away match – Kubala, with two goals, and Di Stéfano, with two more, providing a spectacular reminder of how effective they might have been as partners at Barcelona – Spain fell short.

If Spain left a heavyweight hole in line up of the 1958 World Cup finals, Di Stéfano could regard himself as its double absentee. He was playing for a Spain who were not there; he was *not* playing for an Argentina who were. The various threads of his career as an international player are frayed, and knotted with what in hindsight must have been regarded as moments of regret. Not least because his first impact on country-versus-country football, at the age of 21, had been so emphatic, so precociously successful and so formative.

Photographs from Argentina's expedition to Ecuador for the 1947 Campeonato Sudamericano tell the story of a happy squad, intrepid travellers who enjoyed one another's company in the Majestic hotel in Guayaquil, spent convivial evenings playing cards to the chorus of crickets, and larked around trying on the novelty hats they bought in street markets. For Di Stéfano, the greenhorn of a party that, with José Manuel Moreno among its doyens, seemed to be bridging the best of two generations of excellent Argentinian players, it was an endorsement of his great potential.

His form had obliged the long-serving Argentinian head coach Guillermo Stábile to take him to that Campeonato Sudamericano, his first full campaign in the River starting XI having produced 27 goals. Even so, he had not yet fully persuaded the public, or Stábile, that he had exceptional facets to his game beyond that standout speed, and unflustered finishing, that pushed River to the 1947 league title. But Argentina's successful defence of the continental trophy would mark a significant step in the development of the more rounded, all-terrain footballer he became. Di Stéfano had earned his place, against strong competition at number nine, in Stábile's best side. He would score six goals in the course of the championships, including a hat-trick against Colombia, and returned to Buenos Aires as one of several strong arguments that Argentina should be considered the best-placed national squad to win the World Cup that was due to be staged on their continent, in Brazil, two and half years later.

Argentina never seized that momentum. Quite the opposite. The Argentinian Federation, the AFA, withdrew into a sort of isolation, indignant and perhaps a little insecure. One theory is that General Juan Domingo Perón, a president consolidating his power in the late 1940s, increasing his grip on the levers of propaganda, thought it risky to have a team in national colours fail at a global event of the country's most popular sport. 'Perón was against the idea of

Argentina teams at World Cups,' remembers Norma, Di Stéfano's sister, of the period.

Argentina did not even defend their continental title at the 1949 Campeonato Sudamericano, boycotting the tournament ostensibly because of a dispute between their association and the Brazilian Federation, with whom relations had deteriorated since a nasty, ill-tempered match between the two countries' teams in 1946. That disagreement led in turn to a confrontation between the AFA and FIFA. Argentina withdrew from qualifying for the 1950 World Cup. Nor did the isolationism end there. Argentina's teams remained absent from further South American national championships until the late 1950s, and from the starting grid for the 1954 World Cup, their squabble with FIFA still festering.

The hermit posture sat oddly in some respects with Perón's apparent enthusiasm for other sport, as a centrifuge for nationalism, and indeed as a personal interest, though his own skills were in individual pursuits, like hunting and fencing. Football would be more conspicuously associated with his wife. Eva Perón became the figurehead for amateur youth tournaments to which all-comers, rich and poor, were invited, and the glamorous Evita appeared at events and ceremonies, to be photographed with smiling young players.

The Argentinian head of state, meanwhile, would lead the drumrolling of Argentinian achievements at Olympic Games. His congratulations to Di Stéfano and the other winners of the 1947 Campeonato Sudamericano were certainly sincere, but there is good reason to believe that Argentina, during Perón's first government, turned its back on high-level international football tournaments with Perón's approval, not only because of bureaucratic spats but because the possibility of failure, and a sudden slip down the hierarchy of South America, was real and that might affect national morale. The fact was, the government could not control the whereabouts of the best footballers. Di Stéfano might have been at the vanguard of a gilded generation of Argentinian players, but he had also been one of the Pied Pipers signposting an exit route out of the country. At least half a dozen of the individuals who would have made up the ideal Argentina starting XI in 1950, when Uruguay and Brazil were making their way to the top of the pile at the World Cup, were by then employed in Colombia. They were rebels, and the complications of getting them back into an Argentinian jersey from the so-call 'pirate', Dimayor league they played in were daunting, as FIFA had effectively banned them. Moreover, they were not best loved at home for having left Argentina for El Dorado. Stábile, the national coach, had been among the noisiest grumblers against the mutineers.

From the perspective of an Argentina emptied of Adolfo Pedernera, player of the tournament at the 1946 Campeonato Sudamericano, of Di Stéfano, revelation of the 1947 edition, of Pippo Rossi, of Héctor Rial, who was playing for Bogotá's Santa Fe, and of numerous others who had followed the dollars and anticipated a substantial block on their international careers as a result, it can only have looked a little cheeky when several of them lined up for a team calling itself 'Colombia'.

Unofficial records show that Di Stéfano won four caps for the country he lived in between 1949 and 1952. He tended not to talk too grandly about his appearances in what were essentially exhibition games. The 'Colombia' he played for would be better described as an all-star side picked from the Dimayor league that had ambitiously, and lawlessly, recruited players from all over the world. It was about as Colombian as a mug of Darjeeling tea.

It had an English Midlander on the right side of its midfield and a Mancunian, born in Rangoon, on the left wing.

It did play some high-quality matches, though. There was one against a Uruguayan touring team, some of whose players had participated in Uruguay's victorious World Cup campaign. George Mountford, one of the English players recruited to the Dimayor, and Charlie Mitten, born in Burma because his father was in the British army there, and hired by Santa Fe from Manchester United, were among those tasked with supplying crosses to Di Stéfano and receiving his passes from deep, an experience that Mitten would later relate to his biographer with vivid relish. 'The ground was packed and it turned out to be a heck of a game, very tough and no prisoners taken,' Mitten recalled. 'I had grazes all down my thighs and backside.' He remembered making a pass from which Di Stéfano scored one of two goals that day. Rial, another Argentinian manqué whose dual nationality allowed him to represent Spain once he had moved to Real Madrid in 1955, scored the other.

A Spain national team with added Di Stéfano, Kubala and Rial should have been a productive combination. But Di Stéfano sensed a frailty in the national set-up. He had just begun establishing himself as the finest footballer at work in that country when the Spanish national team were horribly tripped up in their attempt to reach the 1954 World Cup in Switzerland. The task set them looked straightforward: a qualifying group reduced to two teams, Spain and Turkey. At Chamartín, Spain won 4–1. In Istanbul, they lost 1–0, and because ties were not decided on goal difference, a replay took place in March 1954, in Rome. It finished 2–2, extra time could not part the contestants, and so the decision was left to the toss of a coin. Spain called it wrong.

Four years later, with Kubala, Di Stéfano and three years' worth of Real Madrid's European Cup expertise grafted on to the cause, they at least fell short because of bad luck on the pitch. Di Stéfano described 'chances missed by the dozen' in the 2–2 draw against Switzerland in Madrid that left them trailing Scotland in those qualifiers. He later concluded that the Spanish national team were 'always 10 cents short of the full peseta'.

By then, Di Stéfano would have been entitled to feel that his international career, or at least all but the first chapter of it, the half-dozen matches under floodlights at the Sapwell stadium in coastal Ecuador that he played for Argentina, was somehow jinxed. Missing out on the 1958 World Cup hurt. He spent much of the period in that summer on holiday, and claimed he only paid scant attention to reports and broadcast news of the event. That would be out of character for a man so alive and curious about his sport. And he can barely have escaped certain details of what was happening in Sweden.

He had old friends in the Argentinian squad there, like Amadeo Carrizo, the goalkeeper who had come up through the ranks, from fourth team to first team, with Di Stéfano at River Plate. Rossi, his great amigo from River, Argentina and Millonarios, by now forgiven for defecting to Colombia, was barking his amplified orders in Argentina's midfield. Stábile, who had guided the 1947 South American champions, was still their coach.

Perón was no longer the president, though, and any sense of caution he had felt about letting Argentina loose in competitions they might not win was borne out by what happened in Sweden in 1958. 'We were overcome physically,' Carrizo reflected of a disastrous mission. Argentina lost 3–1 to the defending champions, West Germany, in their opener, beat Northern Ireland and then left the tournament following a 6–1 thrashing by Czechoslovakia in the last group match. 'The Germans and the Czechs were so much better prepared than we were, and we had a much older side than theirs,' said Carrizo, 'and we lacked international experience.' Argentina's long abstinence from World Cups had left them behind the rest in terms of preparation.

That abstinence had cost them any lingering chance of Di Stéfano resuming his Argentina career; with no competitions to tempt him back into their colours, saying yes to Spain instead had meant no great dilemma. Even when they were back in the international mainstream, Argentina did not maximise their resources. For 1958, Stábile had wanted to call up a trio of players, Humberto Maschio, Antonio Angelillo and Omar Sívori, who a year earlier had moved to Italian clubs Bologna, Internazionale and Juventus. The AFA insisted Argentina be represented only by footballers at local clubs. And stocks were sufficiently sparse that when injury caused a late replacement striker to be called up, Stábile turned to Ángel Labruna, the last survivor at River Plate of La Máquina. By then, alas, Labruna was in his 40th year.

Labruna represented South American football's sepia past; meanwhile a teenager less than half his age was defining the 1958 World Cup: Pelé, of Brazil, was 17 at the time. It was the summer in which he emerged, his athleticism vividly captured on cinema screens in news broadcasts benefiting from improved technology, the pictures crisper to the eye. The 1958 World Cup was also about Didí, the elegant passer in the Brazil team, whose displays that summer in Sweden made him all the more desirable to Santiago Bernabéu. The fact that Brazil looked so thrilling, so assured, exacerbated Argentina's sense of humiliation. Carrizo described the reception given to the dispirited squad by the public when they landed at Buenos Aires's Ezeiza airport as 'really tough. I'll never forget how bad it felt.'

Playing for Spain, which was by then Di Stéfano's path as an international, could also expose a man to intolerant crowds. Club affiliations were never entirely concealed among Spain's spectators: Suárez, of Barcelona, suffered some jeering at Chamartín while representing his country. But Herrera, HH, had his 'Club España' strategy to resist divisive dynamics when he took over the national squad, bullishly confident that the country had a team strong enough to repeat, in the new European Nations Cup, what Spain's leading clubs had done in the European club competitions. The 'Club España' of 1960 represented two things: an approach to preparation as professional as the day-to-day work the players were used to at their elite clubs, and an effort to galvanise followers across the country. 'The thermometer of support for the national team was beginning to rise again after a long period of apathy and scepticism,' believed Herrera. 'We now simply had to win the Nations Cup.'

Spain, later known as 'La Roja', The Red, had indeed swung into the 1960s in style. Three days before the seven-goal show Real Madrid put on in Glasgow against Eintracht Frankfurt, Di Stéfano, Gento, Del Sol and Pachín had warmed up with a friendly international against England. They won 3–0 against a competitive team including Bobby Charlton, Jimmy Greaves, Johnny Haynes and Jimmy Armfield. For Armfield, the demands of defending against Di Stéfano seemed unique: 'He showed me how important a player's first touch can be,' noted Armfield. 'He had fantastic skill and an ability to bring others into the game, making Gento and Del Sol even more effective performers. He had fantastic control and balance, like poetry in motion. The ball was always right there where he wanted it. He could dribble, he could shoot, he could run forever. He did things with a football I had never seen before, swerving it and bending it.'

Di Stéfano's portfolio of highlights in the jersey of Spain did indeed show off his range. In his third international for his second country – third, if you count the Colombia exhibitions – he scored what he would later call the very best goal of the more than 600 he recorded in his professional career. The venue was Heysel, the opponents Belgium, the marking of Di Stéfano apparently given over to two full-time Belgian sentries.

The filmed coverage of the game seems to be preserved nowhere. Suárez was among those present who agreed that it was indeed a sensational goal, with shades of the acrobatic, heeled volley against Valladolid in his first season with Real Madrid. On this occasion, he connected with a very firm cross, from the right flank, from Miguel, who had underestimated Di Stéfano's speed on the run and so the trajectory meant it arrived when Di Stéfano was a pace ahead of the ball. He had positioned himself, somewhere near the D of the Belgian penalty area, for a flying header. With the ball behind him, his instant, instinctive solution was to flip up his right leg, connecting with the sole of his boot.

'It came off him like a cannonball,' Suárez testified. By the time he landed, from a position some four feet off the ground, the shot had zipped just inside the left-hand post of the Belgian goalkeeper, Henri Meert. Quite apart from the gymnastic excellence, Di Stéfano had to disentangle himself from an attempt a Belgian defender made to grab at him just before he made his horizontal lurch into the air.

He struck a mean dead ball for Spain, too. Some of the 'swerve and bend' so admired by Armfield would hurt Portugal in an all-Iberian match swung Spain's way thanks to a Di Stéfano special free-kick, a shot that curled its way past a defensive wall and keeper Carlos Gomes. That was in only his second international for Spain. No recalcitrant newcomer, Di Stéfano: he had bluntly ordered his Spain team-mate, the Basque man-mountain of a defender Jesús Garay, who regarded himself as expert in such situations, to move aside, so he could take the free-kick.

Any concerns about Di Stéfano's commitment to a Spain under Herrera would be dispelled in the round of eliminators for the 1960 Nations Cup. Spain faced Poland, and in the lead-up to the first leg, in Katowice, the coach felt pleased to see his best footballer taking instructions, even if they were from some of the darker pages of the HH manual. Herrera, informed that Poland had sent spies to watch Spain's practice, told the senior men in the side to pretend to be injured, by limping. He offered a prize to whoever acted most convincingly. They obeyed, though Herrera was self-deprecating enough to report later that the ruse had not really worked. On the day of the match, the Polish head coach, Czesław Krug, remarked to him: 'You've got some very good players, shame they're all injured,' with a knowing chuckle.

Spain fell a goal behind in Katowice, but responded with four, two of them from Di Stéfano, who also scored the first goal of the 3–0 win in the return leg in Madrid. 'The best player in the world showed his unbeatable essence,' purred Herrera. 'In Katowice, he ran for the whole game like a little kid. The Real Madrid contingent wore the Spain jersey with as powerful a feeling as anybody.'

The final, to be staged in Paris, was still 13 months away. Herrera felt bullish, and had time to plan around his Barcelona commitments a scouting trip to the next opposition for his 'Club España'. Spain had been drawn to meet Russia, or the Union of Soviet Socialist Republics, as it then called itself. A resonant quarter-final, a charged event.

Herrera licked his lips. He also had an early clue as to possible bureaucratic challenges that would need ironing out. He asked the Federation to let him travel to Moscow to assess the team of Yashin and company during Russia's friendly match against Poland. He used his French travel documents for the journey. Just as well he had them: a Spanish passport in that period carried on an inside page the words: 'This passport is valid for all the countries of the world except Russia and the satellite countries.'

Spain versus USSR. This was a football contest with all sorts of Cold War complications. Its two legs meant a team travelling from Europe's western extremity to its eastern frontier. Then vice versa. The distances were large, and the relationship between the governments was frosty. They were at opposite poles of the political spectrum. It was President Khrushchev's communists versus General Franco's right-wing dictatorship. UEFA set about smoothing the formalities to allow the parties to travel to the respective legs.

Herrera felt welcome in the Soviet Union. He saw the sights, had a guide and interpreter lent to him and chatted with curious Muscovites in Red Square. His translator told him their main point of interest. 'These people keep asking: "Is Di Stéfano coming?"'

Three weeks later, the question would be: is anybody at all coming?

When the idea of accepting an invitation to the European Nations Cup had been discussed by the Spanish Federation and the Franco government's ministers with responsibility for sport and foreign affairs, the possibility of a USSR versus Spain meeting had been raised. It was viewed in a poor light. At the beginning of July 1958, the Federation received a copy of a letter sent by the Spanish Foreign

Office to the National Sports Delegation advising that 'given the position from the head of government that no sporting encounter between Spain and teams from the Soviet Union be authorised, it is thought appropriate that the Spanish Football Federation not take part in matches for the European Nations Cup.'

That hardline position shifted over the next 18 months. Within the higher echelons of government, there were voices in favour of sporting contact with the Soviet Union. Taking part would accelerate, it was argued, the positive image of Spain internationally, after the isolation and scorn of the 1940s and early 1950s. Di Stéfano's Real Madrid had set an example, in that respect. Their expedition to Yugoslavia, where they thrashed Partizan Belgrade early in their European Cup odyssey, had the pleasing sheen of a triumph over representatives of a nation turning a deep shade of socialist red. Among those lobbying in favour of Spain's participation would be Fernando María Castiella, the foreign secretary and a madridista, who had celebrated the diplomatic benefits of his favourite club's success across the continent, in the Champions Cup, by calling Real Madrid 'the best embassy we ever had'.

By early May 1960, his office was assuming that the USSR–Spain match, for a place in the semi-final of the Nations Cup, would go ahead. His ministry was busily liaising with the Federation, with UEFA and via Spanish embassies in countries where there were established contacts with the Soviet Union, to sort out the paperwork allowing the Spain squad and delegation to arrive in Moscow without difficulties, and to afford the Russian party the same smooth landing when they came to Chamartín in early June to play the second leg of the quarter-final.

Herrera seemed in no doubt that his scouting trip, just ten days before the first leg of USSR versus Spain, would be relevant. He felt confident of the outcome, too, even if he had seen Russia flex their muscles, beating Poland 7–1. He had 'taken notes of the errors committed by both teams and had every reason to write down firmly and optimistically: Spain will knock Russia out'. It can be assumed that, being Helenio Herrera, he would happily have swaggered back into town, his dossier under his arm, to repeat that message, long and loud, to reporters.

The trouble was, reporters weren't allowed to ask. Four weeks before the scheduled match in Moscow, newspaper editors and broadcasters across Spain received a notification from the Ministry of Information that no words from Herrera could be quoted. Censorship could be, and often was, draconian during the Franco dictatorship, but it was unusual for it to extend to banning the words of a loudmouth football manager. However, the issue of the USSR–Spain match had become extremely sensitive at the highest level of government; the Cold War had just entered an especially icy phase.

As Herrera was making his plans to go scouting in Russia, an American pilot was caught spying over Russia. Gary Powers, on a mission for the CIA, was captured when his U-2 plane was shot down in Soviet airspace. By the time Spain's national coach set off for Moscow, a showdown between Soviet president Nikita Khrushchev and his US counterpart, Dwight Eisenhower, with the Powers affair central to it, had ended rancorously. That led to the collapse of a Paris conference that had been set up to reduce Cold War tensions.

Spain's government placed a high value on the approval and support it had received from the Eisenhower administration. Indeed, on 20 May 1960, as Franco and his council of ministers gathered while the Spanish head of state was on a visit to Barcelona, their meeting began with a reading of a message from Eisenhower appealing for allies to stay close and loyal in the light of recent events, the Powers crisis, and Soviet hostility. 'This experience will serve to strengthen the bonds of your country and mine,' he wrote. 'The threat to the free world demands unity and co-operation.' Also on the agenda for Franco and his ministers that day was the quarter-final of the European Nations Cup: USSR versus Spain.

The topic was debated, with determined lobbying on either side. Sport lost, but there was no bullishly defiant announcement of the decision from the Franco regime. Rather, an edict went out to the Spanish media not to cover the story, or preview the match in any way. They obeyed.

The issue had become too freighted with political problems. The rationale may not have been entirely to do with the ten-year prison sentence given to airman Powers, but the chilly climate of East–West relations had a bearing. So too, according to Franco's cousin and trusted general, Francisco Franco Salgado-Araújo, did the state's deep-seated fear of Spanish communism, his enemy during the Civil War. Franco had learned that the Soviet propaganda machine had been using the fixtures for political capital, that Russian radio had predicted crowd rebellion against the Spanish regime at Chamartín. Franco 'was motivated to suspend the matches by the campaign being made on red radio announcing the massive welcome that would be given to the team from Moscow at the Bernabéu, to show the public's repulsion against [Franco]', wrote Salgado-Araújo in diaries published after the dictator's death.

'On top of that, there was the attitude of Khrushchev, demanding that the communists' anthem be played, that the flag with the hammer and sickle be flown which would be exploited by communists in Spain, and agents who would be accompanying the Russian team.'

If that sounds jumpy, there was also, according to Salgado-Araújo's account, a genuine concern that the decision to withdraw would not be appreciated by the Spanish public.

For Di Stéfano and the players, who had assembled in Madrid ready for practice, suitcases packed, their flights to Moscow via Brussels booked, the silence of the press on the story seemed eerie. When it was announced to them that there would be no match it was, goalkeeper Vicente Train recalls, 'just confusing'. Spanish newspapers were obliged to print only a one-sentence statement that the games had been suspended. Abroad, opprobrium. *The Times* of London condemned the Franco regime for an act that 'brought the Cold War into sport' and 'defied Olympic principles'. The innocent Spanish international footballers had been 'coerced' into giving up their aspirations to win the first European Nations title.

From the Soviet Union came anger, and a demand that UEFA take punitive action against Spain. UEFA tried to pursue other options, to rescue the tie: the competition's organisers suggested the playing of two matches, or just one, on neutral territory. The Soviet Union, the wronged party, declined. They were awarded a bye into the semi-final, where they beat Czechoslovakia, on the way to becoming the inaugural European Nations Cup champions, thanks to a victory over Yugoslavia in the final in Paris.

For Di Stéfano, whose Argentina had stopped playing major international tournaments for political reasons, just after he had spearheaded them to the Copa Sudamericano, the curtain had again come down on the possibility of shining at a major international tournament. His Spain had stopped competing in their continental championship, for political reasons, just at the moment when they looked set up for the best opportunity to win a major prize.

Poignantly, the refusenik Spanish national team, instead of voyaging to Moscow and perhaps on to Marseille for a semi-final and Paris for a coronation, filled their time with a friendly tour of South America. It included a match to really pull at the heartstrings of their number nine, as Argentina beat Di Stéfano's Spain 2–0 in Buenos Aires.

Two summers later, he would return to South America, for the swansong of his unfulfilling, frustrating international career. Herrera had been drafted back into service by the Spanish Federation as coach for the 1962 World Cup in Chile; Di Stéfano's goals had propelled Spain through qualifiers against Wales and a play-off against Morocco. But in the last but one preparation friendly, against an Austrian club side in Madrid, Di Stéfano felt an acute pain in the back of his right leg.

Diagnosis proved difficult, and so did his relationship with Herrera. Di Stéfano travelled to Chile with the injury still affecting him. He bought tickets for his parents to fly up from Buenos Aires to Viña del Mar, Spain's group-phase base for the tournament, to see the son who, back in 1947, when he first starred for Argentina, might realistically have aspired to have played in four World Cups by the time he reached the age of 36.

That birthday was imminent. He was not quite the same athlete he had been at 28, or 32, but he was still a match-winner. As the World Cup neared, his fitness would become an issue of conflict with Herrera, whom Di Stéfano thought stubborn in his dealing with the player, and in his ideas of how best to treat the injury that had hampered his movements from the first training session in Chile. Gossip had it that Di Stéfano was unwilling to play because he was fed up with HH. The evidence is that he felt desperate for a cure to his injury. Suárez, his room-mate, found Di Stéfano contorting himself so he could lie with his calf directly under the table lamp of the hotel bedroom in the hope that the heat generated might provide muscular relief. The British journalist Brian Glanville remembers encountering the player's elderly father in Viña del Mar, touchingly clutching a secret liniment, which he was sure could cure his son's pulled muscle. '"Use it, use it!" I tell him,' he reported to Glanville, 'but he won't.'

Alfredo Di Stéfano senior had come up against his son's stubborn streak. Di Stéfano the superstar would not take kindly to Herrera's advice either, clashing with the coach over his strict dietary regimen for the players. Herrera wanted Di Stéfano to lose some kilograms; Di Stéfano thought that by eating too little he was losing musculature, and that was exacerbating the injury, hampering recovery.

His chances of playing in Spain's group matches dwindled. The hope was that by the second round of the tournament, he might be able to take his place in the starting line-up. The fear, after defeat to Czechoslovakia in the first match of the tournament, was that there might be no second round. Spain beat Mexico by a single goal to leave themselves needing a win against Brazil to guarantee progress.

The most telling photograph from that game, Brazil versus Spain, would have been one where the camera picked out two faces in the grandstand. Pelé had been ruled out by a wound inflicted by a Czech opponent in Brazil's previous match; seated not far away, Di Stéfano watched, still troubled by his sore leg. The pair of post-war greats sat, inactive, watching the one World Cup match that might have put them head to head.

Spain took the lead, Garrincha galvanised Brazil, and after two late goals from Amarildo, Pelé's replacement in the line-up, Spain's tournament was over. Spain had found they had less effective back-up for Di Stéfano than Brazil came up with for the absent Pelé. Di Stéfano's only World Cup had ended without his having played a single minute. Pelé, meanwhile, went on to win his second World Cup of his three.

There were no more Di Stéfano caps after that. There was one compensation for a player whose scant list of medals as an international is the looking-glass opposite of his many, many honours with his clubs. In 1963, nearly two years after representing Spain in an official international for the last time, Di Stéfano led out a World XI at Wembley for a match to celebrate the centenary of the English Football Association. He had an unusual role, for him, the captaincy. He led a fine team, in which Puskás played as a substitute, and Kopa and Gento rolled back the years by lining up, as they had for Madrid, on either wing, with Di Stéfano, Portugal's Eusébio and Scotland's Denis Law inside them. Jimmy Armfield captained England and for Armfield 'the photograph I have of my shaking hands in the centre circle with Alfredo Di Stéfano is one of my most prized possessions.'

The following summer, Di Stéfano, about to turn 38, watched from a distance as Spain celebrated winning the second European Nations Cup. There General Franco congratulating the national team for winning a competition he had dragged them out of last time around. The Bernabéu stadium hosted the final. The flag bearing the hammer and sickle flew over Chamartín. Franco stood up in the VIP section of the stadium as the Soviet

Union's national anthem was played in the capital of Europe's most determinedly anti-communist state. The team beaten in the final by Spain were the USSR, in a fixture that four years earlier had been forbidden by the Generalísimo. Times had changed. This was 1964. A new realpolitik shaped East–West politics. The world had moved on.

CHAPTER 14

THE PRICE OF FAME

The world moved on in club football in the early 1960s, too. Hierarchies shifted. Real Madrid were no longer the invincibles of Europe. But by 1963, they had re-established themselves as the supremes of Spain. A third Primera División title on the trot set a new standard for the league: no club had ever achieved three successive championships. They breezed to that title, as easily as they had to the 1961 edition, with an advantage of a dozen points over their closest pursuers, in both cases Atlético Madrid. Barcelona, in 1962, had put up a more sustained challenge, but still fell three points short.

They remained a box-office attraction, second to none. The senior players prepared themselves for another summer on the road as if it was second nature. Part of the job for Alfredo Di Stéfano, Ferenc Puskás and Paco Gento was about exploiting Madrid's global popularity, or – as they would not have put it in the early 1960s – growing the brand.

Lucrative terms had been agreed for a tour in South America. And a return to a tournament Di Stéfano had come to know well, the so-called Little World Cup, a meeting of diverse club teams that had been staged in Venezuela during the later phase of Colombia's El Dorado era, now revived. Millonarios had taken part in it twice in the 1950s when Di Stéfano was becoming their figurehead. Madrid had been involved in 1956; seven years on, they anticipated full arenas and, by the time of the start date, something of a belt and braces approach to the organisation of the event. Initially Benfica and AC Milan, that year's European Cup finalists, had been scheduled to provide some of the prestigious opposition, as were Vasco da Gama, of Brazil. In the end, the Little World Cup had turned littler than anticipated: its champions would come from one of three candidates, either Real Madrid, Porto or São Paulo.

The Madrid squad had flown from Spain, immediately after another close-season tournament in Málaga, and checked in to Caracas's Hotel Potomac two days before their first fixture, against Porto. Some of the players detected an edginess in the Venezuelan capital. 'It was tense and hostile,' recalled Ignacio Zoco. 'At one stage some of us were sitting on the terrace at the hotel and there were these volleys of machine-gun fire, not warning shots but shots that sounded like they were to kill. It gave us all a huge fright. We didn't know who was firing, but it wasn't the police.'

Venezuela was on edge. Elections were due four months later and the government of Rómulo Betancourt, a giant in the country's twentieth-century political history, had enemies, some of whom counted on support from elsewhere in Latin America and the Caribbean. Betancourt had become a significant actor in the theatre of the Cold War, and had played a key role in negotiations around the Cuban missile crisis some ten months earlier. He had made Venezuela a founding member of OPEC, the body representing some of the world's major oil producers, and while he had his champions in the West, leftist groups sought his overthrow. He had survived an assassination attempt in 1960.

Madrid beat Porto 2–1 in their first match of a round robin in which each of the three clubs was to meet the others twice. Di Stéfano played against the Portuguese but by the end of the game felt a sharp discomfort in his back. It was painful enough to rule him out of the next fixture, against São Paulo on Friday 23 August. At half-time in that game, all of Madrid's players began to feel this was a tour they could happily have done without, and not just for reasons of fatigue. The atmosphere around the Universitario stadium was making them uneasy, and they were aware of loud bangs outside the dressing-room. Then they heard more rat-a-tatting. 'We had seen all these guns and now we could hear them going off and it sounded like a battle,' remembers Amancio Amaro, 'it was some sort of political protest, we were told.' Inside the arena, panic had begun to affect spectators, who spilled onto the pitch, confused and frightened.

The footballers were advised to remain in the dressing-room, where they waited for 45 minutes before the second half was allowed to go ahead. Madrid, drawing 1–1 at the interval, conceded a goal after an hour and, their minds not entirely focused, could not find an equaliser.

At dinner in the Potomac that night, the players found it hard to relax. Some of them noted a minor altercation at the doors of the hotel restaurant. A man apparently intent on meeting with the squad had been prevented from disturbing the dinner by the head waiter. Luis Morateja, a Madrid director on the tour, rose from his seat to find out what was happening and was told the Venezuelan intruder wanted to speak with Di Stéfano. In the spirit of cordiality that Real's president Santiago Bernabéu always urged should be an instinctive part of the players' behaviour as touring ambassadors, Di Stéfano sought out the man in the hotel bar after his meal, 'just to see what he wanted'. His sense of etiquette would not extend, however, to agreeing to the stranger's suggestion they take a stroll outside together. Di Stéfano told him he was going straight up to bed.

Two mornings later, the telephone in Room 216 rang at around half past six. Di Stéfano, his back still troubling him, woke and picked up the receiver by his bed. A voice asked him to come down to reception because the local police needed to talk with him. His immediate thought was that some team-mates, emboldened by drink after a longer night than might have been authorised, were playing a prank. He answered brusquely to the effect that they should stop messing around.

The voice on the other of the phone immediately stated that, in that case, the officers would be obliged to come up to his room. In the next bedroom, which had a door connecting to room 216, Pepe Santamaría woke, came through and found his friend in his green pyjamas looking vexed. There was a knock on the door and Di Stéfano, having hastily put a jacket on, answered. His visitors presented him with police identity cards. They were three uniformed men, accompanied by the hotel concierge, whom the players recognised.

This was not a prank, evidently. It was explained to Di Stéfano and Santamaría that Di Stéfano's name had been linked to a drug-trafficking allegation, that they had nothing to fear but he must accompany the officers to police headquarters. He protested that he needed the permission of team management to leave the hotel. He was told brusquely to come downstairs, after being allowed to finish dressing and brush his teeth. A car was waiting at the hotel door and Di Stéfano was ushered firmly towards it, and into the middle of the back seat, a police officer either side of him.

The rough handling he received as he was pushed into the car was the first real clue to Di Stéfano that this was not a simple case of the Caracas CID following up a wild tip-off and eliminating a celebrity from suspicion. 'This is a kidnap,' he was then told, as one of his captors passed a blindfold around his head. It was tied just loosely enough to leave a sliver of a view; he could look directly downwards and see a semi-automatic rifle on the floor of the vehicle.

Although Di Stéfano's abductors were clearly men of violence, during his ordeal they consistently assured him they had no intention of harming him physically or holding him for long. They represented the Armed Forces of National Liberation, FALN, and what they wanted in this instance was to gain attention, publicise a cause. They were broadly loyal to the Venezuelan Communist Party, opposed to Betancourt's governing regime, and their activities were being stepped up as the December elections drew near. The cadre responsible for seizing the world's most famous footballer had recently hijacked a Venezuelan merchant navy vessel, the *Anzoátegui*. Other cells of the organisation had been involved in sabotaging oil pipelines and in gun battles with Venezuelan troops in various stand-offs outside the capital.

The idea of abducting a famous individual, even an entertainer, was hardly novel. By the early 1960s it had become almost a textbook device for leftist revolutionary movements. Di Stéfano's Argentinian compatriot, the motor-racing champion Juan Manuel Fangio, had been abducted at gunpoint in Havana, Cuba, on the eve of the 1958 Grand Prix there, a significant moment in the timeline of the Cuban revolution. Guerrillas loyal to Fidel Castro organised the kidnapping of Fangio, who was released unharmed the next day; Castro would be in power in Cuba the following year, and in the early 1960s his regime was supporting and advising organisations such as the Venezuelan FALN. What better way to captivate the attention of the world's media than to abduct a superstar of the game's most popular sport? At around the same time as the FALN were targeting Di Stéfano in South America, an elaborate plot to kidnap the Benfica star Eusébio, planned by the main pro-independence movement in the Portuguese colony of Guinea-Bissau in West Africa, was only foiled at the last moment.

Di Stéfano's abductors told him the mechanics of their operation had been planned and fine-tuned more than 12 months earlier, when they had plotted to kidnap the composer Igor Stravinsky during a visit he had made to Caracas. They eventually rejected that idea because they feared that Stravinsky, though high-profile enough for their purpose, being older, was too fragile. They were concerned he might become seriously ill, or worse, during the ordeal.

The man they had in the back of their car that August morning, by contrast, was a professional athlete, and a guaranteed newsmaker. And he was tough. A number of legends have grown up around the three days Di Stéfano spent under the control of the Augusto César Ríos Commando of the FALN. Most of them, naturally, come from his own account of how the claustrophobic relationship between the guards and the guarded developed. Yes, he was tough. When he feared, justifiably, that the ordeal might only be resolved in a violent face-off between police and kidnappers, Di Stéfano snapped at one his captors: 'At least give me a gun, so I'm not caught in the crossfire, to be shot at like a rabbit.' He also reported, later, that during one of the very long nights of his detention, he noticed one of the sentries assigned to keep him under constant vigilance might be falling asleep on the job. 'Who's keeping watch on whom here?' he growled at his watchman. 'You on me? Or me on you?'

Even if the fiery would-be revolutionaries of the FALN did have moments when they experienced the gruff side of their captive's character, Di Stéfano's predominant emotions were fear and confusion. As the car carrying him away from the Hotel Potomac sped away from central Caracas, he was told his imprisonment would be finite, brief and accommodating. Yet at the same time, he was being systematically disorientated. At one point the vehicle stopped, he had his blindfold removed and was marched into a flat. Within an hour, other members of the Commando had arrived. Unbeknown to Di Stéfano, there had been a setback in their plans, a failure to abduct one of the Little World Cup tournament's local organising committee members, Damian Gaubeca, who reported armed gunman had attacked him in his office in the Casabara building in Caracas. Gaubeca had resisted being taken hostage and raised enough alarm with his shouts for them to flee.

Back at the Potomac, Santamaría was reporting to Madrid's management, and his fellow players, what had happened. By the time the Spanish embassy in Caracas was contacted, Di Stéfano was being moved on again. He was put into a van, the guerrillas assuming Santamaría would be giving a description of the original getaway car to genuine police officers investigating the case. They reached a farmhouse, outside the city centre, where he was greeted by two young women and with hospitable gestures: they handed him two packets of Viceroy cigarettes and a glass of orange juice. As Amancio recalls, the cigarettes would certainly have seemed welcome. 'I don't know if Alfredo was exaggerating but he said to me afterwards: "Damn it, I hadn't smoked for a whole month before that!" Obviously the nerves turned him back to it.'

His hosts told Di Stéfano he would be with them for a few days. But this farmhouse was not to be his prison. Back into the van they bustled him and, as he detected from behind his blindfold on hearing the sounds of traffic, back into Caracas. They parked, and climbed up two storeys into a small studio-style flat, with a sofa and armchairs but no bed, and a bathroom, the door of which he was not allowed to close when he used it. The door of the apartment remained locked. He was never alone, even if one of his guards had a habit of nodding off on the job.

The propaganda campaign began with a phone call to *Clarín*, a left-leaning Venezuelan newspaper which was the FALN's favoured platform for banging their drum. A special edition of the paper was drawn up for publication on the night of Di Stéfano's abduction. It carried quotes from the chief commandant of the FALN cell, one Máximo Canales, to the effect that the hostage was well, was being treated with every respect and care for his health, and would be released 'soon', and that the group's intention was to draw the eyes of the world to the unhappy political situation in Venezuela. They also pointed to the oppressive posture of Franco's Spain, citing the execution of the Spanish communist activist Julián Grimau earlier that year. The operation to seize Di Stéfano was codenamed 'Operation Grimau' by the plotters.

A caller claiming to speak for the FALN rang the agency United Press International (UPI) several times with updates on the footballer's well-being. Their detailed account of his meals, his activities and his interactions with his captors gave the world's media the human stories that ensured maximum, sustained coverage and at the same time painted a picture of a sophisticated, well-mannered guerrilla organisation. A doctor was available to Di Stéfano, the spokesperson assured UPI; and he had breakfasted on ham, toast and pear marmalade and been offered soup, followed by a paella for lunch.

The spokesperson, a woman whose voice the press agency said they recognised from communications to them during the crisis over the hijacking of the *Anzoátegui*, read a statement from Di Stéfano himself to his family: 'Don't worry, my dear parents and my beloved Sara. I am in good health, nothing bad has happened to me. I am fine and hope to see you soon. Much love, Alfredo Di Stéfano.'

On the first evening of his ordeal, Di Stéfano sat down with Commandant Canales. His first impression of the ringleader of the cell who had undertaken this risky and hugely resonant act was of a very young man. Canales was indeed just 20, fully 17 years the junior of his captive. For the rest of his life, Canales, who died in 2015, would speak of Di Stéfano with the tone of an autograph-seeking fan.

Canales was his nom de guerre. His real name was Paul del Río, and his Cold Warrior credentials were fairly impeccable. His parents were Spaniards, militant anarchists who had fled to Cuba after the Civil War. They abandoned the Cuba of Batista, before Castro's revolution, to settle in Venezuela when their son was four years old.

Del Río, having introduced himself using his alias, talked to the player about the FALN and its aims, explaining its dissatisfaction with the Betancourt regime, and the people's perception that Venezuela's oil resources were being exploited by foreign, Western powers. He also revealed that his guerrillas had infiltrated the national security forces in numbers, an idea that would stick with Di Stéfano and add to his growing concerns. Although del Río repeatedly assured the prisoner his kidnapping would be brief and no harm would come to him, Di Stéfano reported that his 'mind was in turmoil'.

The hours dragged, then the minutes dragged. Di Stéfano, confined in a single room, listened out for every signal of normal life, and thought he heard the chatter of what might be a bar somewhere nearby. When the paella was delivered, he was told, by way of recommendation, it had come from a restaurant in El Silencio, and working from his mental map of Caracas, he tried to calculate his location relative to that district. He considered trying to escape. The flat, he supposed, was one or two floors up from the street; but then del Río said it was on the third floor of a building in the Sabana Grande district of Caracas, about ten minutes from where his team-mates waited anxiously for news in the Hotel Potomac. He thought more than once of making a dash for the window. Fear restrained him. 'I thought they were under orders to shoot,' Di Stéfano later told reporters.

In that state of mind – 'I kept thinking they were going to kill me' – distractions became welcome. He played cards and chess with his guards, and with del Río. Newspapers were brought in every day. They listened to the radio, and placed wagers on horse races ahead of listening to the commentaries. Both del Río and Di Stéfano would later relate that, having no money to use to put down a stake, Di Stéfano thought it only fair that, if he won, he should only take half his winnings off his fellow gamblers. His sportsman's sense of fair play had been stimulated, as had his competitive instincts. In one of the regular updates telephoned to UPI, the agency was told he felt pleased to have picked the right horse in one of the sweepstakes.

His thoughts perturbed, and with no bed to lie on, Di Stéfano scarcely slept. His anxieties only grew on the first full morning of incarceration, 27 August, a poignant date because it was the eighth birthday of his son, Alfredito. In Madrid, Sara received conflicting bulletins, as did the Real Madrid delegation in Caracas. Di Stéfano's parents in Argentina had been listening to the radio when a music programme was interrupted to announce the kidnapping.

Later, the Argentinian embassy in Venezeuela said they had received a call claiming to come from the FALN, which assured them Di Stéfano would be released at some point on the morning of 27 August, just over 24 hours after he had been taken. Norma Di Stéfano remembers that from Buenos Aires, the diplomatic channels seemed a frustratingly poor source of information: 'They said they had things for us but they never materialised. Most of what you could find out about what was happening was from the radio.'

Every hour with no sign of him that day deepened the fears of his loved ones. At one point Di Stéfano told his captors he feared his father, who had a weak heart, might suffer a seizure as a result of the stress and worry. Partly, he hoped the kidnappers' own heart-strings would be tugged. Whatever plans they had for him, they were not altered by any thoughts of Alfredo Di Stéfano junior's birthday party being ruined, or of a suffering Alfredo Di Stéfano senior, a man in his seventies, his health at risk as he frantically sought updates from Argentina's Ministry of Foreign Affairs.

The story dominated world news. Di Stéfano's profile, nourished through the European Cup successes and Madrid's glamorous roadshow of the previous nine years, guaranteed that. Editorials across the Western press placed the FALN firmly in the dialectic of the Cold War. They were 'Castroist terrorists' undermining a Venezuela whose government was striving to maintain a functioning democracy in a perilous, unstable Latin America.

As for the victim, this was a downside of fame that no footballer had ever experienced. Despite some reports which speculated on an FALN ransom demand, this was not an abduction designed to gain money or even to leverage specific concessions from the kidnapper's enemies. It was, bluntly, a publicity stunt, and it was a hugely successful one given the coverage, and the shock value of the headlines. 'Stravinsky Kidnapped!' would have generated a furore, but 'Di Stéfano Seized!' caused a wider sensation, perhaps greater than the abduction of any other contemporary sportsman and all but a few entertainers would have done.

Real Madrid's players had, by the 1960s, developed their own take on the club's embracing of aspects of celebrity culture and had watched Di Stéfano, who had done well out of the spin-offs of being well known, develop a thick skin to its downsides. 'That kind of fame could be a real burden,' Puskás reflected after his retirement, 'even in those days, when the media was not as crazy as it became later.' Puskás was referring to the hangers-on, the opportunists that, moths to flames, gathered with ever greater concentration around the Madrid juggernaut. It could be suffocating. 'You tried very hard to remain approachable, be the "good boy", to keep smiling and remain friendly. But some people out there could be really obnoxious.'

During the crisis in Caracas, the Madrid newspaper *ABC* ran a full-page opinion piece about Di Stéfano, its author the conservative academic and novelist José María Pemán. 'Neither his quality as a sportsman, nor his Spanishness have had anything to do with this operation,' ran his argument. 'The only thing taken into account has been his publicity value.' For that, Pemán apportioned blame squarely on the mass media, and the public's voracious appetites. 'This spectacular operation was actually being prepared by the press for many years, ever since pages and pages of interviews, photos, biographical articles and analyses started being dedicated to him. It's been as good as saying to political gangsters: "Kidnap him!"

'In order to explain this "Operation Di Stéfano" you have to judge not the man but the personality cult around him,' Pemán continued. 'We also have to acknowledge this was never a goal Di

Stéfano ever aspired to achieving for Real Madrid, to be used in an attempt to bring down a state president. It is we, it's all of us, who have effectively kidnapped Di Stéfano, because between us we have all participated in commodifying him, and pumping up the publicity around him. No, this incident would not have been possible without every one of us.'

Di Stéfano knew the benefits of fame, the advertising gigs, the movies. He had recently taken a part in his fourth feature film, the 1962 *La Batalla de Domingo*, directed by Luis Marquina. The film had been a sort of post-modern take on the life of a sporting superstar. Essentially, and in keeping with most of his acting career, Di Stéfano played himself, a renowned footballer, about whom, in this case, a filmmaker had prepared a script. Here's the plot: as the player and the artist start on their collaboration, it becomes apparent the script is misconceived, and a better film will emerge from a more natural, fly-on-the-wall study of the real man behind the star. It's a light, fairly compelling movie, and by the time it was released, one of its episodes had gained an unexpectedly eerie foresight: the scene where the protagonist, the famous footballer, is kidnapped.

Life was now imitating art. In the cramped apartment in the Caracus district of Sabana Grande, the minutes, the hours still dragged. Night fell on Di Stéfano's second day in captivity with the prisoner consumed by fear. On the third morning, del Río appeared again and Di Stéfano saw him take aside one of his fellow guerrillas. He felt certain he heard them talking about his release. This was it, he thought. But when del Río instructed him to change into a fresh shirt, provided by his captors, and wear a hat that could be pulled low to obscure much of his famous face, new terrors overcame him.

Del Río told Di Stéfano his ordeal was over, that his gang would be taking him by car close to Real Madrid's hotel and dropping him so he could rejoin his colleagues on foot. Di Stéfano, forgivably paranoid, envisaged a furore, the possibility of a trick, or a trigger-happy police officer opening fire. Rather, said Di Stéfano, take me to the Spanish embassy, where it was less likely that contingency plans had been made for any handover, with all the dangers that implied. He had no faith in the Venezuelan security forces, having heard from del Río how covert accomplices of the FALN had infiltrated the local police force.

By Di Stéfano's account, the kidnappers accepted that proposal. They also conceded he did not need the crew cut to his thinning hair they had suggested (it was not clear why). They even agreed not to blindfold him, after he protested that, with his hat pulled down tight, he would be kept sufficiently ignorant of the address of the flat that had been his cell. These negotiations suggest a relationship of mutual confidence, and a captive firm and convincing, even bossy, in his dialogue with the young militants. And as they prepared to say farewell to the superstar with whom they had shared 70 hours of close proximity, intense emotions, bets and board games, Di Stéfano was presented with gifts: a small suitcase bearing the insignia of the FALN, and a Che Guevara-style beret. It was almost as if he had become a convert to the cause. They handed him a set of dominos as a memento of how they whiled away their time together. Del Río also gave him a painting, a piece of Commandant Canales's own work.

These tokens of friendship or alliance encouraged Di Stéfano. He volunteered he would say nothing, once he was freed, that would give away his abductors' identities or whereabouts. He assured them there would be no stunts from him at the moment of release.

He was terrified. And that was the point at which he asked that, if they saw police approaching and there was to be gunfire, an armed confrontation, they give him a weapon to protect himself. 'At least then,' he told them, 'I can die fighting back.'

The driver of the car and a designated guard travelled with him for the drop-off. They carried pistols; the prisoner did not. The journey seemed to last an age, taking random detours and a very indirect route around the city before reaching Avenida Libertadores, where the driver stopped, said his goodbyes, and told Di Stéfano he could step out. He leaped towards the pavement and scuttled to crouch behind a tree. To his great relief, the car sped away and, amid the noise of lunch-time traffic along the broad boulevard, there was no crack of gunfire.

After taking a moment to collect himself, Di Stéfano dashed across the road, slaloming between oncoming vehicles to where he supposed he might find the best spot to signal for a taxi. 'I practically threw myself at it,' he later recalled. As instructed, he kept his face obscured by his hat, asked the taxi driver to get him to the Spanish embassy pronto, and felt the rush of more nervous adrenalin when the taxi driver told him he didn't know where that was. Thankfully, the passenger thought he had an idea where to find it.

They located the building quickly. There was a problem. The embassy was closed. On the main doorway a sign read 'Opening Hours 10.00–14.00'. It was now a quarter past two in the afternoon. A frantic Di Stéfano pumped his finger on a doorbell and on seeing, through a grilled gateway, a young couple approach, he shouted: 'Open up, quickly!' The man, a member of the embassy staff, recognised him, and he and his wife apparently burst into tears. They evidently shared Di Stéfano's sense of ever-present danger because once they ushered him inside they told him to stay away from the windows, lest he be spotted from outside, and to open the door to nobody while they went to contact the ambassador.

News of his liberation had by then been broadcast, the FALN having swiftly contacted their preferred media outlets to announce his whereabouts. Muñoz Lusarreta from the Real Madrid delegation called Di Stéfano at the embassy and instructed him to stay put. The same afternoon a press conference was scheduled, and so swiftly was Di Stéfano addressing it, surrounded by cameras and microphones, assuring the world that all was as well as could be expected, that he hadn't had time to change. Perched on a sofa in the embassy in the checked shirt he had been given as part of his disguise by his captors, he made perhaps the most photographed appearance of his life that did not have him in football shorts, and he looked anything but a part of a Real Madrid touring squad. That was the Real Madrid of Santiago Bernabéu, admired for their compulsory smart attire, their impeccable presentation. Di Stéfano was unshaven. He looked like a refugee from a long bar-crawl.

As he addressed the media, he spoke without much elaboration on what had happened. He dutifully thanked the ambassador and said he would not be put off visiting Venezuela in the future because of the ordeal. He attempted a light-hearted joke about having been asked to cut his hair short, its punchline: 'I haven't got much anyway.' What he did not say was that the press conference experience itself was sending a chill down his spine. He felt convinced that, among the reporters lined up in front of him, he saw one of the FALN members who had been part of the gang guarding him. His eyes moved about the journalists, and his eyes alighted on the face of another man he thought had been cooped up with him.

'What is it that people call the condition where a prisoner develops a dependence on his guards?' asks Amancio, remembering the events of Caracas, fully half a century later. 'It's known as "Stockholm Syndrome", I think?' Amancio is not casting any doubt on Di Stéfano's conviction that, even after his three days of captivity were over, the menace felt ever-present. 'In that press conference he didn't dare say anything. There were people in the room who had taken him prisoner. Even on the plane on the way to Caracas, you know, there was a man who kept watching him while he was playing cards. We thought the guy was just a fan. But we saw his picture later in the papers. He *was* one of the ones who had planned the kidnap.'

While Di Stéfano's ardent desire now was just to return as quickly as possible to his wife and children in Madrid, President Bernabéu, in contact with Lusarreta from the Spanish capital, had other ideas. The Little World Cup would not be abandoned. It was a point of principle. Madrid had made a commitment, they were under contract, and moreover, would not let their plans be shaped by an act of terrorism, which had explicitly aimed its anger at Franco's Spain, as well as the government of Venezuela. Real Madrid had not become the world's pre-eminent football club without courage and a deep well of defiance. Their match against São Paulo, scheduled for 30 August, would go ahead; and spectators should expect to see Real Madrid's greatest footballer participating in it.

Di Stéfano did not return to Room 216 at the Hotel Potomac, but stayed overnight at the Spanish embassy, a guest of Ambassador Matías Vega Guerra and his wife, Clara Rosa. He rejoined his team-mates the next day accompanied by two armed officers from the Venezuelan police, and took his place in the dressing-room at the Universitario stadium with a crowd of 35,000 in the grandstands, many chanting his name. His presence for the fixture looked like great bravery and sangfroid. His willingness to be involved, so soon after his sleepless nights in genuine fear for his life, and the jittery aftermath, does speak of his valour.

But his team-mates saw a man distracted, nervous. 'He was not the same until he got out of the country,' says Amancio.

'Make no mistake, this was a thoroughly unpleasant episode,' recalled Zoco. 'He couldn't have his mind on the game after everything that had happened. We saw that straight away, as he sat there in the dressing-room, with these bodyguards on either side of him.'

Di Stéfano started the match, barely more than 24 hours after his release, to a stirring ovation from the audience. His performance was flat, as was the team's, and at the interval, fatigued, he withdrew, replaced by Evaristo. He never felt comfortable with Bernabéu's decision to keep him in Caracas and oblige him to play the last game, and the presence of the pair of secret police officers who shadowed him for the remainder of the tour was far from reassuring. He said he 'didn't really want to be with them. I had no faith in them.'

The fixture finished goalless, which meant São Paulo collected the trophy. Di Stéfano would go home with other souvenirs. There was the painting, given him by del Río, or Commandant Máximo Canales, as he then knew him. The ambassador's wife, Clara Rosa, gave him a parrot, an exotic gift, which would prove somewhat impractical to transport. The poor creature was even less enthusiastic about long-haul aeroplane travel than its new owner. The bird did not reach Spain alive.

Seldom had Di Stéfano felt more relieved to be embarking on a plane, aviophobic or not. Even as he climbed the steps, he became alarmed and mistrustful, confused about who his protectors were, and who had been his captors. An officer of the Venezuelan secret police, accompanying him onto the plane, sidled up close to mutter quietly in his ear: 'Alfredo, you were phenomenal!' It was not a comment about his performances during the matches of the Little World Cup, but about how he had conducted himself during and after his captivity. The freed hostage broke into a cold sweat. Was this man a friend, or a foe? Would he, like the sinister voyeur on the plane into Caracas, who turned out to be part of the plot, be monitoring him all the way home?

At home in El Viso, Madrid, Sara and the children prepared for a reunion they had feared might never take place. They did not do so entirely privately. A photographer and reporters from a glossy weekly magazine had been hovering, by arrangement, from the moment the Real Madrid director and friend of the family Raimundo Saporta arrived to tell Di Stéfano's wife that he was safe and sound. Sara needed reassuring, having had to follow developments via scrappy, incomplete radio reports. So Saporta asked to use her phone so she could hear from high up in government that her husband had indeed been released. On the end of line was General Agustín Muñoz Grandes, the vice-president of Spain, Franco's number two. He confirmed to Sara Di Stéfano that her husband was free and in the safety of the embassy in Caracas.

Friends had visited Sara, offering support through the ordeal, including the Chilean singer, Lucho Gatica, who was close to the Di Stéfanos, and Emilio Mata, Alfredito's godfather, who had seen the boy distraught, apparently refusing to look at his presents on his birthday, a day spoiled by the bad news about his father. Although the photographs that appeared in *ABC* magazine of Di Stéfano's reunion with Sara, the girls and Alfredito are posed, there is a clear, genuine warmth in them, particularly from Nanette, her arms wrapped around her father as she perches next to him on the living-room sofa.

As it turned out, Di Stéfano had not seen the last of del Río, alias Máximo Canales, ringleader of the Augusto César Ríos Commando of Venezuela's Armed Forces of National Liberation. Some 53 years later, for the recording of a film about the history of Real Madrid, sanctioned and overseen by the club, del Río found himself invited to the Spanish capital for a publicity event to celebrate the movie's release. He could hardly be considered a threat at that stage in his life, in his sixties, with his white hair and beard and, indeed, with his status as a respected artist. Del Río's paintings have been exhibited internationally, and a replica of one of his sculptures stands outside the Caracas headquarters of the Venezuelan state oil company, bearing the label, 'Monument to Peace'.

He greeted Di Stéfano in peace, warmly, even effusively. The reply he received would be gruff. 'You made me and my family very frightened,' the captive told the captor.

CHAPTER 15
RUPTURE

Fame may have put Alfredo Di Stéfano in fear of his life in Venezuela. Fame also had its upsides. By the early 1960s, the athlete who had begun the 1950s as a figurehead for industrial action in Argentina, the most conspicuous rebel among the breakaway footballing freelancers who made up Colombia's Dimayor, was topping various unofficial listings of his sport's big earners. *Marca*, Spain's best-read chronicle of the lives of sportsmen, carried their own survey of those, and called him 'the Rockefeller of the game'.

Di Stéfano had begun the year of his abduction a significantly wealthier man still because of his high profile, his marketability, thanks to his participation in an adventurous advertising campaign that was not to everybody's taste. A week or so before Christmas 1962, a women's clothing manufacturer named Berkshire took out full-page advertisements in a number of Spain's national newspapers. They were eye-catching, not just because the face, smiling under a thinning hairline, and the sculpted torso of the world's most admired club footballer were spread across a large area of newsprint. The ads drew attention because, they had turned Di Stéfano androgynous.

The top half of the montage had Di Stéfano with his arms akimbo, wearing his white Real Madrid jersey and his Real Madrid shorts, of which only the top half was visible. Up in one corner of the page ran the words, 'If I were my wife...' Meanwhile the bottom half of the page showed a pair of shapely, feminine legs, the calves coquettishly rubbing together, and at their feet a worn leather ball. Above that image, the rest of Di Stéfano's unfinished quote. If he were his wife, the footballer told readers, he'd 'wear Berkshire tights'. Executives at Berkshire anticipated a stampede to Spain's boutiques and department stores as husbands rushed to buy their stockings in time for Iberia's traditional gift-giving day, 6 January, the twelfth day of Christmas.

On that day, Real Madrid were at home to Atlético Bilbao. Di Stéfano was making his first appearance in the line-up for over a month, having been kept out for an unusually long period by what he suspected was a recurrence of the back problem that had troubled him the previous summer and prevented him from taking part in the World Cup in Chile. Madrid sat at the top of the league, set fair to cruise towards a third successive league title. But some madridistas sounded hostile. Part of the booing might have been motivated by the previous weekend's 5–2 loss at Real Mallorca. Much of it, though, seemed to be directed at Di Stéfano, who was jeered loudly whenever he touched the ball.

The man in women's stockings had been taken badly. The full-page newspaper ads were just one part of the Berkshire campaign. Slots had been bought on national television. Although only a minority of Spanish households had a television set in the early 1960s, more and more people had access to one, owned by someone in the family, or a neighbour, or a local bar, café or restaurant. Television was reaching people. So the Berkshire ad where Di Stéfano, in his Madrid jersey, was seen jogging towards an interviewer had been widely viewed over the holiday period.

The ad's dialogue was brief. The man with the microphone greets Di Stéfano, filmed from waist up, with enthusiasm, as if catching him after a hard training session. 'Here we are, with Alfredo Di Stéfano,' beams the actor playing a journalist, 'the best footballer in the world. He's going to tell us something important.'

'You know what I want to tell you?' Di Stéfano says. Cue the punchline: 'If I was my wife, I'd wear Berkshire tights.' Now for the visual punchline. The camera descends, down to what we take to be the player's legs and his feet. But instead of the muscular thighs that have weathered 18 years as a professional, that have powered thousands of shots at goal, we see a pair of elegant, feminine legs, in dark tights, with stiletto heels on the shoes, and a ball on the ground next to the women's pointy toecaps.

Whether it was the advertisement itself that provoked the derision of some Madrid supporters, or whether they had taken umbrage at the fact Di Stéfano appeared to have spent his weeks off, injured, recording and being photographed for a lucrative and frivolous publicity stunt, the campaign was risqué. The Spain of booming tourism, of the post-austerity, liberated sixties was still the Spain of the sort of conservatism that made the cut of the bikinis being worn by foreign visitors to its beaches the subject of earnest, disapproving discussion.

One conservative, establishment figure certainly found the Berkshire stockings advertisement offensive, and he found it vulgar. That was Di Stéfano's boss, Santiago Bernabéu. Soon after the ad campaign had hit the prints and rolled out on screens the player was summoned to a private meeting with the club president. Bernabéu arranged the appointment in person, appearing at practice, his aspect solemn, his manner abrupt and authoritarian.

When Bernabéu looked like that, those who knew him sensed trouble. 'When he came into a room where we were, whether we were eating or whatever, everyone had to get to their feet,' recalls

Enrique Pérez Díaz Pachín. 'It was as if Franco had arrived. We as players respected it, even liked it in as far as it established status, instilled discipline. But he was strict.'

Image, and the way Madrid's players projected themselves and the club, was a Bernabéu priority. 'The president wanted a great Madrid and a Madrid with a clean image,' added Pachín. 'We even got paid bonuses for good behaviour in the hotels we stayed in, and for when we were allowed to stay in hotels other teams had been prevented from coming back to because they'd got into trouble there, partied, broken the beds, or made a racket. We'd always know we couldn't make noise late at night, never leave the bedroom in our pyjamas, and when we went down to the dining room, we all sat down together, and all got up at the same time. Bernabéu was a stickler for discipline like that: no long hair, and he didn't like moustaches either. You couldn't smoke in front of him, so the smokers had to hide it so he didn't see.'

Even Di Stéfano, a smoker, on and off, for much of his life? 'Even Alfredo,' replied Pachín, 'although with his smoking, I was never sure if he actually inhaled. But he obeyed Bernabéu's rules.'

In this instance, the business of the Berkshire stockings, Di Stéfano had not broken a Bernabéu rule. There was nothing in his contract to prevent Di Stéfano accepting commercial endorsements in his private capacity, largely because there was virtually no precedent for such a lucrative relationship between advertiser and football star as the one he had with Berkshire. The hosiery manufacturers had seen an opportunity that would become second nature to retailers of clothing around the world over the next half-century. Di Stéfano had accepted their 150,000 pesetas, and was not inclined to apologise for that.

The confrontation that followed was of a type. When Bernabéu became angry, the players at Madrid would refer to the episode, the eruption, as a 'Santiaguina'. Di Stéfano described vividly to the journalist Luis Miguel González an early personal experience of a Santiaguina, when the president delivered a tirade at half-time of a match against Rapid Vienna, with their defence of their first European Cup in peril. 'The wind was blowing into his overcoat as he came towards us, so he looked even more like a charging elephant.' On that day, Bernabéu roared at the players, 'You floozies, you're an embarrassment!' The jolt pushed Madrid to scoring the goal they needed to keep the tie alive. Afterwards, the president congratulated the players, telling them, 'You're real men,' and formally withdrew his previous insults.

The issue of the best footballer in the world and his floozy stockings was not resolved as easily. Bernabéu took particular issue with Di Stéfano's having worn a Real Madrid jersey for the advertisements, with the club's badge on his chest, which to the president was compromised by the suggestive legs beneath. He asked Di Stéfano to request that the advertising agency cancel the remaining slots they had booked, both with the newspapers and with the national broadcaster. Di Stéfano said no. The president then took action himself, the campaign was pulled, and Berkshire were compensated from the club's own treasury. The star of the ads kept his fee.

After nearly nine years working with Di Stéfano, Bernabéu and his longer-serving allies among Madrid's executives had come to recognise their figurehead player's wilfulness. They often yielded to it. Di Stéfano had already faced another Santiaguina, again about his decorum, and had answered back. Irritated that the cuffs of the sleeves on his jersey hung below his wrists, he set about them with a pair of scissors, cutting them to a more suitable length. Bernabéu took him aside, emphasised to him the sacredness of the club shirt, and, parsimonious as ever, told him he was generating an unnecessary cost by vandalising the sleeves. Di Stéfano replied, with all his old shop-floor ferocity and indignation: 'I'm the one who wears this shirt and represents this club in it.' Bernabéu apparently left the room, fuming, but offering no further argument.

While Madrid knew Di Stéfano's truculence, they also knew his worth to the club. Adversity stimulated him. The day he was jeered by his home crowd at the Bernabéu for appearing in the ad for women's tights, by midway through the first half the boos had quietened. Di Stéfano scored after 18 minutes to put Madrid 1–0 up against Bilbao. He scored again just after half-time to equalise. Madrid won 3–2, and their totem was back in business, his true business, after a long injury, once again the match-winner, correcting a mid-season wobble.

Goals against Atlético Bilbao carried a special satisfaction. Bilbao were the first club to have interrupted the Madrid resurgence that followed Di Stéfano's arrival, the upstart champions who in 1956 interrupted the sequence of Madrid's league wins in 1954, 1955, 1957 and 1958. They were tough, particularly at their own San Mamés arena. And with Bilbao there was also, for several years, the issue of Di Stéfano's relationship with the press from the Basque region, of which Bilbao is the principal city, an issue that had caused further episodes of corporate discomfort for the Real Madrid board.

In the Basque Country, there was never much kowtowing to Real Madrid. Within Atlético Bilbao, a club with a powerful sense of its locale, a general resentment would be harboured through the years of dictatorship against the capital of Spain, because the Franco regime's restrictions on the official use of languages other than Spanish obliged the Bilbao club to call themselves Atlético rather than use the name they preferred, the original 'Athletic'.

For four years, up in Bilbao, Real Madrid's figurehead player experienced a little of what it felt like to live with a ban on being called by your true name. Between 1958 and 1962, Alfredo Di Stéfano was, in the Basque Country's main newspaper, the Man with No Name. *La Gaceta del Norte* simply refused to print the words 'Di Stéfano', in protest at his perceived arrogance.

At the root of the bizarre policy was a particular incident, following a goalless draw in San Sebastián between Madrid and the Basque region's other leading club, Real Sociedad. Di Stéfano had left the pitch grouchy at the result.

That was not an unusual state of affairs after a setback. He had been in Spain long enough for seasoned sportswriters, as well as colleagues, to have learned that these were not the best moments to engage him in conversation. A reporter from the local *Unidad* newspaper nonetheless went about his work purposefully after the final whistle. Journalists were permitted into dressing-rooms after matches, and needed to gather quotes fairly quickly in order to meet print deadlines for the next day's papers. This one, who went by the very Basque surname Goicoechea, approached Di Stéfano for some post-match words as the player was undoing the laces of his boots. Di Stéfano looked up, gave the reporter a glare and said nothing.

The pressman took it badly. 'Who do you think you are?' Goicoechea asked. 'Some sort of demigod?'

That lit a fuse. Di Stéfano swore at the journalist, who found himself hustled towards the door of the changing-room by Madrid executives and a reporter from the capital. Goicoechea was advised that, after Di Stéfano had showered, the player, the demigod, would be more minded to share his thoughts on the game. But before he left, Goicoechea was reported to have been struck by a flying wet towel, apparently hurled at him by Paco Gento, who had endured a frustrating afternoon on a pitch that the Madrid players felt had been deliberately roughed up in the wide areas to sabotage Gento's runs down the wing.

The hostility, the thrown towel, gave the newsman a bigger story than he had anticipated from a goalless draw, or from a grumbling Di Stéfano even if he had spoken. It would fill many column inches not just in *Unidad*, but across the national press. Invited back into the dressing-room by the anxious Real Madrid staff, Goicoechea sought an apology. Instead, Di Stéfano said to him: 'You're a joke. And so are all journalists.' The newspapers, including *Marca*, reported the tetchy exchange the next day, condemning the player. *ABC* devoted half a page to the controversy.

La Gaceta, a powerful voice in the Basque Country and beyond, went further. It sent a telegram to all other print media. 'Having been made aware of the insolent phrases used by Di Stéfano, I recommend silence across all Spanish newspapers in reporting his sporting activities until he gives a satisfactory resolution to this unjustified behaviour,' wrote *Gaceta*'s editor-in-chief, Antonio González. '*La Gaceta* will be doing so as of today.'

By silence, it meant no mention of the man, whatever he did. *Gaceta* were true to their word. Over time, their 150,000-odd readers learned that to know how Di Stéfano was playing, or even if he was playing, you needed to decipher a simple code. Madrid line-ups would be reported thus: 'In attack, Kopa, Rial, Puskás, Gento, and the *usual centre-forward*.' A Di Stéfano goal? 'A goal by *the number nine of Madrid*.' Some Basque papers followed *La Gaceta*'s lead, and made him the nameless number nine, even when he was performing at his ubiquitous best, man of the match, here, there and everywhere on the pitch. The national dailies did not agree to *Gaceta*'s suggestion, although they stayed interested in the story of his vanished identity up in the north-west. Most of them covered the eventual rapprochement, too, brokered at a formal meeting with *La Gaceta*'s chief football writer José María Unibaso, and involving an apology, fully four years in gestation, at Di Stéfano's home in Madrid.

Di Stéfano could once again be called by his name in the Basque Country from 1962. What he could no longer be called by then was champion of Europe.

Madrid's five-year monopoly on UEFA's captivating flagship competition up until 1960 would be followed by five years of finishing without first prize. Each time, it hurt. No setback hurt more than first losing that title, of no longer owning a competition Madrid had defined from its birth. It was worse because their conquerers were compatriots. In three of the first five glorious years, Madrid had overcome Spanish opponents on their journeys to the European Champions Cup final; they had thrashed Sevilla, edged out Atlético Madrid after a replay and then beaten Barcelona handsomely, defying most forecasts, to make it to Hampden Park and then put on the display widely considered the apotheosis of the club's gilded era.

In the following campaign, the end of their domination of the continent came abruptly. Madrid were drawn to play Barcelona at the earliest stage possible, the last eight, Madrid having earned the title-holder's bye to that round, Barcelona, as Spanish league winners in 1960, having beaten Lierse of Belgium in the first round. Two dramatic encounters lay ahead, a great deal tighter than the semi-finals of the previous season. English referees officiated and, to madridista eyes, both Arthur Ellis and Reg Leafe contributed very directly to the outcomes.

Some of the players involved still mutter darkly about suspicions of an edict from UEFA, issued on the quiet, that the European Cup needed a change of master, because Madrid's ownership of the tournament was in danger of making it repetitive. 'We had meetings together about it,' acknowledges Pachín. 'We all felt something political was going on.' No evidence has ever been produced to support what was just a conspiracy theory, largely based on the mistakes Messrs Ellis and Leafe were perceived to have made in the ties.

Vicente Train, the Madrid goalkeeper, remains adamant, as he told me in 2014, that the penalty given for his upending of Barcelona's Sándor Kocsis late in the first leg at the Bernabéu, by Ellis, was a refereeing misjudgement. The collision, he insists, took place outside the penalty area, besides which Kocsis was already in an offside position. Once Luis Suárez, of Barcelona, converted the spot-kick for his second goal of the match, the away team had recovered from 2–0 down at half-time to 2–2.

So Barcelona took a gleeful momentum to a Camp Nou that, three years after its inauguration, now rivalled the Bernabéu for both capacity and grandeur. On the night of 23 November 1960, a crowd of over 100,000 witnessed a vintage, throwback performance from László Kubala, 33 years old and, compared with Di Stéfano, not such an enduring athlete into his 30s, nor as careful as Di Stéfano at fitting his lifestyle choices to the physical demands of his profession. Kubala was on the comeback. He had been dropped the previous season by Barcelona's then coach, Helenio Herrera.

Camp Nou was also witness in the second leg to a brilliant goal, Evaristo's flying header, a strike to remind Di Stéfano that he was not the only player in Spain given to valiantly flinging himself, horizontally, at crosses that arrived hard and fast at an awkward height. Vicente Train stretched himself to reach the ball first, Evaristo beat him to it, and Madrid fell two goals behind as a result. By the time Canário pulled a goal back, there were just four minutes left of the second leg, not enough for Madrid to force a replay.

Madrid players counted up the errors made by Leafe in Barcelona, and adding them to those committed by Ellis, came to half a dozen reasons, including a Di Stéfano header disallowed for offside, to nourish the conspiracy theories, and to say why their elimination seemed unjust. Spanish newspapers with a Madrid bias echoed those complaints, the prints with constituencies in Catalonia less so. *L'Équipe*, the French sports newspaper, judged Leafe harshly, and even some British reporters expressed sympathy for the manner of Madrid's exit. But by the time he left Barcelona, Leafe would have been forgiven for not extending much sympathy to the dethroned Madrid. Some of their players, including Di Stéfano, harangued him aggressively at the banquet after the second leg.

Barcelona went on to the final. Di Stéfano watched it on television, and saw some evidence that, even if Madrid, winners of the 1961 league title and some 20 points better than sixth-placed Barcelona by the end of its calendar, could still call themselves the strongest team in Spain, they might not be the best in Iberia. Barcelona lost 3–2 in Berne to Benfica of Lisbon, who achieved their first European Cup triumph with an ace still up their sleeve. The Mozambican Eusébio da Silva Ferreira had only just joined Benfica after a tug-of-war with their domestic rivals Sporting as piquant as the joust between Madrid and Barcelona over Di Stéfano. Eusébio did not play in the final against Barcelona. In the next year's Champions Cup, however, he would announce himself as the sport's coming man.

Di Stéfano turned 35 in the summer of 1961. He was still the go-to man for Santiago Bernabéu on important matters of strategy. A year earlier, Di Stéfano had steered the Real Madrid president away from recruiting Helenio Herrera as head coach, and towards Miguel Muñoz, the former Madrid captain, instead. Now he put in a word for recruiting Justo Tejada, a winger with Barcelona, who he knew had itchy feet. The Brazilian Canário, whom Muñoz had turned cold on, was leaving, and his position needed to be filled. Tejada was savvy enough to know who at Madrid had the ear of the boss and contacted Di Stéfano. Di Stéfano in turn mentioned him to Bernabéu, indicated that Tejada's contractual situation with Barcelona was such that he could come without a transfer fee, and saw the president's glee at a possible bargain. In the early 1960s, pressure grew on Madrid's debts, and the loans that been taken out to build the stadium and fund the strongest team in Europe.

Tejada proved a good buy, a wise suggestion by Di Stéfano. He ended up scoring more goals than anybody in the European Cup in 1961–62. By this stage Di Stéfano would not have envied him that as much as he might have in the past. In his mid-thirties, the Blond Arrow was not so frequently zipping past defenders and chasing through balls. Indeed, Madrid under Muñoz looked more like a team lining up in 3–4–3 formation, than the 3–2–5 of the 1950s, with Di Stéfano now part of the midfield, roving as ever, but a number nine acting as a number ten. His reign as Pichichi, leading scorer in the Spanish league, season after season at the end of the 1950s, would not continue into the 1960s. Ferenc Puskás was outscoring him regularly, the Hungarian no longer worried that his friend would take it badly and stop talking to him if he scored too many.

In Europe, Tejada's goals, Di Stéfano's running of midfield, Del Sol's drive, Puskás's finishing, Gento's energy and the defensive command of Pepe Santamaría put Madrid back on their pedestal, and along with another league title, in 1962, they reached a sixth Champions Cup final in seven years. En route to Amsterdam, venue of the final, Di Stéfano collected a hat-trick in a 9–0 thrashing of Danish club Odense at the Bernabéu. For the away leg, a 3–0 Madrid win, some intrepid madridistas had made a banner to display. It featured a human skull in caricature, with the names Ellis and Leafe written next to it.

In the quarter-finals, Madrid met Juventus, the Italian club who nine years earlier had been interested in Di Stéfano; Barcelona had worked at selling him on to them when they held a portion of his ownership rights. Juve had since recruited the next best Argentinian striker to make his way to Europe, a feisty competitor, Omar Sívori. The two legs turned into a duel between the pair. Di Stéfano's goal won the Turin match, Sívori scored the only goal of the game in Madrid. A replay, staged in Paris, went Madrid's way, 3–1. The winners gained international praise. *Tuttosport*, the Italian newspaper, lauded Real's 'rational football', while the *Corriere della Sera* gave high grades to 'old Di Stéfano' and for the marking job Pachín did on Sívori.

Madrid strolled through their semi-final, 6–0 aggregate winners against Standard Liège, a rout that began with Di Stéfano plunging to reach a ball at the far post, another photogenic moment. Sliding along the ground at the Bernabéu, he ended up in a crouching position, right arm raised in celebration even before the ball crossed the goal-line, a defender prone and forlorn behind him and the light catching, or rather brightly illuminating, the bald patch on the back of his head. He may not have been 'old Di Stéfano', as the *Corriere* bluntly called him, because the athlete could still lurch at speed to the far post, but his face wore symptoms of creeping middle age, wrinkles on the forehead, thinning hair.

At Amsterdam's Olympic stadium, Madrid were undone by a phenomenal young athlete. In the years ahead, Benfica's Eusébio and Di Stéfano would form a mutual appreciation society; and over the next decade Eusébio would come closer than anybody to challenging Di Stéfano's long-standing record of 49 goals in the European Cup. In Amsterdam, fast, strong and with a powerful right foot, Eusébio, then 20, presented his credentials as the leading attacking footballer in Europe.

Madrid had arrived in the unfamiliar role of challengers. Benfica were the defending champions. The old guard fought back. Madrid led 2–0 early on, Di Stéfano setting up Puskás for the first, and the Hungarian, his fellow 35-year-old, scoring the second with a shot from distance. Benfica, coached by the wise Béla Guttman, found their way back in, Di Stéfano constrained by the marking of Domiciano Cavém, whose goal ten minutes before half-time brought the scores level at 2–2. Puskás restored Madrid's lead quickly, then hit the post. On the hour Mário Coluna made it 3–3 and in the final 30 minutes the dynamism of Eusébio settled the destination of the European Cup. Madrid's two-goal lead finished up a two-goal deficit, at 5–3. 'Eusébio launching bombs from out of the area,' recalls Vicente Train, the Madrid goalkeeper. 'He had a kick like a mule.'

There were gripes about the referee, the Dutchman Leo Horn, particularly for the penalty awarded to Eusébio – 'that was a bit unfair,' believes Vicente – after a challenge from Pachín, and even more for the penalty not awarded when Di Stéfano tumbled in the area with 11 minutes to go. Di Stéfano had paused, facing goalkeeper Costa Pereira, and was then brought down. Horn apparently later explained that he thought Di Stéfano's deliberate hesitation had been designed to provoke a foul. 'Alfredo wanted to gobble up that referee,' recalled Del Sol.

The grumbling went on into the night, exacerbated by the evidence offered by those who had watched on television. Pictures were being transmitted with greater clarity thanks to increasingly sophisticated broadcast engineering, and many viewers believed the Eusébio penalty had been incorrectly judged by Horn. After what had become Madrid's standard interrogation of the referee at the post-match dinner in Amsterdam, the irate players went out on the town, the younger singletons in their own group, Di Stéfano and Santamaría with their wives, who had travelled to the Netherlands to watch the match.

What happened next Di Stéfano would later describe as being like a scene from the Wild West. Apparently a group of men, speaking Spanish, approached the two couples and became a little over-friendly in their remarks to Sara Di Stéfano. So Di Stéfano and Santamaría took their wives back to their hotel, ready to abort the excursion. They ran into team-mates, including Pachín. So, with their wives safely in their rooms, they went out again, and bumped into the same party of rude revellers who had caused offence. Di Stéfano identified the man who had spoken inappropriately to Sara. A fight broke out, Di Stéfano delivering a head-butt at one stage in the scuffle.

Around them, bedlam. Santamaría grabbed at a chair that an assailant was about to use as a baton on Pachín's head. Surreally, out of the corner of his eye, with glass bottles flying about the bar, liquor spilling across the floor and causing the fighters to slip over, Di Stéfano saw a couple smooching, apparently unconcerned with the brawlers. Somebody shouted that the police were on their way, and the Madrid players were ushered to an emergency exit.

The tale, as Pachín remembers it, testified to the musketeer spirit of the Madrid team. It was not so edifying for the image of the Real Madrid ambassadors, of whose decorous behaviour abroad Bernabéu made such a high priority. It turned out that the group with whom the deposed European champions had been scrapping were Spaniards. They had been at the final, as spectators, and felt angry at the outcome and with referee Horn. Hear, hear, said the Madrid footballers. There was even some amiable chatter as the would-be warriors came together again on an Amsterdam street, weapons discarded, rage stilled, sleep beckoning.

That episode, and the ire at another European Cup lost, was not yet the rage of a man fearing the dying of the light. Di Stéfano's Real Madrid would still be Di Stéfano's Real Madrid for another two years. They would win another pair of Spanish titles, enjoy another two seasons in which Di Stéfano maintained his record of always reaching double figures with his tally of league goals for Madrid. But in 1962–63, he did miss more matches than usual with aches and strains, an alert to Madrid's management staff that his game needed to be tailored to preserve his stamina. Those around him sensed a club in transition. 'In football, you can maintain talent, but physical assets decline,' reflected Pachín. 'That's the unforgiving reality. Alfredo Di Stéfano and Ferenc Puskás were not indestructible.'

Viewed from the back of the formation, signs of deterioration could be detected. 'Great teams have a duration of three years, maybe four,' said Vicente Train, the Madrid goalkeeper through what would, according to his theory of three- or four-year cycles, count as the third great Real Madrid of the Di Stéfano era. 'And then there's the agony.'

Managing transition was tricky for President Bernabéu. He sold Del Sol to Juventus because the club needed liquidity. They missed the electric charge the midfielder had given the team, even if players like Ignacio Zoco and Amancio Amario, Spanish recruits, promised an exciting future.

The Amsterdam hangover carried over into the next European Cup, with a brusque first-round elimination, Madrid going down 1–0 in Anderlecht after having only drawn with the Belgian club in Madrid, where a Di Stéfano header put Madrid in front for the last time in the tie. After that, he would get one more crack at the Champions Cup.

Look for evidence of waning powers in Di Stéfano's determined, purposeful march to the 1964 European Champions Cup final in Vienna and it is not to be found on the scorecards. A month after he was incarcerated in a flat in Caracas with gun-wielding kidnappers, he was delighting Glasgow again, as he had in the Match of the Century at Hampden, combining elegantly with Gento to set up a chance squandered by Amancio in Madrid's first match of the 1963–64 campaign against Rangers. Puskás won a tricky first leg in Scotland with the only goal, late on. In Madrid, Puskás scored a hat-trick in a 3–0 win.

If the Galloping Major could still gallop at 37, so the Blond Arrow could still be stiletto-sharp. Di Stéfano scored in both legs against Dinamo Bucharest to book Madrid's place in the last eight. His skill with a dead ball took Madrid past Milan in the quarter-finals; he scored from a direct free-kick, and effectively set up Amancio for the first goal of a tie won 4–3 on aggregate with another hammered free-kick when the Milan goalkeeper could not hold on to it. In the semi-final, Zurich were beaten home and away, Di Stéfano scoring in each leg.

In the middle of March 1964, Di Stéfano struck a hat-trick at the Bernabéu stadium in a league game against Real Murcia that put the club at the top of the Spanish table. They stayed there until the season's end, an eighth title in the 11 years of Di Stéfano's Madrid. And on 27 May 1964 they lined up at the Prater stadium in the Austrian capital, Vienna, for the seventh final featuring Di Stéfano in the nine-year history of the European Cup.

When Madrid lined up, Di Stéfano was not entirely confident about their mood, and had doubts about their preparation. He had also detected an unusual anxiety about Bernabéu ahead of the game. The president had visited the players the evening before and pressed Di Stéfano about tactical ideas, plans, suggestions. The opposition, Internazionale, from Italy, had a coach who was very well known in Spain from his work at Atlético Madrid, at Barcelona and with the Spain national squad, where he and Di Stéfano had experienced their ups and downs. Helenio Herrera, 'HH', expert at exuding confidence, had given his customary impression that he had a masterly surprise planned.

'As soon as we had beaten Zurich, HH was talking to all the media,' recalled Ignacio Zoco. 'We all knew that was his way of deflating the opposition, behaving like he was a wizard of the game.' HH's Inter certainly had some zip, and pace going forward. What had Real Madrid in answer to that? They had their concentrated experience. 'Let's say that the team who were on the up at that time were Inter,' says Amancio Amaro. 'They were the favourites. We had a team where the years were, little by little, beginning to show in key places, in the spine of the team, with Alfredo, Pancho Puskás, Pepe Santamaría.'

As he prepared for the final, Muñoz, the head coach, now long into his service in the job, seemed to Di Stéfano to be excessively concerned with one player from Inter instead of the team as a whole. That was the Inter left-back, Giacinto Facchetti – fast, forward-thinking, feared. Di Stéfano suggested to Muñoz, his former colleague, that he try something proactive, by switching Amancio, who could trouble opponents on either flank with his speed, to the left so that Facchetti felt obliged to follow him there, enabling Madrid to make more use of their right flank, which Facchetti would not be so free to patrol. Muñoz heard the idea and rejected it. The suggestion did not become a strategy.

Madrid, up against a well-organised Inter back line, did not impose themselves on the final. To Di Stéfano's growing irritation, they were often outnumbered in midfield. He endured some suffocating attention from Inter's Carlo Tagnin and Armando Picchi. HH was winning the tactical duel even before Sandro Mazzola put Inter a goal ahead just before half-time.

After Aurelio Milani had scored a second with a long-range shot just after an hour, Di Stéfano thought it time to have his say. He jogged to the touchline to speak with Muñoz. He repeated his idea of a tactical switch, something that might alter the dynamic against an Inter equipped with plenty of tools to make safe a two-goal lead. Muñoz reacted badly to being told what he should do. The two men swore at each other.

Quite how much that brief, heated dialogue had a bearing on what unfolded over the next few days would be disputed. But after the pungent exchange of views, the clock ticked down on Di Stéfano's last half-hour of competitive football as a Real Madrid player. Those 30 minutes featured Puskás thumping an effort against the frame of the Inter goal; they featured hope, when Madrid pulled a goal back with 21 minutes of the final left. That turned to despair thanks to an error from Di Stéfano's great ally and friend, Pepe Santamaría. Mazzola pounced on the mistake for 3–1. Goodnight, Vienna.

The Madrid squad returned to Spain, and Di Stéfano felt livid. He anticipated the press would take a fin-de-siècle tone, drawing attention to the age of certain players. The newspaper *ABC*'s account of the game included the wistful sentence: 'The fact that Di Stéfano could not take charge, for the first time in a final, made it almost inevitable Madrid would lose.' Most players expected some reshaping of the squad's personnel that summer. 'We had begun to think that, if we lost in Vienna, Puskás might be replaced,' recalled Zoco, 'and that was a worry because he was so loved. The real surprise came just a few days later.'

The players could not start their holidays because they still had a pending Copa del Generalísimo semi-final replay, against Atlético Madrid, to fulfil. They reported for practice the day after returning from Austria and Di Stéfano discovered he had not been included in the line-up; nor had the goalkeeper Vicente Train. Di Stéfano asked Muñoz why, and felt the answer was evasive, prickly, something along the lines of 'because I haven't called you up'. He saw Muñoz chatting with a senior director the same day and became concerned. His contract, which had been renewed annually for the previous five years, was due to expire in June. He took his anxieties home with him and paced about, thoughts churning.

He was asked to see the president in his office the following Monday. Bernabéu offered him a new contract, but it was unlike any of the Madrid contracts Di Stéfano had signed, with ever higher salaries, since 1953. The talks about the next deal never even reached discussions about money. Bernabéu told Di Stéfano he wanted him to remain at Madrid but not as a player. He had read an unfavourable technical report from the coach Muñoz, which was in part guiding his decision. But, the president insisted, Di Stéfano must stay, doing for the club 'anything he wanted'.

The vagueness of the job description offended the player. He took from it an implication that Bernabéu considered ending his playing career as more important than thinking precisely about what use his skills might be put to in the service of the club. Doing 'anything he wanted' sounded like doing nothing. 'What Alfredo wanted was to keep playing,' remembered Zoco. 'He could have been technical director, or anything like that,' Amancio understood of the offer.

Di Stéfano said no, feeling resentment at Muñoz for his role in the rupture, and indignation at the coach's suggestion, to Bernabéu, that chronic back problems were restricting him physically. He also felt disappointed by the president, a sentiment that stayed with him for a long time. Bernabéu tried once more, at a meeting at the president's home, to persuade him that a role at the club outside the playing staff was his best course of action. He heard the same negative response.

By then, Real Madrid's greatest ever footballer was thinking practically, endeavouring to take control of his situation, pondering his next move and how to manage the exit. He wrote to Bernabéu emphasising that in no way should his refusal to take up alternative employment at the club be deemed 'an act of rebellion', and insisting that his imminent departure need not yet be made public.

Bernabéu, who never again offered Di Stéfano a role at the club of any sort – although he allowed the Real Madrid stadium to be used for a testimonial match three years later – wrote back. It was a letter that praised the player's contributions to Madrid's unprecedented successes of the previous decade, but also contained the odd sharp line of scantly veiled criticism: 'Everyone at Madrid has almost always lived alongside one another happily,' wrote Bernabéu. 'Our successes have been collective, and made possible by the loyalty of all to each other, and by discipline, crucial in any group, because without it nothing would be achievable, and real chaos would be caused if everybody only ever did what they as an individual wanted to do.'

What the footballer being sacked wanted was simply to go on being a footballer. There were other club presidents and chairmen keen to facilitate that. Di Stéfano was tempted by an offer from Glasgow Celtic, but more convinced by entreaties to go and live in Barcelona, the city he once supposed would be his home in Spain. He received an offer from the Catalan club Espanyol, where, irony of ironies, László Kubala, with whom he had imagined in the long summer of 1953 he might be forming a dazzling partnership at Barcelona, was coaching and playing. He accepted, and the family, of whom the youngest, Elena, was now six years old, moved to Catalonia.

An era had ended. The next one began with a twist. Di Stéfano's first match in the league for Espanyol was at home, in the Barcelona suburb of Sarrià , to Real Madrid. 'That made me feel really strange, seeing Alfredo in a blue-and-white striped jersey, no longer a team-mate,' remembered Zoco. 'A good friend, so loved by all of us, now a rival. It was really odd, and for him, too. I'm sure he suffered.'

By the end of his league debut for Espanyol he did suffer. Di Stéfano, who had just turned 38 years old, reminded his Madrid colleagues early in the game that he could still smack a fierce free-kick. It drew a good save from Madrid's goalkeeper. Espanyol took the lead. But their new superstar began to tire as the contest went on. Di Stéfano failed to dispossess Puskás in the build-up to the Hungarian's winning goal, for 2–1, and left a live television audience across Spain with a poignant image. Amancio, lithe and slippery, skipped away from Di Stéfano with the ball, and the older man tried to grab at his jersey, flailing at it desperately.

'I saw him grabbing at the back of opponents' jerseys a few times when he was at Espanyol,' said Pachín, a little sadly. 'In his whole life until then I had never seen him doing that. But you get to an age when you can't do what you used to. Just think of the sheer number of matches Alfredo had played by then.' The tally of matches from his Madrid years alone comes to over 500, games played all over the world, on long tours, and competitive matches in Europe's leading cup and perhaps its best domestic league.

He had his moments at Espanyol, added another 11 goals to his Spanish league account in two seasons there, but among his former team-mates a consensus formed, watching him wind down his career at the city of Barcelona's lesser club, that 1964 had been the appropriate time to stop playing for Madrid. 'He didn't like it, but I think the big man, Bernabéu, was probably right,' said Pachín. 'Alfredo did suffer pain in his back. And Alfredo was never going to be a man to say to himself, "I'll just plant myself here in midfield, and spray passes around." No, he wanted to run and run, and the legs can only take so much.' The all-terrain, total footballer that Di Stéfano had become from his early 20s was not about standing still and spraying passes. The towering statistics bear witness. In the 510 Madrid matches he played, there were 418 Di Stéfano goals, a few of them poached around the six-yard box, but no one ever described him as a mere goal-hanger.

Bernabéu did not travel to Madrid's opening game of the 1964–65 league season. It may have been because Di Stéfano playing against Real Madrid was bound to draw uncomfortable attention. It may have been because it was still summer, and the Madrid president liked to spend time in the warmer months on his boat on the Mediterranean. The vessel, a gift from grateful Madrid directors, had been called *The Blond Arrow*. In 1964, after the breach with Di Stéfano, a new name was soon painted on the boat's bow, *Marizápalos*, in honour of María Bernabéu, the president's wife, with whom he had a long but childless marriage.

Bernabéu and Di Stéfano became estranged, embittered towards one another over the circumstances surrounding the player's departure. They had almost no contact. But four years after Di Stéfano had left Madrid, the silence would be broken, though the relationship hardly repaired. Di Stéfano sent a telegram to his former employer. It referred back to the vague offer of a non-playing position at Madrid, and it was candid.

'Through the years, we haven't really spoken,' wrote Di Stéfano. 'I take most of the blame. I was a phenomenon and a rogue. If I didn't agree with you it was because I didn't want it to be thought I was looking for a gift job. I have always worked hard for what I earn, and I took the view I would be doing something false to please you. I was disillusioned, and nobody helped my morale. As a father you let me down. You have not had children, and that shows. Fathers always forgive.'

If the tone was elegiac as well as viperish, it was because Di Stéfano was saying goodbye. The telegram started: 'Don Santiago, I'm going to my country now. I don't know if I will be back soon.' He signed off like this: 'If I don't come back, I leave with you my fond memories. *Un abrazo*, a hug, Alfredo.' The boy from Barracas had decided to return to his native Buenos Aires. He had a job offer that was anything but vague, but it was for a job that was famously demanding.

CHAPTER 16

ALFREDO THE SECOND

Alfredo Di Stéfano, of Espanyol, kicked his last ball as a professional as he was about to turn 40. It was 1966. That May, Real Madrid, still coached by his nemesis Miguel Muñoz, at last won a European Cup final in which Di Stéfano was not on the scoresheet. That July, Argentina at last made it past the first stage of a World Cup, during which their finest former player filed opinion pieces from the Wembley press box for the Spanish press agency, EFE. Di Stéfano seemed to enjoy the journalism, less so some of a tournament he found to be of variable quality, the football often too negative for his tastes.

Retirement, after the best part of a quarter of a century of the routines of practice, the adrenaline of match day, the bonhomie, and the delivering of bollockings in the dressing-room, had left a gap in his life. But the close company of like-minded colleagues would be maintained, especially over the summers, holidaying with the families of two of his closest friends from Real Madrid. The Di Stéfanos would continue to travel down to the Andalucía coast, around Marbella, with the families of Pepe Santamaría and Isidro Sánchez.

Those vacations were a fixture in the calendar. The children played, the fathers talked shop. As Quique Sánchez Flores, Isidro's son and Alfredo Di Stéfano's godson, recalled: 'What Alfredo loved was to sit around a table with his friends and chat about football.' In the summer of 1966 he spoke with his friends about the ways he could stay in the sport. The punditry was a sideline. He wanted to coach. The instinct had hardly been latent. Those who shared a pitch with him for Madrid, well used to being castigated and cajoled, recognised the manager within.

The difficulty might be to marry his high standards with the lesser capabilities of younger mortals. 'My father always used to tell me, "The worst thing with Alfredo is that he is so demanding,"' said Quique. 'He'd say, "The rest of us could not keep up to his level. That was impossible, we weren't capable of doing everything very well all of the time." He was a real, driven perfectionist.' As Quique grew up, he would come to know Di Stéfano as an encouraging mentor; later the adult Quique saw day to day for two years his godfather, the professional coach using the carrot as well as the stick, skilfully: 'As a coach, he had a good combination of three tones, if you like: the stern, the sympathetic and the humorous.'

He needed to be in football. What the Di Stéfano of his early forties was not going to become was a full-time househusband, primary carer of four children, with two more, Sofía and Ignacio, to come by the time he was making a very fine reputation in management. 'Like a lot of us who are in love with our professions, he was never one to take charge of family life at home,' Quique observed. 'He wasn't a close father, or very protective of the children. Sara was the matriarch, and she took care of all of that.'

Sara worried about her husband in his new career path. Quique recalls that his own mother, Carmen Flores, a hugely successful singer and dancer and a very close friend to Sara, would sometimes light candles at the family home to coincide with a match involving a team Di Stéfano was coaching. When her son asked why, Carmen would explain that Sara had asked her to, to bless the outcome.

It became a ritual. Sara Di Stéfano's prayers did not bring a great deal of luck during her husband's first gig as a coach. He was offered the manager's job at modest, provincial Elche, of Spain's Primera División. He liked the president, he knew the goalkeeper, Manuel Pazos, the Madrid team-mate he had consoled after Pazos's errors cost Madrid two points at Valladolid during Di Stéfano's first season in Spain. He accepted the Elche job as a taster of what management was like. The sampler ended after half a season, following some boardroom upheavals and only 3 wins out of 14 games. Elche survived in the top flight in 1967–68, but Di Stéfano's best contributions there would only be seen clearly in hindsight, in the progress made by two or three younger players he had hoisted up into the first team.

He had a gift for identifying talent, and knew it, a knack for assessing in a teenager his grown-up potential. He had an appetite for scouting, too, which was part of the appeal of the second managerial post he accepted, from a club much more grand than Elche. It was a club with a developed competitive hierarchy of youth teams, a structure he admired and whose byways he knew intimately. They played in the league he had grown up in. The only awkward aspect of this offer to manage in Argentina was that it came not from River Plate, his alma mater, but the institution with whom River shared the most intense rivalry, Boca Juniors.

Leaving his family in Madrid, Di Stéfano flew to Buenos Aires, having sent his part conciliatory, part caustic telegram to Santiago Bernabéu at Real Madrid, saying he was off home, to Argentina, with no clear idea how soon he would be back. He can hardly have hoped to be so successful, so soon.

Boca finished top of Argentina's Campeonato Nacional in Di Stéfano's first full season as a coach. He made a firm imprint on the side. The Boca of that championship are remembered as attractive to watch, innovative in that Di Stéfano revised some tactical orthodoxies, prioritising creativity from deep midfield, encouraging his central striker to move laterally. The Argentinian columnist Roberto Fontanarossa wrote: 'Di Stéfano built a Boca team that seemed tailored to the tastes of River Plate supporters, a team light on its feet, flexible, balanced and constructed around positive possession of the ball and skill rather than battling and combativeness, the basic attributes of Boca's heritage.'

His River Plate past, as Norma Di Stéfano, his sister, remembers, 'was not a problem' for Boca supporters when he was appointed their club's coach. Once they started consolidating a position at the top of the league, it became irrelevant. Besides, Di Stéfano's career as a player in Argentina had reached its abrupt full stop 20 years earlier. For a generation of Boca fans, he was better known as Di Stéfano of Madrid, a faraway ambassador of Argentina's native excellence.

Norma and Tulio, his brother and sister, enjoyed having him around, the fact he sometimes stayed at the family house in Flores. He worked hard, spent a great deal of time watching the Boca youth teams, using his sharp eye to recommend players to promote from the junior ranks. River Plate did not much enjoy Di Stéfano's return to the city. Boca sealed their title with a 2–2 draw at River's Monumental stadium in the derby.

Celebrations over, Di Stéfano moved on. While he was in Argentina, Sofía, his fifth child, had been born in Madrid; he felt he ought to be closer to his family, but not secure enough of a long-term future for them in Argentina to move them all there. He could afford to be choosy. The Boca success had identified him as a coach with prospects, as well as a name that would always guarantee interest from supporters and fascinate ambitious club presidents and directors.

His next employer, Valencia, approached Di Stéfano out of the blue. One day in 1970 he and Sara happened to be dining in a restaurant in Madrid at the same time as a group of their directors, and one thing, namely a bottle of champagne sent over by the club president to the Di Stéfanos' table as a courtesy, led to another. By the beginning of the 1970–71 season he was at work in Spain's third city. He was intrigued by the possibilities. The Valencia he knew as a player were a club who, in a good season, could finish in the top three of the Spanish league, and had a habit of successful runs in the Copa del Generalísimo. He liked their fame for cultivating classy young footballers. He rubbed along well with Julio de Miguel, the urbane president who had ordered champagne for him and his wife without being pushy or ostentatious about the gesture.

So began a long love affair with a city and a charismatic football club. Or, if not a love affair, a long relationship of highs and lows, break-ups and let's-start-agains. 'The bond between Valencia and Alfredo was always a special one – one of those where you say: "I love you but at the same time I hate you a little bit too,"' smiles Quique, who played for the club with his godfather as head coach at a time when the vicissitudes of that bond were dramatic. 'It was a love-hate relationship between him and the club. But with more love overall than hate.'

The love blossomed best at the beginning. Valencia's 1970–71 Primera División title was an extraordinary coup. The coach was still a relative novice in the job. Valencia had finished the previous campaign fifth in the table. There had been no lavish recruitment of players to usher him in, no champagne signings, apart from the famous manager, from President De Miguel.

The players greeted their new coach with curiosity. As the midfielder, Sergio Manzanera, recalled when we met in Valencia, where he has since built a successful second career as a dentist: 'There was surprise in the sense he didn't have much experience as a coach. He came aged 45; he'd been playing until he was nearly 40. But there was also the Di Stéfano persona. That raised our expectations. He seemed very sure of himself, at least from the outside.'

Manzanera, a teenager whom Di Stéfano had recommended Valencia recruit from nearby Levante, would find that the public Di Stéfano, forthright and fierce, was one man; the other, private Di Stéfano behaved differently. 'Once you knew him, at close range, you saw a very affectionate person, quite the reverse to the image of a hard character. But you had to be quite humble with him to start with to know that side of him.' Manzanera, 19 and nervous, felt humble. Indeed, he felt jittery to the point of near-paralysis. Speaking 45 years later, he remembered vividly the moment his boss's reassuring sensitivity settled a teenager's anxiety.

'I used to get so stressed,' Manzanera said. 'Really, I was a very nervous individual. Before matches I'd be vomiting in the dressing-room. That was just in our pre-season. But Alfredo saw something was up and came to see me.' At that point, Manzanera admits, he burst into tears. 'I was crying. You know, he really didn't mind seeing that, not at all. What I came to realise was that he could be a very warm person, but that not many people dared to let down their guard with him. He was sympathetic if they did, if you said honestly to him, "Listen, I'm having this or that problem." He and I got on very well. He had wanted me to come to Valencia, from a lower division. He helped me gain confidence, showed faith in me, and was quite protective.'

Out on the training pitch, the Di Stéfano tongue had not suddenly softened, however. His *rioplatense* accent had never been diluted in his 11 years in Madrid, and having been back in Buenos Aires for the best part of a year with Boca, he was speaking football in pure South American. His players were obliged to do their own glossing of any jargon they did not recognise, invectives included. Manzanera accepted that his new mentor was an intense, irascible, driven martinet when standards were not being met. 'He could get very angry about losing, and it was just the same in practice. He insulted us, told us where to go.'

As it turned out, Valencia did not lose too often, and where they were going, after a stuttering start, was up and up. With an eerie inevitability, Di Stéfano's first league fixture as Valencia head coach took him to the Bernabéu stadium, a head-to-head with Muñoz, still coach at Real, and a 2–0 Madrid win. The third match of the campaign was lost at home to Sevilla. Then things changed. The Luis Casanova arena, as the Mestalla was then named, turned into a fortress. A young, unstarry team, emboldened by the coach with the superstar backstory, began to creep up the league table.

Valencia beat Barcelona, pacesetters in the first half of the season, at Camp Nou. They developed an identity, but not one that could be neatly attributed to the specific dogmas of their coach. As at Boca, he encouraged a talented passer, Pep Claramunt, to use his forte as a distributor of the ball from the base as much as from the apex of midfield. Yet this Valencia were not designed chiefly to enchant the neutral spectator. 'We were a young team. Nobody imagined us at the top of the table,' said Manzanera. 'Our game wasn't great, exquisite football. It was practical, even, you could say, a bit primitive. What Alfredo instilled in us was a consistency, a real battling quality, he taught us to fight for every ball.'

Valencia put together a run of seven matches without conceding a goal, and by the middle of the season, they sat joint second, a point behind Barcelona. Real Madrid came to the Luis Casanova and lost 1–0, the first in a series of eight games undefeated for Valencia. 'We had a powerful defence,' explained Manzanera, 'and we were quick on the counter-attack. Óscar Valdez, the striker, had speed and I was pretty rapid. But look at the end of season figures and you see our top scorer had only eight goals. We were not a high-scoring team. But nobody scored many against us either.'

After the penultimate round of matches the league table showed that while Valencia had Spain's meanest defence, they were much less potent up front than Barcelona, Atlético Madrid and Real Madrid. But those three all looked up at Valencia in the table. Di Stéfano's rugged pupils sat top, with one match to go. A win away at Espanyol would guarantee Valencia the league title for the first time in 24 years. Less than two points, and either Barcelona or Atlético Madrid could leapfrog them. To the delight of Spanish television executives, who had cameras readied in two cities for the dramatic denouement, Barcelona were away at Atlético Madrid for their last fixture. A draw between those teams and Valencia would win the title even if they lost in Sarrià, home of Espanyol, by dint of the goal-average tie-breaker.

At the Di Stéfano home, Sara lit candles. In Sarrià, Di Stéfano lit cigarettes. According to *ABC*'s reporter, he smoked his way through 30 during the make-or-break 90 minutes. His players did little to ease his nerves. Espanyol scored, from a set-piece, the sort of goal Valencia's drilled defenders had all but immunised themselves against through the previous eight months. 'Alfredo was on edge, certainly,' remembers Manzanera, 'and as it was a goal from a header from a corner, even worse. He blamed one of our midfielders.' The blaming, come the final whistle, would have been explosive, expletive.

As the minutes tick-tocked down, Valencia losing, Di Stéfano turned to the crowd. Fans with transistors radios reported to him that with five minutes left in Madrid, Atlético and Barcelona were drawing 1–1. Valencia supporters had travelled in their thousands to the Espanyol game, a four-hour drive up the coast. When the final whistle blew, the players and their head coach knew for certain the outcome at Atlético because of the pitch invasion by valencianos. Their club had lost, but they were gleeful – Barcelona and Atlético had shared the points in the capital and the championship was won.

The victorious coach was nearly knocked over in the frenetic kerfuffle of fans and exhausted players. The league hierarchy had been bowled over. Valencia, without a title for close to a quarter of a century, were champions again, with their squad of little-knowns and local lads. Di Stéfano looked like a Midas. In his first season in Spain as a player, he had won Real Madrid's first title for a generation. In his first full season as a coach in Spain, he had done the same with Valencia.

After that the sport's gravitational forces began to pull. Valencia pursued Real Madrid doggedly the following season, to finish second, and made it to a second successive Copa del Generalísimo final. In 1971, they lost the Cup final to Barcelona, in 1972 to Atlético Madrid. 'Valencia were not a club that spent much money at that time, and though we were still competitive, we started to drop down after three years together,' recalls Manzanera.

Di Stéfano grumbled about slender budgets, but also recruited resourcefully. He looked beyond the orthodox sources for fresh talent, pushing for the signature of the first winner of the new African Footballer of the Year award; Salif Keita, a

Malian, joined Valencia from Marseille. It was a shrewd move for a gifted and soon popular player, but one who had needed to hear reassurances from Di Stéfano that he would not find Spain a backward, racist country.

The Valencia of the early 1970s made no more sustained challenges for the title, reached no more Cup finals. In 1974, Di Stéfano, thanked for his work, was looking for another job. Valencia would later be offering one; they would come back to him again and again. 'Eventually he started saying to Valencia presidents, whenever they sacked him: "Okay, call me again when you need to win something,"' smiles Manzanera. 'Every time, the way he left Valencia was the wrong way,' believes Quique. 'He gave a lot to the club and in the end perhaps the recognition of Alfredo there was not as great as he deserved. Sometimes he used to say: "Valencia is the best club, with the worst directors."'

He served several different juntas at Valencia, and worked under some very unreliable employers indeed between his first two spells there. Di Stéfano did not have a regular agent for most of his professional life, and although in the 1950s agents were not so ubiquitous, by the 1970s many coaches and managers had a delegated representative, to seek out work and negotiate terms for them. Di Stéfano might have been better advised with some of his choices as he passed his 50th birthday. He took on jobs that sounded promising, even prestigious, and they turned what had been a coaching highway of a career into a series of nasty hairpin bends.

There was Sporting Clube de Portugal, who never paid him a penny, by his account of the escapade, for the several months he was there as head coach, failed even to honour his Lisbon hotel bill, and then sacked him as he was about to board a flight, with the team, to play a match in the Algarve. He promptly got in his car and drove straight home to Madrid, pausing only to stop and make a brief phone call to Sara. It began with a growled, single word: 'Chaos!'

A brief stint at Rayo Vallecano had many confusing days. Coaching Castellón, of the second division, looked like a low point, because of the club's status, but he enjoyed the place, its proximity to Valencia, and the colleagues there. Di Stéfano later reflected on his experiences coaching around the provinces, and in Lisbon, as educative. He worked with footballers who struggled to make a living, who would sheepishly tell him they had missed practice because they could not afford petrol or their bus fare. He had no reason not to believe them. He felt old hackles rise, remembering the indignation he knew as a young footballer in Argentina, at the time of the players' strikes, the resentment he felt about wealthy directors, about mismanagement, at the exploitative face of the sport.

Sometimes, he gave out money from his own pocket to players in penury. Some of colleagues from his years as a very handsomely remunerated footballer used to joke about Di Stéfano's careful spending, his meanness at the card table or the bar. Others describe his generosity. 'When my parents separated in the 1970s,' Quique reports, 'it was a difficult time and the Di Stéfanos were very generous, economically, in helping my mother when we needed help.' The Sánchez Flores parents – Isidro, the former Madrid player, and Carmen, the singer who had put her performing career partly on hold to raise a family – were both good friends of Alfredo and Sara Di Stéfano.

As a child, Quique valued the couple's support, and their attention. 'Sara used to send me all these things from Valencia, scarves and things, so I grew up with the club Valencia very present in my life. Sara was thoughtful in that way, a strong character, and in control.' He smiles, before adding: 'Alfredo admired her strength, but he did have this nickname for her, later on. He called her "Thatcher", as in Mrs Thatcher.' As in Iron Lady.

Sara Di Stéfano lit many evening candles, and said many prayers for her husband the coach, the man always answerable for defeat, only vicariously credited in victory. Meanwhile, if Di Stéfano himself still held a candle for the job that logic said he should have been offered by the middle of the 1970s, he kept it private. But Real Madrid did not offer him a managerial position after he won a major league, Argentina's, at his first attempt. Nor did they ring him when he won Spain's championship in improbable, impressive circumstances with Valencia. There was a belief, an assumption, that Santiago Bernabéu, the Madrid president who had once been like a father to Di Stéfano, would never consider the possibility, because of the breach between the two men in 1964.

Bernabéu died in 1978. But the next tempting call came not from his successor as Real Madrid president but from Valencia. Di Stéfano took up the position of head coach there for a second time, though with a much altered set of players. The Valencia of the late 1970s were flashier than they had been, with a penchant for footballers who had dazzled at World Cups. The Argentinian, Mario Kempes, top goalscorer and champion at the 1978 tournament, led their forward line; behind him, Rainer Bonhof, a stylish member of Germany's midfield, with a doctorate in direct free-kicks.

The previous season Valencia had won the Copa del Rey, as the main domestic cup was known after Franco's death and the restoration of the Spanish monarchy in 1975. So for 1979–80 they entered UEFA's Cup-Winners' cup, not quite as prestigious as the Champions Cup, but still an exciting, glamorous, pan-European competition – close enough to what had been Di Stéfano's kingdom as a player.

Valencia reached the Brussels final, where their opponents would be Arsenal. Di Stéfano spent much of the day of the game feeling angry, and raging against distractions caused by what he viewed as typically excessive late-twentieth-century commercialisation of his sport. An unedifying row about boot sponsorship was disrupting preparations, with players arguing about their right to wear the branded boots they endorsed. Di Stéfano ordered some agents to leave the hotel premises. His stress levels would rise further when, after 90 minutes, and extra time, Valencia and Arsenal could not be separated. The final would go to a penalty shootout.

Sara Di Stéfano and the children were among the spectators in the Heysel stadium. No candles, just prayer. Her husband later described the experience of watching penalties, from the manager's bench, as akin to giving birth. On the night, he was the coach with the easier pregnancy. Saves by the Valencia keeper Carlos Pereira won the Cup. Just ahead of the spot-kick lottery Pereira had been advised by Di Stéfano to dive to his left against the left-footed Arsenal penalty-takers. The counsel turned out to be wise.

Valencia finished sixth in the league, insufficient to keep Di Stéfano there for the next season. He had been sacked for the second time by a Valencia he had guided to a prestigious title. But he did not wait long to be offered his next big job. It sounded even better. He was invited to coach what at the time was probably the best club squad assembled anywhere in the world.

The offer came from his old club, from the place he had started, to work at the ground where he used to go as a young fan before he was ten years old. River Plate wanted their Blond Arrow back, their treacherous rebel, 31 years after he walked out, fully unionised but chasing big dollars in Colombia. Di Stéfano the manager assessed the

1981 River squad and saw a line-up full of champions, a mirror of the team that had triumphed in Argentina, for Argentina, at the previous World Cup. This was not coincidence. The Argentinian Federation had ordered that, with one or two exceptions, players expecting to represent the country at the 1982 World Cup should be employed with clubs in Argentina, not abroad. At River were Kempes; Daniel Passarella, the Argentina captain; the national team goalkeeper Ubaldo Fillol; in all over half a dozen men who had won a World Cup or would go on to do so in 1986. There was a downside. The national squad players would be required to train with the national coach, César Luis Menotti, three or four days a week.

In Passarella, Di Stéfano found a like mind. His captain was tough, sometimes suspicious of those around him, but he and Di Stéfano worked well together. The River team, though, very often looked like less than the sum of its illustrious parts. River's Kempes was not the dashing Kempes he had relied on at Valencia. Di Stéfano fell out with the playmaker Norberto Alonso, and would be booed at the Monumental for leaving Alonso out of the starting line-up. 'That was a brave thing to do because Alonso was an idol for fans,' recalls Julio Olarticoechea, a midfield player in that River team and the Argentina side.

For Olarticoechea, Di Stéfano's appointment 'made an impact because of the figure he was'. He found him, as a coach, less a man of details than one of drive and determination. He could be quite sparing with his words, stern at times, humorous at others. He acted out the caricature of his grouchy reputation. A running joke, when the River squad travelled together, would be to watch Di Stéfano's reaction when he was served coffee at whatever hotel or café they visited: the players anticipated a grimace or a cartoon splutter if the coffee tasted sub-standard.

His more serious complaint was that the brew of River's squad was wrong. The stars were both too numerous and too absent, because of their commitment to work with Menotti so intensively. 'He didn't like interference. He wanted our dressing-room to be sacred, and ours alone,' Olarticoechea told me in Buenos Aires, 'and he was a very different sort of coach to Menotti. He didn't do a lot of work on specific tactical plans, but he was a good motivator.'

River, given they had such a high proportion of the leading Argentinian players, had been expected to win all the competitions they entered. But the quality of many of their performances made their triumph in the Nacional, the league that ran from September to the end of the year, seem fortunate. They may have had the great Di Stéfano in the dugout, and the spine of the Argentina national team on the pitch, but they did not have Argentina's outstanding, match-winning individual. The 20-year-old Diego Maradona, on his way to becoming the finest Argentinian since the Blond Arrow, was at Boca Juniors. Maradona's three goals in the two Boca–River derbies in the 1981 Nacional, one of them a superb direct free-kick, made Di Stéfano's job awkward.

River did win the title. 'It was close, and we didn't always play the football we should have been capable of,' said Olarticoechea, who scored, along with Kempes, in the final play-off matches against Ferro Carril Oeste that gave Di Stéfano his satisfying, uniquely symmetrical record as a coach in Argentina's elite division. In two attempts, he had achieved two league titles, one with each of the behemoth clubs of Buenos Aires, Boca Juniors and River. He would go back to the city in 1985 to add a third title as coach of Boca, who by then had lost Maradona to the Spanish league.

Di Stéfano returned to Spain in the middle of 1982. Events pushed him there. There was the family, of whom the youngest,

Ignacio, was ten, and the oldest, Nanette and Silvana, were into their twenties. Argentina was suddenly at war, over the sovereignty of the Malvinas, or Falkland Islands; Spain seemed a more stable place. Most of all, he had received an overdue call. It was *the* call. Real Madrid needed a new head coach, and they asked their most successful alumnus to be the man.

It felt like a homecoming, a prodigal son's long anticipated reunion, 18 years after his last match as a Real Madrid footballer. It felt ceremonial, cathartic when Di Stéfano, before signing his contract in front of photographers, visited María Bernabéu, the widow of the former president.

Twenty thousand madridistas turned up to watch his first practice session. He surveyed the players there, and the list of those due to join, and had worries and a sense of déjà vu. Man for man, the River Plate he had been employed by months earlier looked a much better resourced squad than the Real Madrid he had taken over; just as it had been when he was a player. The River Plate whose red stripe he wore was a River still equipped with some of the cogs and pulleys of La Máquina. That always seemed to him a finer model than the Real Madrid whose team he joined in the early 1950s.

The perfect storyline, where the great former player turns out to be the great coach at the club that he defined, does exist. It happened for Johan Cruyff at Barcelona, Kenny Dalglish at Liverpool. Di Stéfano the manager very nearly made Real Madrid great again, from his dugout. He fell short by very narrow margins.

Madrid, who had finished third in the Primera División but won the Cup in 1981–82, had five competitions to aim for the following season, with Di Stéfano, white-haired and portly, as their new guide. They lost the first, the Supercopa, a two-legged play-off against

Real Sociedad badly, with a 4–0 defeat in an away leg disfigured by violence off the field, in the crowd, and two Madrid red cards.

That was December, just before New Year. By the end of April, having led the league table for most of the season, they went into the last weekend ahead of Athletic Bilbao by a single point and with a goal-average advantage over the Basque club. Madrid's last fixture, poignantly for Di Stéfano, was at Valencia, a Valencia carrying a fear of possible relegation. Madrid lost, 1–0. Athletic did not slip up, so the title went not to the Bernabéu but to the Basque Country.

Two silver medals, then, but three trophies to go for still. Madrid had reached the European Cup Winners' Cup final, via some gruelling tests, notably against Italy's Internazionale in the quarter-finals. In the Gothenburg final, they had to play Aberdeen, managed by a young Alex Ferguson. After 90 minutes, it was 1–1. The Scots scored in injury time. Madrid were runners-up. Again.

Another day, another cup. Di Stéfano's long season had also included a run all the way to the final of the Copa del Rey. Madrid met Barcelona in Zaragoza. As against Aberdeen, it was 1–1 going towards the 90th minute; this time, agonisingly, the 90th minute marked full-time. Barcelona had scored with less than 60 seconds left.

Four silver medals, one chance left at gold. The now defunct Copa de la Liga, a shorter competition, held the two legs of its final at the end of June. Madrid had reached it. It would be another Barcelona versus Madrid showdown. Two Argentinian managers squared up: Menotti, the former Argentina manager, was coaching Barcelona. His compatriot Maradona scored Barcelona's goals in both games. Madrid had come back from 2–0 down to draw 2–2 at the Bernabéu. In the deciding leg, they went 2–0 down again at Camp Nou. This time they could only manage one goal in reply.

Five competitions, all them fought to the very brink, finished up yielding five runners-up positions. A cruel karma had visited Di Stéfano's first season as Real Madrid head coach. As a player he had won five European Champions Cup finals with Madrid on the trot. As a coach, he had lost five grand finales in seven months. 'You know, that was so close to being Madrid's greatest season ever,' goalkeeper García Remón reflected. 'Instead it is remembered as quite the opposite.' Catchphrases would be coined about that season, including a sobriquet for the coach. Di Stéfano, the player who usually finished first in everything, was now 'Alfredo II', Alfredo the Second, because second was where the Madrid he managed finished in everything they tried.

Alfredo II's second season coaching Madrid also ended without a major trophy. But it is remembered for something else, his promotion of a group of younger players from the Madrid youth academy to the first team, most of whom would go on to define the club's next decade, and would be known as La Quinta del Buitre, the Vulture Squadron. His sharp eye had not discovered the potential in the likes of Emilio Butragueño, nicknamed the Vulture, but his confidence that the young striker and other tyros would respond well to being promoted to the seniors proved an excellent intuition.

'He wasn't a bad judge or teacher, Alfredo,' says Amancio Amaro, who coached Castilla, the Madrid feeder team, at the time, liaising with Di Stéfano about which players to fast-track. Di Stéfano would manage some members of La Quinta del Buitre again, when they were established seniors, but it was only for a matter of months in what was essentially a caretaker role, a second spell as Madrid head coach in 1990. He finally won a trophy as Real Madrid coach that year, the Supercopa, a cup which counts as slightly more than ceremonial.

After the Alfredo II episode, the near-miss season and the blank one that followed, he coached at Valencia for a third time, with the task of bringing them up into the Primera División. He succeeded in that. Alfredo the Second, now in his sixties, won the second division. His godson Quique was playing at Valencia by then, part of a team who were galvanised by their coach, and often entertained by his sense of fun.

Quique recognised Di Stéfano's relish at being on the practice ground every day. As for other aspects of coaching, Quique wonders how much Di Stéfano actually enjoyed it: 'That I am not so sure of. I am really not. I believe he loved watching football, playing it of course, and when he could no longer play, observing it. What I am not clear about is whether coaching was ever a vocation for him. He had a different sort of talent, and more as a player than as a coach. To be honest, I think that whether he had had his coaching career or not, he would have been equally happy in his life.'

EPILOGUE

On the first weekend of March 2016, in the upper tier of the south grandstand of the Santiago Bernabéu stadium, supporters of Real Madrid displayed a series of banners, painstakingly prepared ahead of a league match against Celta Vigo. They were sufficiently large so their words could be read from every other point in the arena and, above all, by the 11 Madrid players on the field. Around 25 people stood to lift up the first sheet, its letters printed in three-foot high, black block capitals on white background; the same number heaved up the next line. A dozen madridistas clutched the edges of the last banner, which simply carried the name, in royal purple: 'Di Stéfano'.

He was being quoted. 'To wear this badge,' read the lines above, 'you have to soak the jersey in sweat.'

The message cited a phrase Alfredo Di Stéfano once muttered, with his sternest face on, to a new player at the club, Amancio Amaro, well over half a century earlier, an admonishment which has become part of the folklore of the club. None of the disgruntled madridistas who devoted their free hours to printing the quote onto long canvases were old enough to have ever seen Di Stéfano perspiring on the pitch at the Bernabéu. But they would not call themselves true madridistas if they did not believe a biting remark from Di Stéfano might still act as a powerful reprove; not quite as alarming as seeing him, broad-shouldered, fiery-eyed, planting himself directly in front of you, but the next best thing.

Di Stéfano, even after his death, remains Madrid's standard-bearer. He lived long enough, by a few weeks, to have seen the club he transformed win a tenth European Champions Cup, a landmark Madrid achieved in May 2014. As a player, it took him five years to accumulate Madrid's first five; the post-Di Stéfano Madrid needed fifty to win the same number. Granted, the competition and the sport changed a good deal in that half-century, although the rate of its evolution was probably never as rapid as in the 1950s and early 1960s, the era when Di Stéfano was its catalyst.

Di Stéfano, Pelé, the late Johan Cruyff, Diego Maradona, Lionel Messi. Debates about football's greatest individual since the Second World War tend to centre on that quintet, the last four's candidacy aided by the evidence of a great deal of film and television footage in colour, by their participation in World Cup tournaments and, for most of them, a high profile nourished and maintained by their appeal to advertisers and sponsors. 'Pelé had a whole army of people marketing him,' a member of Di Stéfano's family remarked to me, not with pronounced bitterness, but to highlight a distinction, the difference between a superstar of the tail-end of the sport's sepia age and an icon whose portfolio of skills and triumphs can be shown off in full technicolour.

Luís Figo, Zinédine Zidane, Brazil's Ronaldo, David Beckham, Kaká, Cristiano Ronaldo. In the new millennium, Di Stéfano, or 'Don Alfredo' as he was often known in his stately years, would dutifully welcome the stellar footballers of a new century to the club he transformed. He held a position as honorary president of Real Madrid from 2000, appointed to it by the ambitious president Florentino Pérez, a successful construction magnate who as a child had watched Di Stéfano play at Chamartín, and set about trying to do for modern Madrid what Santiago Bernabéu, with Di Stéfano his most important ally, had done in the second half-century of the club's history.

As Don Alfredo, Di Stéfano would come on stage at the Bernabéu to shake hands and approve the brilliance of Madrid's latest figurehead recruit. Every time, the audience were invited to listen to the echoes. In the summer of 2000, Pérez signed Figo, a dashing Portuguese winger-cum-creative playmaker from Barcelona, a Barcelona who did not want to lose Figo; here was a sharp business coup to evoke Madrid's seizing of Di Stéfano from under Barça's noses. Twelve months later, ahead of Real Madrid's centenary, Zidane was formally handed his Madrid jersey by Di Stéfano, a world record fee having been paid to Juventus for a footballer who, at 29 years old, would conventionally have be deemed, if not beyond his peak, certainly not building up to it. But the elderly man presiding over Zidane's arrival stood as a reminder that class is ageless. Di Stéfano was 29 when he won his first European Cup, and an evergreen 34 when he lifted his fifth.

When the honorary president of Real Madrid handed Ronaldo, fresh from winning a World Cup with Brazil, his white jersey, Pérez had just completed a deal to bring the gifted centre-forward to Spain from Italy's Internazionale. The selling club felt miffed because the player had forced his exit from Inter, amid threats not to attend training or to play if his Italian employers did not let him leave. He was labelled a mercenary in much the same way as Di Stéfano had been when he left River Plate more than five decades previously. When Real Madrid triumphantly introduced Beckham as one of their own, as heavy an emphasis would be placed by the club's executives on the photogenic English footballer's fabulous freight of merchandising potential as on his ability to curl a pass and bend a direct free-kick. The Blond Arrow, grey and a little stooped, greeted the Blond Advertising-Magnet at a glitzy unveiling, broadcast live across the world. Di Stéfano would have been forgiven for reflecting how Beckham could make front-page news for wearing a sarong, four decades after Di Stéfano had caused a national stir for publicising a brand of women's tights.

The Brazilians Ronaldo and Kaká brought Ballons d'Or with them to Madrid. They, like Beckham, never managed to win a European Cup with Real. The Di Stéfano era set standards beyond modern reach. Many of his goalscoring records endured well over half a century, and only after Cristiano Ronaldo, a driven, dynamic Portuguese, accepted the white Madrid number nine jersey from its most celebrated wearer did the club have a man on their staff capable of scoring at a sustained goals-per-game ratio to compare with Di Stéfano's blitzes through the first half of his Madrid odyssey.

As honorary president of Real Madrid, Di Stéfano earned a comfortable stipend. The club he had defined looked after him through the last 15 years of his life. But to report he passed through his autumn years in gentle repose would be to mislead. The honorary president could still turn into the ornery presiding judge. One highly decorated Madrid player of the modern era testifies to being button-holed and harangued outside the home dressing-room by a bilious septuagenarian. From his seat in the stands, Di Stéfano had watched the player offer a performance without what he deemed the necessary work-rate and tactical intelligence. The offender had worn the Real badge, and not sweated through the jersey. Di Stéfano gave him an earful.

Don Alfredo was liable to forget his obligations to Madrid's sense of its own grandeur and decorum from time to time. Photographers commissioned to record the tableau portraits of Di Stéfano with dignitaries at official Madrid photocalls tell of having to airbrush their images to remove from his hand a cigarette. He had never been one to stand on ceremony. He could go off message. Journalists asking Di Stéfano, the first serial winner of the Ballon d'Or, the sport's version of an Oscar, who he ranked as the best player of all-time, or of the current time, would hear him veer away from the narrative they wanted. He would not name-check Cruyff, or Maradona, or Cristiano Ronaldo. He instead recited the names that were the poetry of his teenaged years: 'Muñoz, Moreno, Pedernera, Labruna, Loustau. Pick any of those you want'.

Muñoz. Moreno. Pedernera. Labruna. Loustau. River Plate's La Máquina, the one line-up in his career Di Stéfano had to struggle, and to wait, to earn his place in, his original standard-bearers from his Argentinian golden age. Although Spain was home for more than half his life, and the country he represented most in an unfulfilling international career, Don Alfredo never forgot he was once Alfredito, the boy from Barracas. There was the way he spoke, for a start, in a voice peppered with the phrases and the timbre of Buenos Aires. Of a Monday, meeting friends in Madrid, he was as ready to talk about the match he had watched that weekend, via satellite television, in the Argentinian top division, as about whether Real Madrid's players had sweated for the badge.

In retirement, he kept the company of several old friends from Madrid's golden era, at the headquarters of the club's veterans' association, where he served for a period as president, with an office in the lower ground floor of the Bernabéu stadium. There was some nostalgia when they got together, though he was not easily drawn into championing his own epoch as the definitive good old days, into saying that, back then, games were always tougher to win,

319

goals always harder to score, or to grumble that the moderns were spoilt and indulged by comparison with his generation.

Sara, Di Stéfano's wife, died in 2005, and Di Stéfano was admitted to hospital at the end of that year for a heart bypass operation. He lost his eldest daughter, Nanette, who had become his principal carer, to illness in 2012, by which time he had formed a close relationship with a woman some 50 years his junior. Gina González, a Costa Rican who came to Madrid as a journalist soon after the turn of the millennium, had been working with Di Stéfano on a proposed memoir, organising his diary, before, to the discomfort of his remaining five children, many of his friends and the Real Madrid hierarchy, they announced their engagement in the pages of Spain's *El Mundo* newspaper. Di Stéfano sensed there would be disapproval. To which, as one close friend of his put it to me, he responded as Di Stéfano would on being told what not to do: he was defiant. 'Let the madman do his own thing,' he told *El Mundo*. 'I have been widowed for eight years, and I am young at heart.'

The story did not end happily. Di Stéfano's children, Silvana, Alfredo, Elena, Sofía and Ignacio, made a legal application that their father's 'means be protected' and his deteriorating health be examined to determine his capacity to make independent judgements. In May 2013, a Madrid court passed the custody of the 86-year-old Di Stéfano, by then reliant on a wheelchair to move about, to his children, though not before González had called a press conference in which she told reporters he had effectively 'been kidnapped', prevented from communicating with her.

Di Stéfano was surrounded by his children when he died, on the afternoon of 7 July 2014. He had been rushed two days earlier to Gregorio Marañón hospital in Madrid having collapsed, suffering serious heart and respiratory problems after celebrating his 88 birthday with his family.

His body lay in repose at the Santiago Bernabéu stadium for two days before his burial in Almudena cemetery in the Spanish capital. Six weeks later, Real Madrid began the season of their defence of their tenth European Cup. Ahead of their home leg of the Spanish Super Cup against Atlético Madrid, an outsized white number nine jersey was spread across the centre circle of the Bernabéu, and to the sound of a string quartet and then the still of a minute's silence, spectators were invited to look upon a display of the titles Di Stéfano had brought to the premises in his time as a player and as a coach.

Each of the trophies was set out on a broad, tiered podium. There were the two Ballons d'Or, and a uniquely smelted prize called the Super Ballon d'Or, given to the greatest of the twentieth century's European Footballers of the Year. There was his Copa del Rey, an Intercontinental Cup, and, his yield from his last adventure in management, the Spanish Super Cup. There were the eight league championship trophies. There were the five European Cups. In the minute's silence, there seemed barely enough time to count them all up.

ACKNOWLEDGEMENTS

As well as the people cited in the text who gave their time, knowledge and shared their recollections generously, I'm grateful for the guidance and help of Fernando Macua and Luis Castiblanque at the Asociación de Ex Jugadores del Real Madrid, of José María Otero, Diego Torres, Andres Burgo, Pato Nogueira, Sid Lowe, the Mittens Jonathan Wilson and Stephen Burgen.

Andrew Goodfellow, at Ebury, and David Luxton, my agent, came up with the idea, and Laura Horsley, at Ebury, took it forward with care, professionalism and patience. Thanks also to Valen Simpson and Chris Moar Aguiar for their many hours transcribing interviews and their research; to my son, Michael, for his expertise in Catalan and Portuguese; to the helpful staff at the Hemeroteca Municipal in Madrid and the Biblioteca Nacional in Buenos Aires, and to the sharp eyes of Catherine Beckwith, Steve Dobell and Howard Watson for spotting errors.

BIBLIOGRAPHY

ABC, *El Real Madrid, Campéon de Europa* (Planeta, 1993)

Adamson, Richard, *Bogotá Bandit* (Mainstream, 1996)

Arias, Inocencio F., *Los Tres Mitos del Real Madrid* (Plaza, 2002)

Armfield, Jimmy, *Right Back to the Beginning* (Headline, 2004)

Burns, Jimmy, *Barça: A People's Passion* (Bloomsbury, 1998)

Campomar, Andreas, *Golazo! A History of Latin American Football* (Quercus, 2014)

Candau, Julián García, *Bernabéu, El Presidente* (Espasa, 2002)

De la Plaza, Luis Prados, *Real Madrid Centenario* (Silex, 2001)

Di Stéfano, Alfredo, with Relaño, Alfredo and Ortega, Enrique, *Gracias, Vieja* (Aguilar, 2000)

Estévez, Diego Ariel and Lodise, Sergio Alberto, *110, Más de un Siglo Rojo y Blanco* (Continente, 2011)

Fabbri, Alejandro, *Historias Negras del Fútbol Argentino* (Capital Intelectual, 2008)

Fontanarrossa, Roberto, *No te vayas, Campeón* (Sudamericana, 2000)

Franklin, Neil, *Soccer at Home and Abroad* (Stanley Paul, 1956)

Frydenberg, Julio, *Historia Social del Fútbol* (Siglo Veintiuno, 2011)

Galeano, Eduardo, *El Fútbol a Sol y Sombra* (Siglo XXI, 2015)

Glanville, Brian, *Football Memories* (Virgin, 1999)

Gomez-Santos, Marino, *Conversaciones con Santiago Bernabéu* (Renascimiento, 2014)

González, Luis Miguel, *Alrededor de la Historia, Memoria Gráfica del Real Madrid* (Everest, 2002)

González, Luis Miguel, *Las Entrañas del Real Madrid* (Esfera, 2014)

Granado, Alberto, *Con el Che por Sudamérica* (Marea, 2013)

Guevara, Ernesto 'Che', *Diarios de Motocicleta* (Planeta, 2005)

Herrera, Helenio, *Yo Memorias* (Planeta, 1962)

Kopa, Raymond, *Kopa* (Jacob-Duvernet, 2006)

Lorente, Rafael, *Di Stéfano Cuenta su Vida* (Sáez, 1954)

Lowe, Sid, *Fear and Loathing in La Liga* (Yellow Jersey, 2013)

Luque, Xavier G. and Finestres, Jordi, *El Caso Di Stéfano* (Península, 2006)

Mangriñán, Juan Vicente, *Como El Blanco Azahar* (Centre de Estudis Vallers, 2011)

Matthews, Stanley, *The Way It Was* (Headline, 2000)

Montoliú, Pedro, *Madrid Bajo la Dictatura* (Sílex, 2010)

Neira, Jorge Mario, *Las 1001 Anécdotas de Millonarios* (Zeta, 2013)

Peucelle, Carlos, *Fútbol Todo Tiempo* (Dictio, 2011)

Pérez, Alberto, *La Retransmisión del Fútbol en la Radio* (CIDIDA, 2014)

Pinedo, Carlos, *El Real Madrid en Europa 1955–2014* (T y B, 2014)

Puskás, Ferenc, *Puskás on Puskás* (Robson Books, 1998)

Ramos, Ramón, *Que Vienen los Rusos!* (Comares, 2012)

Relaño, Alfredo, *Memorias en Blanco y Negro* (Corner, 2014)

Relaño, Alfredo, *Nacidos para Incordiarse* (Planeta, 2012)

Ribeiro, Péris, *Didí, O Gênio da Folha-Seca* (Gryphus, 2014)

Rippon, Anton, *European Cup* (Mirror Books, 1980)

Santacana i Torres, Carles, *El Barça i el Franquisme!* (Mina, 2005)

Santander, Carlos Fernández, *El Fútbol durante la Guerra Civil y el Franquismo* (San Martín, 1990)

Semprún, Martín, *Santiago Bernabéu, La Causa* (Primer Plano, 1994)

Townson, Nigel (ed.), *Spain Transformed* (Macmillan, 2010)

Viñolo, Juan Soto, *Los Años 50* (Esfera, 2009)

Wilson, Jonathan, *Angels with Dirty Faces* (Orion, 2016)

Wilson, Jonathan, *Inverting the Pyramid* (Orion, 2008)